Keeping Up with the Joneses

Keeping Up
with the Joneses

Envy in American Consumer
Society, 1890–1930

SUSAN J. MATT

PENN

University of Pennsylvania Press
Philadelphia

10 9 8 7 6 5 4 3 2 1

Published by
University of Pennsylvania Press
Philadelphia, Pennsylvania 19104-4011

Library of Congress Cataloging-in-Publication Data
Matt, Susan J. (Susan Jipson), 1967–
    Keeping up with the Joneses : envy in American consumer society, 1890–1930 /
Susan J. Matt.
        p. cm.
    Contents: City women and the quest for status — Envy in the office — "The prizes of life
lie away from the farm" — From "sturdy yeoman" to "hayseed" — Coming of age in
consumer society.
    Includes bibliographical references and index.
    ISBN 0-8122-3686-6 (cloth : alk. paper)
    1. Social values—United States—History.   2. Envy—Social aspects.   3. Social status—
United States—History.   4. Consumption (Economics)—Social aspects—United States.
5. Social change—United States—History—20th century.   I. Title.
HN90.M6 M37 2002
303.3'72'0973—dc21

                                                                                2002029110

For my parents,
Barbara Jipson Matt and Joseph Matt,
and
for my husband,
Luke O. Fernandez

Contents

Introduction

In 1897, readers of the *Saturday Evening Post* encountered
the story of Mary, "a very pretty girl of sixteen," who was
the daughter of "a man in moderate circumstances." "Oh!
If I only had a pair of diamond earrings!" said Mary to her
mother. She confided, "I believe I should be perfectly happy
if I had them. You don't know, mama, what a beautiful pair
Esther Haley has. All the school girls envy her." After some
quiet consultation, Mary's parents decided to buy her the earrings, with the hope of teaching her that "happiness does not
consist in fine jewelry, but in a contented and cheerful spirit."
While she was initially happy with her new acquisition, Mary
soon tired of the jewelry. She began to compare herself with
the wealthy young women of her acquaintance who sported
diamond bracelets and who were far "more richly dressed"
than she. "At first this made her envious; but . . . she was both
good and sensible. . . . gradually she began to see that, as she
could not have all she wished, it was better to put a limit to
her desires at once." She came to realize that "It isn't what we
wear that makes us happy; it is the contented spirit within."
Guided by this new insight, Mary gave her earrings back to
her father. She told him, "I find now . . . that I was unhappy,
not because I had no diamonds, but because I was daily
breaking the tenth commandment, and guilty of covetousness. . . . So, if you please, I'll do without them, and be content with old ones, which are more appropriate to your means,
dear papa." At this, Mary's parents wept with joy, happy that
their child had gained such wisdom so early in life.[1]

Mary had learned a crucial lesson, one widely taught in
nineteenth-century America: Envy is the enemy of contentment and must be conquered. She had learned that there were
some items, like diamond earrings, which were inappropriate
for people of modest incomes. Men and women of moderate

means should not expect to own the same things as wealthy folks did and should conquer their desires for such luxuries. Rather than act on their envy and struggle to change their condition, they must learn to be contented with their divinely appointed lot in life, no matter its limitations. To envy the rich and to emulate them was to rebel against God's wisdom and to commit a grave sin.

A quarter century later, this evaluation of envy and emulation had been supplanted by a radically different understanding of the emotion. A 1923 editorial in the *Ladies' Home Journal* captured the new attitude. The magazine congratulated American women for dressing well. It offered particular praise to those women of humble origins who still managed to attire themselves with style and flair: "whatever their background, they seem all to be inspired with what we are told is a typical and somewhat standardized American desire to 'look like a million dollars.' " The magazine queried, "Is it all a wicked scramble to look rich? Is it an immoral stampede to find and worship the false gods of fashion?" The editorial writer thought not. Instead, he concluded, the desire to appear as well dressed as the rich was a sign of "innocent vanity—wholesome ambition to look one's best, to achieve beauty and distinction, to assert good taste and cultivated selection in clothes." The editorialist celebrated the fact that "shopgirls in Salt Lake City" were more fashionably dressed than "some duchesses in London." Rejecting the idea that individuals had to dress in a manner that reflected their economic position, the *Journal* encouraged women in their desire "to look like a million dollars," regardless of their income.[2] Stylishly attired women of moderate means no longer ran the risk of being condemned for their envy and emulation; instead, they were congratulated for their judgment and taste. Their clothes, modeled after those of the upper classes, were no longer a sign of dishonor and moral transgression but were lauded as visible symbols of their aspirations. Envy, which thirty years earlier had been considered a grave sin, was now regarded as a beneficial force for social progress and individual advancement.

This book traces how envy came to be so radically redefined and what this change meant to middle-class Americans.[3] It examines the process by which it became acceptable for middle-class men, women, and children to envy and pursue the possessions of the rich. This transformation in envy's meaning and legitimacy was significant because it was part of an emerging emotional and behavioral style that supported the expansion of the consumer economy. America could sustain a full-fledged consumer economy only after men and women had overcome their religious reservations about materialism and had developed an emotional style that emphasized the value of pleasure, indulgence, and desire and downplayed the importance of restraint and delayed gratification.

This emotional and behavioral model is widely evident today.

Modern Americans take for granted that all can legitimately pursue their consumer desires, that they need not repress their envy, but can instead gain satisfaction by acting on it. They unquestioningly accept the notion that ownership of particular luxury goods like diamond earrings is not the exclusive right of the upper classes. While this book focuses on how it became acceptable for middle-class white consumers to envy and emulate, the same transformations would also affect expectations about working-class and African American consumer behavior. Gradually, men and women of all ethnic and racial groups and all economic levels, with the exception of the very poor, have been urged to see themselves as full-fledged consumers with legitimate desires.[4]

This book focuses on the years between 1890 and 1930 because it was during that period that the modern understanding of envy emerged. The social and economic backdrop for this development was the expansion of the consumer economy. Department stores, mail-order catalogs, mass-circulation magazines, movies, and advertising developed and offered new provocations for envy. People could see with unprecedented color and clarity the desirable goods that they could not always afford. The consumer economy, however, also provided new ways for Americans to express, and sometimes resolve, their envy. The mass production of imitation luxury goods allowed the middle and working classes to emulate the upper-class styles they admired. While people have experienced envy throughout history, the expansion of the consumer economy multiplied the occasions for the emotion and offered new ways to assuage it.

In the late nineteenth and early twentieth centuries, Americans who found their appetites for luxuries whetted, and who tried to emulate the wealthy, encountered strong opposition. Until the 1910s, clergymen, magazine writers, and social reformers attempted to control envy and emulation in order to preserve a moral economy and a conservative, hierarchical social order. They praised the virtue of contentment, which they considered to be envy's opposite, and counseled the bourgeoisie to be contented with their circumstances instead of yearning for their neighbors' possessions and privileges. Magazines, newspapers, fiction, and sermons repeated this theme again and again. As essayist Agnes Repplier recalled in 1923, "The virtue most deeply inculcated in our nurseries was content."[5] Moralists told the middle class that they should forgo the glittering bounty that stores and catalogs so temptingly displayed. They warned of the moral perils of materialism and urged their readers and listeners to keep their gazes focused on heavenly prizes instead.

In the second decade of the twentieth century, a far-flung group of advertisers, economists, sociologists, journalists, and consumers spread a new view of envy. They repudiated the doctrine of contentment and rejected the notion that there were divinely ordained limits on what members of each social class should possess. They instead argued that people should act on their envy and fulfill their desires. By 1926, as one essayist noted with evident dismay, the tenth commandment had been completely redefined. The new version of the commandment was: "Thou shalt not be outdone by thy neighbor's house, thou shalt not be outdone by thy neighbor's wife, nor his manservant, nor his car, nor anything—irrespective of its price or thine own ability—anything that is thy neighbor's."[6] While the editorialist lamented this change, most Americans considered it in a more benign light. During the 1910s and 1920s, the phrase "keeping up with the Joneses" came into popular use. Devoid of moral opprobrium, the phrase implied that envy and emulation were normal and widespread social instincts rather than sinful and dangerous passions.[7]

The belief that envy was an acceptable emotion to act on took root in the 1910s and 1920s for a number of reasons. First, the growing abundance of goods fundamentally changed the way Americans thought about the emotion. When there was only a limited supply of goods, one person's gain was another person's loss. In such a situation, envy could lead to resentment and disorder, for it might cause people to struggle over a scarce supply of goods. The result would be social conflict, hostility, and strife.[8] At the turn of the century, however, such conditions of scarcity were disappearing. As they strolled through department stores or paged through catalogs, bourgeois Americans saw vivid proof that the limited goods economy was quickly becoming a thing of the past. All around them they observed a proliferation of items in a range of prices. There were the expensive and sometimes rare ornaments of the rich, but there were also less expensive, mass-produced goods, which, while not always identical to the possessions of the wealthiest classes, were often credible reproductions of them. Newspaper editor William Allen White described this new age of plenty in his memoirs:

Mass production was accumulating and distributing wealth by some inner automatic process quite beyond government and law, as though the mass of machinery on this continent was one vast machine which was spewing out of its hopper a glittering shower of goods, chattels, and material hereditary appurtenances which were being carried by tubes and wires and shafts and funnels and trolleys to all parts of the earth, to all estates and conditions of men; distributing it by some prescience accurately, if not quite justly, to the homes of the multitude.[9]

With such plenty available to so many, commentators of the 1910s and 1920s expressed less concern about envy, for there seemed to be enough of the world's riches to go around. No longer did envy inevitably lead to hostility and strife; instead, in a world filled with mass-produced goods, it was at the very least a harmless emotion and some believed even a beneficial one.[10] In fact, many commentators concluded that when men and women acted on their envy of the wealthy and emulated upper-class ways of life, they brought about social progress rather than social destruction. When they made luxury purchases, they raised their standard of living and spurred economic growth. In many minds, these benefits seemed to outweigh the social and moral dangers of envy.

In addition to being swayed by the new abundance they daily saw around them, advertisers, journalists, social scientists, and consumers of the 1910s and 1920s were influenced by Darwinian theory, which seemed to endorse movement, change, and competition, as well as by new psychological theories of the self which maintained that certain human emotions and instincts— like envy and competitiveness—were natural and sometimes ungovernable. The emerging field of sociology also offered new perspectives on the way larger social and economic environments shaped human interactions and personality development. These novel and generally nonreligious interpretations of human behavior and social life were joined by a growing secularism in American society, particularly in the wake of World War I.[11] Together these intellectual currents undermined the belief that God had planned the social world, had carefully chosen the place and role of each individual, and would reward those who were humbly placed in this life with riches in heaven. As a columnist in the *Saturday Evening Post* wrote in 1925, "It may also be that the most momentous economic fact in the history of mankind was the decline of religious faith in the last century—faith looking to all rewards and amends hereafter. Naturally, as this faith was lost, people more and more would demand their compensations here, upon this earth." The promise of heavenly riches was losing power as a balm for the envious.[12]

As a result, a secularized vision of the marketplace emerged during the 1910s and 1920s.[13] Commentators repudiated the idea that there were divinely ordained limits on what each class should consume and instead encouraged all to pursue what they desired. Religion no longer dictated marketplace behavior, and envy and emulation were no longer sins. This vision continues to influence consumer behavior today: Modern Americans receive little criticism when they express their envy and strive to possess the luxuries of the rich. Some commentators even maintain that envy and invidious comparisons are driving forces of economic activity and middle-class social life, suppositions that would have appalled nineteenth-century social observers.[14]

In addition to describing and explaining this key shift in the meaning of envy, this book illustrates the fundamental link between the history of the emotions and the history of social, economic, and cultural life. Historians have often resisted studying the emotions, believing them to be the ephemera of history, too personal and private and bearing little relation to larger social developments. It was, however, the conditions of American public life which provoked envy, and it was in turn this envy, and the emulation it inspired, which supported the expansion of the consumer economy.

By probing the emotional experiences of Americans, much can be learned about the social conditions of turn-of-the-century America. It is, after all, the recognition of inequality that produces envy.[15] Perhaps in democratic societies that celebrate the idea of equality, citizens are more conscious of inequities and more envious than elsewhere. Certainly in the nineteenth century the American bourgeoisie were acutely aware of the material differences that separated them from the upper classes, and these differences rankled. At the same time, they were also aware of the material chasm between their own standard of living and that of the working classes, and they jealously guarded the privileges and possessions that distinguished them from those lower down. A democratic culture had conditioned Americans to expect equality. A liberal social order had spread the belief that, through struggle and competition, anyone could get what he or she longed for. The distance between Americans' expectations and their actual social and material circumstances produced envy. Envy was a response to the unrealized promise of equality; the emulation it inspired was an imperfect attempt to fulfill that promise.

The outcry over envy also illustrates the contested nature of liberal capitalist values. While many have assumed that the tenets of liberalism had become a staple of American cultural and social life by the late nineteenth century, the widespread condemnation of envy, emulation, and the desire for advancement offers powerful evidence to the contrary. Not all in American society welcomed striving and struggle. As late as the first decade of the twentieth century, many continued to believe that individuals should know their place and should not attempt to leave it.

The history of private emotions illuminates and intersects with public realities in other ways as well. Envy often spurred spending, and such spending supported the expansion of modern consumerism.[16]

In exploring the link between envy and spending, this study bridges the scholarship on the history of the emotions and the history of consumerism. There have been many rich examinations of how particular consumer institutions have developed and how various groups and individuals acted within or responded to these institutions.[17] Little historical research, however, has been done to uncover the connection between changing emotional norms and the growth of the consumer economy.[18] While the expansion of the consumer economy depended on the creation of department stores like Macys, Wanamaker, Bonwit Teller, and Marshall Fields, catalog houses like Sears and Montgomery Ward, and advertising firms like the J. Walter Thompson Advertising Company, it also depended on a transformation in attitudes and emotional codes. America's development into a nation of consumers was not possible until the longings of middle-class people for the luxuries of life were recognized as legitimate and encouraged.

As Americans redefined envy and devised new rules about how to express it, they also revised their understanding of what it meant to be contented, and this new meaning supported the emerging consumer ethic as well. In 1909, a commentator in *Harper's Bazaar* said of the traditional meaning of contentment, "To be contented with what you have, translated, usually means to be contented with what you have not."[19] By the late 1910s and 1920s, contentment meant almost the exact opposite: To be contented or satisfied meant to have exactly what you wanted, to lack nothing, and to envy no one. Accordingly, Americans began to seek contentment not by conquering their envy and accepting their deprivations but by pursuing all that they lacked and longed for.

The process by which it became legitimate for members of the middle class to act on their envy and to consume as the upper classes did was halting and uneven. Different groups within the middle class faced varying degrees of criticism in response to their envy. Today men and women of all ages and from all regions are recognized as potential consumers with acquisitive tendencies, but this was not the case in 1890.

At the turn of the last century, bourgeois women found that clergymen, editors, and moralistic writers considered their envy to be far more reprehensible than the envy of men. Women were commonly idealized as pure creatures who should have little involvement in the commercial world. Their desire for material goods and social prestige seemed out of keeping with their image of innocence and natural virtue. Women who acted on their envy and attempted to raise their status were roundly condemned. For example, in 1891, Edward Bok, editor of the *Ladies' Home Journal*, counseled envious women: "If you do not possess all the things you would like to have, it is very poor policy to idly wish for them." Bok claimed that the woman who longed for things she could not own harmed herself because such longings made her "dissatisfied with herself, unpleasant to her friends, and . . . old before her time." Bok had even harsher words for those women who dared to act on their envy and who emulated upper-class styles. "I can conceive nothing so well fitted to the term *disagreeable* as a woman who pretends to be what she is not, to clothe and carry herself in a manner unbecoming to her circumstances, and in other ways spoiling herself for her family and friends by being a sham."[20] Turn-of-the-century moralists like Bok were convinced that if a woman succumbed to her envy, she would soon engage in other types of immoral behavior that might threaten family peace and welfare and endanger female purity. Such moralism attempted to limit women's market participation and circumscribe what they could legitimately buy. A new vision of women as creatures with at least some legitimate economic instincts and competitive tendencies began to gain power in the 1910s and 1920s. Many commentators came to regard women's envy as a natural part of femininity and considered their emulative purchases to be a harmless way to resolve material inequalities.

Middle-class men encountered a different set of expectations and emotional prescriptions. Bourgeois men, long perceived as naturally ambitious and competitive, found it somewhat easier to express their envy and generally faced less censure when they did so. Nevertheless, they had to learn the socially sanctioned modes of emotional expression. In the context of the burgeoning corporate economy, the amount of envy and individualism that men should display was hotly debated. How much initiative and competitiveness should men show? When did envy hurt one's job performance? By the 1910s and 1920s, consensus seemed to form around the notion that envy in the workplace might be counterproductive, interfering with the smooth operations of a coordinated team effort. As one executive noted, rather than being a "sour-face, shriveled-up, envious and jealous pull-back," the ideal worker should pull "together with . . . [his] fellow-creatures."[21] Yet despite restrictions on emotional expression in the workplace, men found much encouragement for their envy outside of it. They were encouraged by ads, business writers, and their peers to act on their envy and display their ambitions by purchasing prestige goods. By acquiring and displaying well-cut suits and fine cars, bourgeois men could engage in subtle competition and one-upmanship with coworkers. Through such actions men gradually redefined success. Increasingly, the successful and enviable man was defined as much by the things he owned as by the position he held.

Other factors besides gender influenced emotional prescriptions. Moralists and reformers of the late nineteenth century believed that individuals' desires should be appropriate to their geographic location. Accordingly, men and women who lived on farms were expected to remain free of desire for the luxuries of city life and to protect themselves from the contaminating influences of urban commercial culture. Despite these expectations, farm youth often found themselves longing for the fine clothing and glamorous entertainments that seemed to abound in cities. President Theodore Roosevelt noted in 1908, "There is too much belief among all our people that the prizes of life lie away from the farm."[22] The idea that urban life was superior to farming was first regarded as heresy in a nation long wedded to a powerful agrarian mythology. Consequently, those farm people who wanted urban amenities were criticized for betraying national ideals. Eventually, however, country people found their desires for urban standards of living accepted and encouraged. In the 1910s and 1920s, reformers concerned with the conditions of farm youth came to believe that they must introduce urban styles and standards of living to rural districts if they ever hoped to assuage the widespread envy and discontent and stem the rural migration. These reformers welcomed rural men and women into the fold of consumers and encouraged them to indulge their desires and consume as urban people did.

Americans coming of age in the late nineteenth and early twentieth centuries were maturing in the midst of this cultural flux. They heard competing messages about how they should behave. Educators and moralists attempted to restrain their envy and limit their involvement in the marketplace, while parents, peers, and merchants often encouraged their desires. Drawn more to spending than self restraint, American children grew into adults who held a strong faith in the power of material goods to transform social identities and who were thoroughly schooled in the emotional style of modern consumer behavior. They believed that longings should be fulfilled and that envy and competitiveness were emotions easily resolved through purchases. Their children and grandchildren continue to follow the same emotional code today. When they envy the clothes, houses, and cars of the upper classes, they no longer worry that their emotions may represent moral transgression. Instead, they feel entitled to pursue these luxuries of life for themselves.

1. City Women and the Quest for Status

In 1900, a *Ladies' Home Journal* columnist inquired, "How much time do we give to studying our fashionable neighbor's hat, or to making cheap, sleazy imitations of her Doucet confections?" Convinced that her readers undoubtedly devoted too much time to such activities, she questioned further, "How much of that discontent . . . found in our faces has grown out of years of craving for more costly clothes than we can afford?"[1]

The columnist had put her finger on a central and, to some, a troubling reality of middle-class urban social life. Bourgeois women often seemed to be beset by envy. Living in America's expanding cities, where the pace of social life seemed to be ever accelerating, many women felt themselves to be engaged in a race for status. They longed for the prestige and belongings of wealthier women and frequently tried to imitate upper-class styles of dress and decor. Through emulation they hoped to assuage their envy of more affluent women and to distinguish themselves from those lower down on the social ladder.

Women in the late nineteenth and early twentieth centuries received condemnation for their envy and emulation, but their daughters and granddaughters in the 1910s and 1920s received encouragement and enjoyed praise for such behavior. That transition, from a cultural climate which made women feel ashamed of their envy to a culture which encouraged the emotion, represented a key shift in the American emotional style. It was the rise of this more liberal attitude toward pleasure and indulgence which helped to sustain the expansion of consumer society in the twentieth century.

Consumerism played a central role in bourgeois women's quest for higher status at the turn of the century. While their class position generally depended on some factors outside of their control—such as their husbands' or fathers' occupations—consumer spending was one very visible marker of social status which women themselves could control.[2] Bourgeois women were acutely aware of the social significance of possessions and often were convinced that they might elevate their status, and that of their household, by duplicating the spending habits of the wealthy women they envied.

Women living at the turn of the century found that they could learn far more easily and quickly about the fashions and fads of the elites than earlier generations of aspiring women. While middle-class Americans had long been avid consumers, enviously aware of upper-class styles, the expansion of the consumer economy between 1890 and 1930 heightened their familiarity with elite styles and also heightened their desires, thus multiplying the occasions for envy.

For example, the growth of urban department stores allowed middling folk to have new knowledge of the comforts of the wealthy. As Daniel Boorstin has pointed out, before the emergence of these stores, "common citizens might spend their lives without ever seeing a wide array of the fancy goods that they could not afford." When department stores opened their doors during the late nineteenth century, members of all classes suddenly could see luxury items that previously had been the exclusive domain of the wealthy. This greater visibility of alluring, often expensive, consumer goods increased opportunities for envy. Michael Schudson has remarked that department stores did not democratize luxury so much as they democratized envy.[3]

As the possessions of the wealthy become more publically known, the new consumer culture made them more central as standards of taste as well. Across the nation, women in cities and towns and on farms paged through issues of mass-circulation magazines like the *Ladies' Home Journal, Woman's Home Companion*, and the *American Magazine*, studying their fashion sections, home decor features, and advertisements. As movie theaters became widespread in the early twentieth century, women from all across the country were entranced by the same film stars and glamorous images projected on the silver screen. These diverse media instructed women from Montana to Massachusetts about what was fashionable and current. This widely disseminated consumer culture standardized tastes: It led women separated by vast geographical distances to measure themselves and their possessions against the same ideals, and it prompted them to long for similar goods. In the midst of the emerging commercial culture, middle-class women in metropolis, hamlet, and on the open range were united in their consumer desire and envy.

Many urban women sought to assuage their envy through emulation. This was an important strategy for women who wanted symbols of an elevated social status but who could not afford the actual goods that the upper classes possessed. Women sometimes tried to create imitation goods by hand and sometimes purchased them. Those women who tried to replicate the possessions of the wealthy with their own handiwork might make their own rugs, tablecloths, and curtains in an effort to create a home that resembled those of the wealthy. They might sew dresses modeled after gowns worn by affluent women. After 1863, women could more easily create by hand the garments that they envied, for it was in that year that the Butterick family introduced clothing patterns, affordably priced for households of moderate means. Inexpensive magazines, such as the *Delineator*, *Harper's Bazaar*, and the *Designer*, also began to carry patterns and became popular in the last decades of the nineteenth century and the first years of the twentieth. The widespread availability of patterns meant that a greater number of Americans could keep abreast of changing styles and more easily attire themselves after the manner of the rich (Figure 1).[4]

As a result of mass production, machine-made imitations also became increasingly accessible. Some scholars have maintained that the technologies of mass production which allowed consumers to emulate upper-class styles did not develop accidentally, but instead were a response to women's envy and aspirations.[5] Because industry was responding to shoppers' demands for cheaper versions of luxury goods, women could buy imitation silk clothing instead of real silk, machine-made laces that were reproductions of handmade lace, rhinestones marketed as substitutes for diamonds, machine-made carpets designed to resemble more costly hand-loomed rugs, and replicas of silver vases rendered in a cheaper metal.

Another aid to the envious was the rise of chain stores that distributed mass-produced goods and provided women across the country with access to identical garments and home furnishings. In 1886 there were only two chains with five stores between them. By 1912, this number had climbed to 177 chains, with 2,235 stores, and by 1929, there were around 1,500 chains controlling 70,000 stores. In the 1920s, the J. Walter Thompson Advertising Agency reported that twenty department chain stores, with 739 outlets, were

Figure 1. A 1924 ad for Butterick patterns promised women that they could sew garments which would be the equal of Paris high fashions. Used with permission of the Butterick Archives, McCall Pattern Company.

doing a combined business of $768 million.[6] The expansion of the consumer society thus not only increased the provocations for envy but also offered new ways to assuage the emotion.

The City Home: The Crucible of Envy

In 1891, Helen Jay, writing in the *Ladies' Home Journal*, recalled the envy and anxiety she sometimes felt as she compared her possessions with those of other women. "I did not like to invite to my plain house the friend who had married a merchant prince, because I feared she would miss the luxuries of her costly environment. I had no Persian rugs, no Satsuma teacups, no Oriental hangings to show her, and the fact both distressed and mortified me." As Jay made clear, there was much for women to envy in the material world of turn-of-the-century America. It would be impossible to catalog all of the objects that excited their envy. Nevertheless, there were particular types of goods which middle-class women seemed to particularly covet and to which they gravitated in their quest for higher status.[7]

Many women expressed envy when they saw the homes of richer women. A well-furnished house reflected the homemaker's taste and refinement, while a shabbily decorated home implied some fault in its caretaker. As Thorstein Veblen observed, the home was a means of displaying "vicariously" the male breadwinner's pecuniary power. Having a sparsely or unstylishly furnished home reflected poorly not only on the woman of the house but on her husband and on their social position as well. Because the appearance of their homes helped to shape their social identities, middle-class women often compared their own houses and furnishings with those of others. In the course of visiting friends' houses, hotels, or estate sales of the wealthy, middle-class women acquired an education in interior decoration. They kept abreast of national decorating trends by perusing advertisements and studying pictures that magazines like the *Ladies' Home Journal* supplied in features entitled "The Ideal Kitchen," "Inside of a Hundred Homes," or "Looking into Other Women's Homes."[8] Such contact with upper-class styles led many middle-class women to develop tastes beyond their means.

When women saw elegant decor in the homes of the affluent, and then considered their own homes and limited budgets, they were often beset by feelings of dissatisfaction, inferiority, and envy. One such moment was vividly described in a fictionalized episode published in 1890 in the Methodist Episcopal journal, the *Christian Advocate*:

Mrs. Canary had a nice little home of which she was very proud. Her parlor was neatly carpeted and curtained, and each article of furniture in it had a history. The wood was all black walnut, but the style of the several pieces was various. . . . All about the room were evidences of Mrs. Canary's industry, courage, thrift, and taste. No wonder she was a proud and happy woman. She deserved to be.

It was a sad evening for Mrs. Canary, when, upon invitation, she went to dine in the city with her old friend and schoolmate, Mrs. Camp. . . . Her house was furnished with such luxury and style as was quite new to Mrs. Canary. Everything that furniture and upholstery, guided by a cultivated and exact taste, could do to make rooms beautiful and attractive was done. . . .

. . . when she went back to her cozy little home, it seemed mean and cheap and almost contemptible. She was tempted to despise herself for having taken so much comfort in it. That rag carpet that had cost her so much time and labor before it went to the weavers, how coarse and ugly it was! How much nicer would be a lignum or even an oil-cloth. The odd pieces of furniture, how inelegant, and lacking in style. Her home-made adornments, how the beauty faded from them![9]

In measuring her house against larger social standards, Mrs. Canary suddenly realized its shortcomings. It was not equal to her friend's house because of its homemade and inherited furnishings, and it marked her as inadequate as well. The sting of having less was clearly painful. Helen Jay confided that she too had experienced anxiety and envy when she realized that her home marked her as inferior. "When calling on a friend I mentally compared her household with my own, and wondered how I could create, from my own limited resources, the things of beauty by which she was surrounded."[10]

Such comparisons were not merely the stuff of magazine articles. In 1885, Mara Millar, the young bride of an affluent Kansas judge, fell into the same trap of comparing her furniture with that of an acquaintance. After seeing her friend's belongings, she decided that she must go on a shopping spree. "Once I had seen a wedding present for one of my friends, a folding bed with a long mirror in its front. My soul would know no rest until I possessed one of my own." She found and purchased a similar "golden oak" bed. "Then it occurred to me that the new bed and the old furniture would laugh at each other." To prevent such a clash of styles, she had the junk man gather up her husband's heirloom furnishings, and she replaced them with newly purchased chairs and tables that matched the golden oak bed. To complete the effect she also purchased a "white velvet carpet strewn with huge pink and yellow roses and cream velvet curtains with gold fringe." When her husband came home to find the new furnishings, he was displeased and tried to find ways to limit her spending.[11]

While women like Mara longed to create a rich domestic environment throughout their houses, there were particular furnishings which they believed to be essential to a refined household. Many women coveted pianos and carpets, believing that these items would create the elegant atmosphere for which they yearned.

Pianos were perhaps the most crucial piece of furniture for aspiring families.[12] Faith in their refining and status-raising potential was remarkably widespread, as merchants and social scientists discovered. This faith was demonstrated in an oft-repeated anecdote that circulated in the advertising industry: A department store in New York City had a surplus of inexpensive pianos. The store launched an ad campaign in the newspapers but could generate little interest in the cut-rate instruments. It was only when the advertising manager revamped his campaign that he was able to sell the pianos. Rather than concentrating on the instruments themselves, his new campaign focused on the enviable social benefits that they could provide. The headline of his new ad was, "Make your daughter Mary a lady." According to one source, "The copy pointed out that music was the soul of culture and perhaps the finest of the social graces, that it was the duty of parents to provide their daughters with a musical education." So powerfully did this pitch appeal to consumers' aspirations that the pianos sold out within twenty-four hours. In a 1912 article in the journal *Advertising and Selling*, Edward Babcox reported that it had been the Wanamaker store in Philadelphia which was overstocked with pianos. After running the "Make your daughter Mary a Lady" ad, the store was able to sell its entire stock of 275 pianos for $240 apiece in just three days. Whether it took one day or three for the pianos to sell out, demand for pianos was high among envious consumers who hoped that with the instrument they might create a refined domestic space in their houses and foster in their children the talents and sensibilities necessary for social success.[13]

Pianos were both a signal of cultivation in the present and an investment in the future social status of one's children. Survey findings supported the idea that families from all classes viewed pianos as important symbols of status. In studies conducted between 1903 and 1905, interviewer Louise

Bolard More found that the "most common ambition" of mothers on the Lower East Side of New York was to own a piano. In a market study conducted by the J. Walter Thompson Agency, middle-class families who did not own a piano but who were considering buying one most often wanted a piano so that their children could learn to play. A secondary motive was the simple desire to have a piano in the house, presumably for purposes of display.

Pianos were most common among wealthy and middle-class families living in cities, yet families lower down the status ladder also possessed them in large numbers. According to the Thompson study, 81.0 percent of the very affluent and 72.7 percent of the middle class surveyed owned pianos, as compared with 52.9 percent of the lower middle class. At the turn of the century, the most prestigious and desirable type of piano to own was a grand piano, and not surprisingly, the largest number of grands were found in the homes of the urban upper class. Less affluent families and small-town or farm families were more likely to own square pianos or uprights. Upright pianos, designed for consumers with moderate incomes and introduced to America in the 1860s, were not as elegant or as expensive as grand pianos, yet they offered middle-class and working-class families a means of emulating the wealthy. Families who purchased uprights might feel that they had raised their social status and made an important investment in their children's futures.[14]

Harriet Lane Levy, the daughter of a prosperous San Francisco merchant, recalled the satisfaction that her family gained from the possession of a piano. They had been so proud of the instrument that they created a special room for it. "The music room," she remembered, was "redolent of gentility; indeed, it was something to say [to guests], 'You will find her in the music room.' " The piano itself, a Steinway square piano, was also a source of pride, because it set the Levys apart from their neighbors and friends. "Of all our friends, we alone possessed a piano that fitted into an architectural frame, and we waited for our friends' unfailing exclamations of surprised approval."[15] Many American families longed to appear refined and to gain the admiration of their friends. Aware of the status connotations of pianos, middle-class families eagerly pursued them—and the prestige that they promised.

Another furnishing that many bourgeois women believed would lend an air of elegance to their homes was a well-made and distinctive carpet. Like Mrs. Canary, who came to despise her homemade rag rug after visiting her friend's more elegant home, and Helen Jay, who was embarrassed because she owned no Persian carpets, middle-class women were aware that fine rugs eloquently communicated high social status.

At the turn of the century, children whose parents could not afford Brussels carpets were known to lie and claim that their families actually possessed them. Those households lucky enough to own them sometimes experienced what William A. White termed a "sinful pride" in them. In the early twentieth century, Oriental rugs gradually gained cachet and supplanted Brussels carpets as the floor covering of choice for aspiring families. Joseph Appel, the director of publicity for the Wanamaker Department Stores, described the typical female consumer's desires in 1911: "She wants a beautiful home, rich Oriental rugs, exquisite tapestries and curtains, good furniture." But not all could have what they desired. Only the most affluent families could easily afford imported carpets. In 1921, researchers for the Thompson agency discovered this as they interviewed rug dealers in major cities. Time and again, dealers noted that it was the wealthiest families who invested in Oriental rugs. They described their clients as "well-to-do people," a "very intelligent class of buyers" and "discriminating people." A St. Louis dealer broke the purchasers down into several categories, among them the "wealthy, educated class [who] buys very expensive Orientals including antiques, as objects of art because of their beauty." Another market for the rugs was the newly wealthy who "buy rugs because it's the thing to do,—to give them social prestige."

In addition to those who could actually purchase the rugs, there were many families that wanted Oriental carpets but could not afford them. One dealer reported that "everyone would like to own an Oriental rug if they could afford it," while another told researchers that "Oriental rugs are universally desired but can't be purchased by people with limited means."[16]

Middle-class women of limited means were acutely aware of what their homes were lacking. They followed closely the changing spending habits of elite women and these patterns informed their own tastes and expenditures. When bourgeois women purchased fine carpets, pianos, or beds, they displayed both their familiarity with the status connotations of home furnishings and their social aspirations. As they struggled to create a domestic environment similar to that of the elites, they were also struggling to create for themselves a more elevated social identity. Their envy and desire to emulate were powerful fuels for consumption, a point that becomes even more clear in the context of women's fashions.

Fashion

In 1912, columnist Juliet Virginia Strauss observed that "the oldest and plainest and 'sensiblest' of us" experienced "the quick envy of other women's clothes" and the "determination to have something as fine or as pretty or as stylish as her neighbors." She believed that the demand for particular fashions was based on emulation, noting, "It is a great business of imitation, this dress business."[17] The pressure to imitate high fashion was growing at century's turn because clothing was becoming an ever more important social marker in urban America. In the nation's swelling and increasingly anonymous cities, judgments about people's background, position, and prospects were gradually depending less on close acquaintance and more on appearances. As Thorstein Veblen noted in 1899, "the only practicable means of impressing one's pecuniary ability on these unsympathetic observers of one's everyday life is an unremitting demonstration of ability to pay."[18]

Clothing became only more important as a marker of status in the twentieth century, as Hortense Odlum, the first female president of Bonwit Teller, indicated in her autobiography. There she laid out her philosophy on clothing, declaring, "We live in a competitive world. . . . we have to accept it." To succeed in such an environment women needed to dress well because "in this age in which life moves at double-quick time, when we haven't the leisure to evaluate people slowly and carefully, when we meet hurriedly and make decisions quickly, first impressions are tremendously important. In a less accelerated day, we had perhaps a sounder basis for judging people. Meeting fewer people we knew more about their inheritances and their backgrounds." She contrasted that bygone era with her own life in a bustling city where "we are apt to be called upon to form opinions of a dozen or more persons of whom we know absolutely nothing but how they look and speak. It may be a false way to judge, but there it is."

In such an environment, where a fashionable appearance could do so much for one, the lack of stylish clothing was hard to bear. Odlum described how she had felt when she could not afford fine clothing and had to make do with cheaper attire. In the 1910s, as a young wife with little money, Odlum had purchased an inexpensive black chiffon dress, which she described as "shoddy" and "ugly." She wore the dress to a formal dinner and felt profoundly self-conscious and inferior. Odlum had to wear the black dress for many years, and she remembered what that "terrible dress did to my spirits every time I put it on." Eventually she was able to afford more fashionable clothes, and her new garments gave her great self-confidence. She explained the effect of good clothes on women's psyches: "The right clothes mean an added zip to life, a heightening of the woman's belief in herself, —youth and gaiety and happiness. When she knows she's well dressed she can be sure of herself, unselfconscious, friendly and at ease."[19]

Many women attached even greater social importance to good clothing. Fashionable attire did more than make women feel "at ease" and "friendly." It also gave them the opportunity to be on equal footing with the more afflu-ent when they ventured into public. In turn, when they were forced to wear unfashionable clothing in public settings they found themselves feeling at a social disadvantage. When well dressed, "I feel equal to meeting anyone," confided a twenty-eight-year-old women to psychologist G. Stanley Hall in 1905. A twenty-year-old woman agreed that when she wore good clothing, "I have a feeling of equality." Another twenty-year-old woman claimed that with the right clothing she "mingle[d] more freely with others," while a nineteen-year-old reported, "I feel able to meet any person" when well dressed. In a similar study, a twenty-year-old woman told psychologists Li-nus Kline and C. J. France that "if I could have a fine dress on [at a party] I should have a grand time, should feel like suggesting new games and in gen-eral taking the lead." On the other hand, "if I were obliged to wear an old dress to a party my whole evening's enjoyment would be spoiled." These young women articulated the prevalent belief that dressing as stylishly as the upper classes gave them social power and conferred on them a measure of social equality. They felt equal when they could dress as their neighbors and social betters did, and envious when they could not.[20]

In 1912, reformer Ida M. Tarbell summarized the attitudes of young women like these, noting that envy and a desire for social equality moti-vated many women when they were shopping for clothes. "It sounds fantas-tic to say that whole bodies of women place their chief social reliance on dress, but it is true. . . . If you look like the women of a set, you are as 'good' as they, is the democratic standard of many a young woman." Tarbell be-lieved that these attempts to gain equality through imitative dressing were misguided: "The folly of woman's dress . . . lies in the pitiful assumption that she can achieve her end by imitation, that she can be the thing she en-vies if she look like that thing."[21]

Despite such warnings, many envious women believed that they might gain equality with elite women through imitation. Emulation became a common tool for those trying to assuage their envy and gain social equality. A columnist in the *Ladies' Home Journal* described the emulative consumer practices of her day, observing, "I see feathers and laces and embroideries and garments rich or trying to seem so, worn by graceful young women who are in [narrow] circumstances." She believed such attire sprang from women's tendency "to envy the rich—to long for a taste of the refining and beautiful refreshment which we are inclined to think belong to the wealthy ones."[22]

When it came to clothing, many women went to great lengths to appear as the "wealthy ones" did. Virginia Durr and her mother felt it necessary to dress like upper-class women, and hired an affordably priced seamstress to create fashionable garments for them. They were not always convinced, however, that their seamstress's creations measured up to more expensive apparel. Durr, born in 1903, left her Birmingham, Alabama, home in her late teens to attend the National Cathedral School in Washington, D.C. There she met girls who were far wealthier than she. "All my friends in Birmingham and the girls at the Cathedral School were richer than I was. . . . I was always conscious of not having the money that other girls had." This fact was particularly evident to her when she compared her own dresses with those of the wealthier girls. "Their mothers would go to New York every fall to buy their clothes. I always had somebody come in for three dollars a day to make mine. Mother had good taste, but we were keeping up with the Joneses at great effort—trying to make a fifteen-dollar dress look like a hundred-dollar one."[23] It was difficult to cover up deep status and income differences with imitation goods, yet despite the shortcomings of their copies, families like the Durrs continued to emulate, believing it necessary to at least try to keep pace with those above them.

Women who could not hire seamstresses to make imitations of high fashion often turned to retail stores, which offered factory-made apparel. By the late nineteenth century, manufacturers had begun to aid the envious by copying expensive garments designed for elites and translating them into more affordable garments priced for women of moderate means.[24] Tarbell described this process as she traced the path of a style through the streets of New York and the city's status system:

The French or Viennese mode, started on upper Fifth Avenue, spreads to 23rd St., from 23rd St. to 14th St., from 14th St. to Grand and Canal. Each move sees it reproduced in material a little less elegant and durable, its colors a trifle vulgarized, its ornaments cheapened, its laces poorer. By the time it reaches Houston St. the $400

gown in brocaded velvet from the best looms in Europe has become a cotton velvet from Lawrence or Fall River, decorated with mercerized lace and glass ornaments from Rhode Island. . . . The very shop window where it is displayed is dressed and painted and lighted in imitation of the uptown shop. The same process goes on inland.[25]

These mass-produced and readily available "knock-offs" offered aspiring women a new way to satisfy their hunger for clothes of distinction.

Bourgeois women eagerly purchased these replicas, which were generally available at their local department stores. This is what Mara Millar did when she began to feel envious of the rich and famous women she observed. Millar was a lady commissioner to the Columbian Exposition of 1893, and in that capacity she came in contact with many celebrities. After meeting the Broadway star Lillian Russell, Millar longed to look like her. "When I first saw Lillian Russell," she recalled, "she was wearing a dark blue serge tailor-made [suit] with a pink linen shirtwaist and a high boned collar restricting her lovely throat. Her large black picture hat, loaded with flowers of all hues, filled me with covetousness." Millar realized that nothing that she possessed would allow her to dress like Russell, for she owned neither a tailor-made suit nor a hat. To remedy this problem, Millar had "a hurried consultation with Marshall Field's" and probably used their in-house tailoring and millinery services. The result, Millar reported, was that "I emerged three days later" with clothes "just like . . . Russell's. I felt and hoped that I looked like her."[26]

Many bourgeois women were attuned to the smallest details of high fashion, and they envied and emulated not just dress and hat styles but also the accessories of the wealthy and famous. At the turn of the century, factories began to mass-produce elite accessories, and women of all classes began to pursue and enjoy what had formerly been the luxuries of the rich. Silk stockings offer an example of a widely envied good that became accessible to women of virtually every income level as a result of mass production. Over the span of two decades, all classes of American women came to wear silk hosiery, once a symbol of privilege and luxury.

At the turn of the century, only the elite wore silk stockings, and most women made due with lisle or cotton hose. By the 1910s, however, middle-class women began to emulate the stocking styles of upper-class women. A *Journal* editorialist described the growing passion for silk among women of all classes. She had seen so many silk stockings "on exhibition on the legs of women climbing off and on the street cars. I have seen young women whose husbands were working on low salaries—arrayed in silk stockings and pumps." The editorialist was convinced that the popularity of silk stockings sprang from envy. "Now this was merely the effort to carry out somebody else's ideal. Some other woman, whom these girls envied or whose way of living embodied their ambition, wore silk stockings and pumps."

Although silk stockings may have started out as "somebody else's ideal," in the twentieth century they became an item to which middle-class and even some working-class women felt entitled. Those women who could afford real silk stockings purchased them; an even greater number of women contented themselves with artificial silk. Between 1914 and 1923 the consumption of silk and artificial silk stockings increased, and cotton hose gradually but decisively fell out of favor. During this span of nine years, silk hosiery production increased by nearly 27 percent and artificial silk hosiery production increased by 417 percent. By 1920, not only middle-class white women but also working-class white women and African American women came to see silk or pseudo-silk stockings as a necessity. Albert Atwood reported in the *Saturday Evening Post* that "in a canning factory in New York state last summer every girl wore silk stockings, though any sense of fitness and desire to get the most wear out of a garment would have abolished silk stockings from such a place." Many of the girls had forgone meals in order to afford the hosiery. Atwood reported that as a result of this widespread desire for silk only one-quarter of the cotton stockings sold in 1914 were being sold in 1920.[27]

To aspiring middle-class women, stockings, dresses, pianos, and carpets all seemed to be important status-marked possessions which, if purchased, would allow their owners to stand on equal footing with the upper classes. For this reason, many women acted on their envy and made emulative purchases. Yet the actual social effects of such imitative spending were at best ambiguous. Women felt more equal when they dressed and looked like the wealthy, as G. Stanley Hall's subjects testified. Yet feelings and symbols of equality were not the same as actual social and economic equality. Perhaps the most poignant proof that merely imitating the attire of the elites would not bring greater wealth and higher status was the image of working women, clad in silk hose, laboring at a cannery. Women, buying on the basis of envy and hoping for advancement, ended up with the stockings but not the status of the elites whom they longed to equal.

Figure 2. Phoenix Hosiery promoted a vision of material democracy in this 1922 ad. Used with permission of the Kayser-Roth Corporation.

Status Anxiety: The Threat from Below

There was other evidence that the democracy based on identical fashion and furnishings was incomplete. Mass production had made it possible for women with widely differing incomes to purchase similar rugs, pianos, dresses, stockings, and a host of other items. Yet not all welcomed this new availability of goods. Status-conscious women who worked to resemble social elites expressed their discomfort and resentment when women lower down in the class hierarchy imitated them. Members of the middle class not only imitated the styles favored by those above them on the social scale, but they also worked to differentiate themselves from the social classes below them. In turn, upper-class women worked to separate themselves from their bourgeois imitators. As mass-produced goods became more common and it became easier for all classes to possess what previously only the wealthy could afford, the need to distinguish oneself from the crowd became all the more important for those in the middle and upper echelons of society.

Dorothy Rodgers, wife of the Broadway composer Richard Rodgers, recalled her fears of being lost in the mass. In the 1920s, as an affluent unmarried woman in New York, she frequently attended dances. As she prepared for these events, she and her friends sometimes felt anxiety about their gowns. They had to avoid buying what they called a "Ford." This was a "dress so chic that it could easily turn up on at least two or three girls at the same party. Today such a thing would be highly unlikely, but then Paris was the center of the fashion world, and we all wore copies of French dresses—knock-offs that could be had in a wide price range." Like the car, a "Ford" dress carried connotations of mass production, relative cheapness, and lack of distinction—qualities which status-conscious women desperately wanted to avoid.[28]

Rodgers and her set were not alone in their fears. Across the country women expressed the same status anxieties. Sociologist Newell LeRoy Sims in his 1912 study of the social life of an Indiana town reported that the "critical" and "intellectual" women in the town expressed "a strong desire to be different from the common herd. While conforming to fashions in general they don't want to have, and do 'what's common.' Among women, especially, in respect to dress you hear them say: 'Oh, everybody wears that and I wouldn't have it for anything.' In this there seems to be a sense of superiority; a desire for distinction or for preservation from being lost in the mass."[29]

Advertisers and market researchers were also well aware of these status anxieties. The J. Walter Thompson agency documented this attitude as it conducted market research studies for the Kent-Costikyan rug company. The agency was exploring whether a market existed for a significantly cheaper Oriental rug that might be priced to compete with American-made carpets. Dealers who were interviewed worried that the rugs would be all too popular and would therefore threaten the prestige of Oriental carpets. A representative of the rug department at the Jordan Marsh store told interviewers that the introduction of a cheaper Oriental rug "would be a bad thing . . . because Orientals would lose their distinctiveness." A decorator concurred, noting that "the best trade would not want Orientals if they became too common."[30]

Consumers showed their anxieties about overly common styles even when they were making small and seeming inconsequential purchases. For instance, women preferred imported or very expensive domestic toiletries precisely because fewer people could purchase them. Officials at Chesebrough Pond's discovered this in 1923 when their sales began to slacken. Historian Kathy Peiss has described how Pond's, a popular cold cream for women since the early 1910s, began to be considered too common and cheap and therefore less desirable than higher-priced facial creams like those of Elizabeth Arden and Helena Rubinstein. Market researchers noted that the costliness of other creams was regarded as an indication of their social prestige, while the low price of Pond's creams and their "enormous popularity had brought them loss of caste; they lacked exclusiveness, social prestige." Investigators who worked undercover behind department store cosmetic counters reported that there was "a distinct feeling in the Fifth Avenue store that Pond's creams lacked prestige and 'smartness.' "

If the desire to separate oneself from the herd through consumer practices was evident in the decline of Pond's, the widely held need of consumers to align themselves with the upper classes was evident in its market resurgence. As a result of its dwindling cold cream sales, Pond's unveiled a new series of ads designed by the Thompson firm. The ads contained endorsements from women "of great wealth and social position," "society matron[s]," and women known for their "lineage and beauty." The positive consumer response to the campaign suggests that many shoppers were seeking prestige and social differentiation. In the wake of the new marketing, sales for one of the creams increased 45 percent over the previous year, and sales for the other cream increased 17 percent.

The Pond's campaign also illustrates the increasing importance that brand names came to play in the struggle for distinction. Bourgeois women believed that not just specific consumer goods but particular brands of goods were essential to social prestige. Cold cream might give consumers an enviable complexion, but some creams might make individuals feel more enviable than others. Just as merchants and advertisers had hoped, the connotations of the brands often eclipsed the nature of the goods themselves. For instance, while women undoubtedly purchased cold cream first and foremost for their skin care needs, those who purchased a bottle of cold cream from Helena Rubinstein or Elizabeth Arden might consider themselves to be in an altogether different category from women who merely possessed a bottle of Pond's.[31]

Middle-class and upper-class women used their knowledge of brand names as a means of navigating the status system. Across the country, women trying to fashion an elite image for themselves and their households concurred that certain brands were to be avoided because the lower classes purchased them. J. C. Penney's stores offer a case in point. In the eyes of many bourgeois and upper-class women, the chain sold goods they considered cheap and catered to a clientele they considered déclassé. These women told researchers that they disliked the Penney stores because too many women of lower status shopped there. Their perceptions were grounded in fact, for surveys indicated that while only 2 percent of the most affluent class shopped at Penney's, 30 percent of each of the lowest two classes studied shopped there. When asked why they did not shop at Penney's, consumers often reported that the goods available there were "below" their "prevailing standards." Other reasons consumers gave included their perception that the "range of selection was too narrow and too low in price" and their dislike of both the "style of Penney's goods" and the "appearance of the stores." All of these factors combined to make many consider Penney's a "cheap" store. Even those who shopped at the chain reported that they occasionally worried that the style and quality of goods was too low.

As shoppers discussed Penney stores with researchers, they provided evidence that there was a consensus among the nation's elites as to what was and was not acceptable and fashionable; all seemed to agree that Penney's goods lacked prestige and style. A shopper from Ashtabula, Ohio, believed that "Penney's hats and more expensive ready to wear [are] not good enough for most women" she knew. Another Ashtabula resident chimed in, "It's all this town can afford—a low class store," while a wealthy woman in Little

Falls, New York, was equally dismissive, noting that "Penney's is a popular store with the hands in father's mill."

Status-conscious consumers avoided Penney's not only because the lower classes shopped there but also because they wished to avoid overly common styles. Each Penney store might stock dozens of the same garment, and when a good became too common, its social value fell. Many chain stores encountered resistance precisely because they offered standardized and therefore undistinctive goods. "Most chain stores are considered cheap," said a Rome, New York, resident, while another reported, "Chain stores are so standardized—styles copied, can get no originality." Some women objected to Penney's and other chains because "everyone has seen the clothes if you buy here" and presumably everyone could guess both the brand and price of specific pieces of apparel. In order to escape the overly common styles sold at area chains, many women avoided Penney's and shopped at stores some distance from their homes. "Goes out of town for range of selection and style" was a common report of investigators.[32]

There was and is an inherent tension in the American status system. Middle-class people often wanted to look like those above them, yet those higher up did not want to look like the bourgeoisie and so constantly sought out new styles. The tension became acute with the increased availability of mass-produced imitation goods. No longer could possessions be used as clear signals of social position. By providing affordable dresses, hats, carpets, and pianos that imitated elite styles, the new system of production threatened the exclusivity of the upper-class lifestyle.[33]

This new situation, which allowed the middle and working classes to act on their envy and to possess garments and furniture that resembled those of the upper classes, troubled many elite Americans. Not only did they try to differentiate themselves from those below through careful consumer spending; they often tried to discourage envious bourgeois and working-class consumers from making emulative purchases.

Controlling Envy: Contentment, Sincerity, and Purity

Between 1890 and 1910, essayists, clergymen, and editorial writers vehemently attacked urban women's envy and emulative spending habits. They believed that covetousness was a grave sin that could lead women and their families down the road to ruin. They repeated traditional Judeo-Christian condemnations of the emotion. They also offered strenuous opposition to the expanding consumer economy, believing that it fostered immorality. Some historians have slighted this opposition, maintaining that American moralists and religious leaders generally accepted the new consumer ethic.[34] The countless condemnations of envy offer compelling evidence that there was strong and sustained resistance to the expanding consumer economy and deep concerns about its moral implications.

Most of the writers who condemned envy and consumerism had been born before the Civil War. They had grown up before the advent of department stores, mail-order catalogs, and mass-produced goods. Accustomed to a somewhat simpler material life, these writers watched with alarm as the nation and its mores were being transformed. Accustomed also to a material divide that separated and clearly distinguished one social level from another, these moralists lamented the accessibility of dresses, lamps, sofas, and carpets that enabled envious men and women to hide their actual economic circumstances and that threatened to obliterate class and status differences.

This generation of moralistic writers lauded emotions and virtues that would discourage envy. One key virtue that they ceaselessly extolled was contentment, which, they maintained, was the opposite of and the antidote to envy. For centuries, the idea of contentment had been a part of Christian theologians' discussions of inequality, and it was central to their efforts to mollify the dissatisfied. Moralists of the nineteenth century frequently referred specifically to Saint Paul, who instructed men and women that whatever they had, whatever their condition, "therewith to be content."[35]

The doctrine of contentment that clergymen, editors, and writers preached was predicated on the hoary idea that hierarchy was natural. The centerpiece of this tradition was the concept of the Great Chain of Being, which held that God had made all creatures and had designed for each a special niche in his hierarchy which they should happily accept. This divinely ordained system existed not merely in the natural world but in the social world as well. Social conditions were God's will; indeed, many moralists referred to social position as the "dispensation" or "appointment" of Providence.

Often moralists relied on natural imagery to support their claims that God had willed the order—and the inequalities—of the social world, pointing out how every creature had been expressly shaped for a particular duty and destiny. Bees, birds, roses, and trees were not all equally grand, but each had a valuable role to fill. Elzira A. Whittier, writing for the *Christian Advocate* in 1895, offered a poetic explanation of this philosophy as she told the

story of a humble violet growing beside a "haughty oak." The oak wondered
how the flower could be content with its lot when it continuously saw the
oak's grandeur. The flower explained:

We each have our place on earth to fill,
And I am sweetly content
To waft my fragrance o'er land and sea,
For I'm on that mission sent.[36]

Like the violet, individuals should realize that everyone had a divinely appointed role to fill and should accept its privileges, obligations, and shortcomings with grace and serenity. Envious men and women who longed to
leave their current position and raise themselves socially should recognize
that this was contravening God's plan and his wisdom. They should strive to
live contentedly in the position God had chosen for them rather than struggling against it and disrupting the order of the world.

Many of those who expounded on the virtues of contentment addressed
women specifically. Nineteenth-century gender ideals held that women
should be serene, desireless, moral creatures who obeyed God's will. Nevertheless, it was clear that women often failed to live up to this ideal and
that they were in fact filled with strong desires and dissatisfactions. To
remedy this, moralistic writers tried to teach women how to cultivate contentment within themselves. First, envious bourgeois women should develop an outlook that would allow them to accept their deprivations and
suppress their envy. As Edward Bok, the conservative editor of the *Ladies'
Home Journal*, explained in 1891, "If you do not possess all the things you
would like to have, it is very poor policy to idly wish for them. A woman is
happy just in proportion as she is content. . . . Contentment is a wonderful
thing to cultivate."[37]

A more concrete model of contentment was provided in the story of
Mrs. Canary, the woman who had been envious of her friend's house. She
was ultimately able to find happiness with what she had and resist emulation. The narrator reported that Mrs. Canary struggled to suppress her envy:
"She fought out her battle and conquered. She accepted with cheerfulness
the allotments of Providence to her, and settled down into a deeper content
than she had ever known before." The key to this happiness, Mrs. Canary
discovered, was recognizing class boundaries and not overstepping them.
She must stay in her own circle: "She insisted that she was happier in her as-
sociations with friends of like financial position with her own than with

those whose resources were very much larger than hers or very much less. Her standards in these must be her own, and for her own peace she must adhere to them."[38] The essay idealized a segregated social world, where all knew their places, and where interactions between classes were limited. In such a world, there would be stability, harmony, and happiness for all.

Those who espoused the doctrine of contentment tried to shape their words and lessons to resonate with the concerns of middle-class women. Moralists often relied on the idea of heavenly rewards. If the envious believed that a more just distribution of goods awaited them in heaven, their envy would be neutralized and they would be contented with their earthly deprivations. To make these celestial rewards worth waiting for, writers frequently described them in intriguingly material terms, portraying heaven as a home filled with desirable knick-knacks and furnishings. Ann Douglas, in *The Feminization of American Culture*, discussed similar mid-nineteenth-century celestial imagery, terming it the "domesticization of death."[39] By the late nineteenth century, however, heaven was not merely a domestic environment; it was a consumer environment. Moralists told women that a luxurious, well-furnished house in heaven would compensate for the humble homes that many occupied on earth. The *Christian Advocate* offered such imagery as it told of a woman walking on Fifth Avenue who proclaimed to her friend:

I will show you the house I am building sometime. It has a large picture gallery hung with so many beautiful pictures. There is a music room in it, with an organ and a piano. . . . There is in it a library. In the historical alcove are all the histories I have ever read. In the astronomical alcove is stored all I know about the stars. . . . There is a chapel, too, in my house. . . . In that chapel I keep all the sermons I have ever heard, all the religious truths I have garnered, all the Bibles I have owned, some of them worn with long use and blotted with tears. I have lace curtains at my windows and the patterns in them are the poetical fancies that have come to me, the beautiful thoughts I have read in literature.

The woman confided that she would be able to take the house with her to heaven because "it is builded on everlasting foundations." It existed not on earth but in the woman's heart and soul. The narrator noted that while the woman possessed only modest means, "she has found the secret of tranquility and content," presumably for all eternity.[40]

In a similar vein Margaret Bottome, a *Ladies' Home Journal* columnist, proclaimed that those in "humble, mean environments" should imagine "the beauty of their surroundings" in heaven: "Daughters, will you not expect that God will show you, so to speak, one beautiful room after another? . . . If the different experiences of God are the different rooms, some are in very small houses living in only a few rooms, while others have such large and wonderfully furnished rooms. Let us be rich!"[41] Women had no cause for envy, for the very things they coveted in life would be theirs, at least metaphorically, in the hereafter. To combat the lure of worldly goods that might divert Christian women away from their faith, those who wrote of heaven tried to make it compelling to the imaginations of readers living in an expanding consumer society. Possibly Christianity's traditionally immaterial rewards could only compete with material life if they were translated into glittering visual images.

Accompanying the call for contentment and the promise of rewards in the hereafter were pleas for sincerity in self-presentation. If a woman genuinely tried to cultivate a contented spirit, she would be happy with her station in life and not try to hide her true condition or rise above it. She would not attempt to dress "up" herself or her home in order to pass for a member of a higher class. Instead, she would embrace her status and all of the material symbols that traditionally accompanied it.[42]

Editorialists and ministers believed that women who attired themselves with imitations of high fashion, paste jewelry, and cheap laces and who decorated their homes with fake mahogany and mock velvet were insincere dissemblers. Recognizing that it was tempting and increasingly easy for urban women to try and pass themselves off as members of a higher class, these critics urged women to make their apparel and their homes "sincere" and reflective of their true station in life. Edward Bok intoned, "I can conceive nothing so well fitted to the term *disagreeable* as a woman who pretends to be what she is not, to clothe and carry herself in a manner unbecoming to her circumstances, and in other ways spoiling herself for her family and friends by being a sham." Besides being morally dishonorable, such imitative dressing was useless. "No woman ever successfully pretended to be what she is not. Nature is always more true than artifice, and *will* show herself. The woman who dresses above her station always shows her level in her actions, to say nothing of her taste in dressing." Instead of engaging in such "humbug" and deception, women should proudly embrace who they actually were. "You have been placed in a certain position in life. . . . Instead of trying to cover your real position with sham, why not adorn it and make yourself envied for your own qualities if not for your possessions. . . . To strive to be what you are not, is as unworthy of you as it is useless."[43]

A young woman who was striving to be what she was not, who wore imitation pearls, imitation turquoise, and other faux jewelry in an attempt to look like Ethel Barrymore earned columnist Alice Preston's ire. Preston advised the girl to exchange these imitation goods "for one genuine, guaranteed article, if it is only a currycomb or cake of soap that pretends to be no more than it is. . . . Say and do and think sincere things only, wear sincere things only. . . . Let us begin by giving up all the false or insincere material things."[44]

Women who persisted in dressing above their station were guilty of not one transgression but two. Moralists claimed that such women were telling lies about themselves. In 1904, Orison Swett Marden, a prolific author of books on character, success, and morals, warned, "Dressing or living beyond one's means is nothing less than absolute dishonesty. . . . If you are wearing clothes that you cannot afford they are perpetual witnesses against you. They are labeled all over with falsehood." Addressing himself to young women, he wrote, "If your jewelry, your carriages, your furs, and your costly gowns tell me that you are rich, when you live in a poverty-stricken home, and when your mother is obliged to make all sorts of sacrifices to enable you to make this false display, you lie just as surely as you would if you should try to deceive me by your words." In Marden's view, clothing and possessions should serve as unambiguous badges of class status. To wear elite styles when one was not affluent was to be an imposter.[45]

It was not just those who overdressed themselves who were dishonest, however; critics believed that families who lived in pretentious houses were also telling lies. A columnist in the *Ladies' Home Journal* argued that "there is no reason why a small house should be built of the same material as a palace or a public building. It is a vulgar desire to be something which one is not, that leads to most of the architectural mistakes we see."[46]

This belief that a dress or a house could tell a lie, and that clothing and decor should reflect a women's actual economic conditions rather than her aspirations, reveals a great deal about the way in which mainstream American writers conceived of feminine identity. Ideally, a woman's self was not an image which she constructed and presented to the world; it was an unchanging and unchangeable set of qualities with which she was born. While moralists generally seemed comfortable with the notion that men could create their own social identities, they believed that women could not and should not. Women were to be serene, unchanging, and without desire.

Convinced that women's identities should be static, these writers nevertheless were forced to confront the reality that it was becoming easier for women to fashion the selves which they presented to the public world. In many ways the fear of insincerity that they articulated was a response to a new system of production and new habits of consumption that they could not control. Historian Karen Halttunen has shown the widespread fear of hypocrisy in mid-nineteenth-century America, which developed in response to the increasing anonymity of American urban life.[47] By the end of the century, there were even more opportunities for artifice and insincerity. Cities were becoming even larger, filled with strangers who were unaware of each other's true economic circumstances. Individuals might easily lie about their backgrounds and claim greater wealth and standing than they actually possessed. Additionally, there were new aids for artifice. Magazines and newspapers told readers what the wealthy wore and how they furnished their houses, while mass-produced imitation goods offered aspiring people new ways to obscure their true station and live as elites did. Anxiety about sincerity sprang out of the unprecedented availability of goods that could assist a woman in changing her identity.

While aspiring women may have believed that their attempts to equal the social elites were legitimate, in the minds of the upper classes this undertaking was morally suspect. Commentators believed that envy and emulation could lead to insincerity and dishonesty, which in turn could lead to even more serious behavioral and moral pitfalls. Moralists who instructed women to control their envy often reminded them of their financial dependence on men. If a woman envied a dress, a rug, or a piano and hoped to purchase it, she frequently had to turn to a man for the money to do so. Commentators warned that reliance on men for money could easily lead to financial ruin for the man and the whole household or to moral ruin for the woman herself.

Turn-of-the-century commentators often maintained that women were the main impetus behind spending in a household. They worried that women's expenditures were frivolous and motivated chiefly by a desire to compete with other women. *Journal* columnist Ruth Ashmore asserted, "Many a business man can trace his downfall to the diamond earrings for which his wife or daughter begged so hard."[48] Other moralists claimed that extravagant spending on items of home decor led to financial ruin. A *Journal* editorial told of a couple who had moved to an area full of socially ambitious families, with the young husbands all employed in the lower echelons of white-collar professions. The wife quickly became swept up in the whirl of pretentious social events and competitive decorating schemes, and the couple descended into debt. The husband finally decided, against his wife's wishes, that they must leave "this fashion and social ambition atmosphere." He declared, "We will have done with tawdry finery, and the aping of vulgar imitation, and live simply and truly."[49] In this cautionary tale it was only the prudence of the virtuous husband that was able to curb the seemingly insatiable appetite of his emotionally vulnerable and socially ambitious wife.

Women's excessive and competitive spending threatened not only a household's finances but its tranquility and stability as well. An underlying theme in many cautionary tales was that women who thought too much about keeping up with the neighbors were overly involved in public life and insufficiently attentive to their domestic roles. In Agnes Surbridge's 1904 novel, *The Confessions of a Club Woman,* Johnaphene Henning moved with her husband to Chicago. Johnaphene had aspirations, but her prospects were limited by her marriage and position. "Had the fates been kind, I should have been in the smart set of which I read so much, with money, a carriage, social position, admirers. . . . Instead I was the insignificant married woman, the wife of a grocer, the mother of two babies at an age when society girls were still enjoying themselves, with no outlook on life, no future." Johnaphene, however, was soon rescued from social obscurity. She made the acquaintance of a leader of a fashionable women's club. Her rise through the ranks of this club "necessitated several new gowns and hats, and I learned the gentle art of running up a bill at the shops." Her husband was displeased to discover her new spending habits and even more incensed by her increasing devotion to her clubs. They took her away from the family and distracted her from her wifely duties. He asked her to quit the organizations, but she would not.

Johnaphene continued in her quest for social recognition, investing in fashionable gowns and accessories and spending ever more time away from home. So consumed with ambition was she that she was willing to risk almost everything, neglecting her children, who took ill, and her husband, who threatened divorce. As her family teetered on the edge of disaster, Johnaphene finally came to her senses, curtailed her club activities and ambitions, and returned to the home fires. Her envy and her desire to rise to the top of urban social life had brought her to the brink of ruin and dishonor. Her longing for social recognition and her desire to outshine other women bespoke a nature overly attuned to public life and insufficiently attentive to domestic joys. To safeguard family life, women like Johnaphene needed to keep their desires in check and their eyes studiously fixed on the hearth and home rather than on the passing fashion parade.[50]

Essayists went further, asserting that envy could completely corrupt a woman's character. Eager to have what she envied, but without financial resources of her own, an envious woman might turn to a man for help. Such financial help had its price. Journalists and reformers implied that unmarried women might have sex, and even become prostitutes, in exchange for finery. In many of the scenarios that moralists provided their middle-class readers, it was single working or working-class women who lost their virtue, but the cautionary tales still served to show the middle class just where unchecked envy could lead.

Laura Smith, a writer for the *Journal*, circumspectly warned girls not to accept gifts from men. "Above all, never allow a man to make you presents of articles of clothing, no matter how plausible his reason seems to you or how badly you want the article."[51] She did not say explicitly where such actions could lead, but others were more blunt. Ida Tarbell informed her audience outright of the evils that accepting gifts from men could cause: " 'I wanted the money,' I heard a girl arrested on her first street soliciting tell the judge. 'Have you no home?' 'Yes.' 'A good home?' 'Yes.' 'For what did you want money?' 'Clothes.' " Tarbell told of another girl, a "pretty sixteen-year-old" who had proclaimed, "Gee, but I felt as if I would give anything for one of them willow plumes." She had left home "with a man, because he promised her silk gowns and hats with feathers." Tarbell believed that these girls' experiences represented a larger social evil: "This ugly preoccupation with dress does not begin with the bottom of society. . . . it exists at the top and filters down."[52]

Because the "ugly preoccupation" with fashion existed at all levels of society, some held the enviable upper classes to blame for the moral downfall of the lower classes. Columnist Juliet Virginia Strauss speculated on how the sight of rich women's opulent fashions affected poor women. The rich woman attending the theater "costumed to the limit, . . . hair elaborately dressed, her fine wrap slipping from her shoulders, the grand hat nodding its trailing plumes," was unaware of how her display affected the poor girls who observed her: "That very hat, that very opera cloak may tonight turn the balance against that young girl's virtue. She may decide that the world is well lost if only she may look, for once in her life, like that rich woman in the box." Strauss claimed that the "noticeable dressing" of the wealthy was the cause of the "prevailing evils" in society.[53]

Although Strauss condemned rich women for inciting immoral behavior, it was far more common to blame poorer women for their envy and their promiscuity. Reformer Reginald Kauffman's 1914 book, *The Girl That Goes Wrong,* was a case in point. Kauffman offered a series of sketches based on interviews with prostitutes in several American cities. In a chapter titled "The Girl That Wanted Ermine," Kauffman recounted the story of Letty Dowling. Letty's bourgeois parents lived beyond their means and inculcated expensive tastes in their daughter. When Letty was a small child, her mother had decided to buy her costly clothes, declaring, "I guess that anything that's good enough for a Fifth Avenue girl isn't any too good for my daughter." When Mr. Dowling died some years later, Mrs. Dowling frittered away the pensions he had left the family. Although the money was disappearing, Letty's expensive tastes were not. She saw everywhere around her luxury and wanted it for herself. One night she walked by a well-dressed woman in a restaurant and "in passing, surreptitiously touched, with longing fingers, the ermine boa" which the woman was wearing. Her envy was observed by an older man who sent her his card and later offered to buy her a similar ermine set. At first Letty refused his offer and instead implored her mother to buy it for her, complaining, "I'm ever so much worse dressed than the other girls." Her mother, however, had no money to spare. Not long after, Letty had sex with the man, received the ermine set in exchange, and began a career of prostitution.[54] Such reports warned women of the perils of envy and served as a stark reminder to parents. Parents must inculcate tastes appropriate to their children's actual economic conditions; if they did not, their offspring would grow up to be like Letty. Possessing elite tastes and little in the ways of funds, they might find that the only way to fulfill their desires was through immoral means.

Between 1890 and 1910, women, regardless of their class position, were idealized as the virtuous guardians of social morality. Yet commentators sadly noted that women could also cause moral ruin by provoking or acting upon envy. Essayists and reformers hoped that women would be more prudent in acting on their longings if they knew what consequences their desires might have. As long as they were dependent upon men for their spending money, they would always be vulnerable. The way to protect morality and prevent sin was to teach women to repress their desires.

The Gradual Acceptance of Envy

In 1938, a quarter century after the appearance of these cautionary tales of good girls turning bad because of their love of finery, fashion designer Elizabeth Hawes observed that the conventional wisdom of her day held that every woman was entitled to finery: "The proudly American clothing boast is that *all* American women can have beautiful clothes."[55] Hawes's statement illustrates the transformation in opinion that occurred during the 1910s and 1920s. Social mores had changed so much that by the time Hawes wrote, envious women were no longer expected to cultivate contentment and sincerity or to practice emotional repression. Instead, the new wisdom held that regardless of social position, all women were entitled to indulge their desire for the luxuries of the rich.

This belief spread. Old habits and moral concerns did not disappear completely, but there was widespread evidence of a changing culture. Some commentators claimed there was more envy than ever before; whether or not that was true, there was certainly a greater tolerance for envy and emulation.

Sociologists Robert and Helen Lynd claimed that there was more envy and more striving in the 1920s than in previous decades. They interviewed longtime residents of Muncie, Indiana, about the changing social structure of the town. From these interviews, the Lynds concluded that in the 1890s members of different classes "lived on a series of plateaus as regards standard of living; old citizens say there was more contentment with relative arrival." Some residents recalled that rather than feeling deprived if they could not afford the lifestyle of the elites, "it was a common thing to hear a remark that so and so 'is pretty good for people in our circumstances.' " In contrast, by the 1920s, citizens no longer seemed satisfied with "relative arrival," with merely attaining the plateau. Instead, the Lynds reported, "the edges of the plateaus" had been "shaved off, and every one lives on a slope from any point of which desirable things belonging to people all the way to the top are in view."[56] This not only was true of Muncie but seemed to be the case across the country. A *Journal* columnist used similar alpine imagery in his description of American women's aspirations in the 1920s. "I see the woman of England gracefully reposing on a thousand-year-old lawn, I see the women of America, with nails on the soles of their Parisian shoes, climbing the rough sides of a mountain which has no summit."[57]

In spite of such compelling descriptions of the social landscape, it is difficult to conclude definitively that women were *more* envious, dissatisfied, or acquisitive in the period 1910–30. Already between 1890 and 1910, middle-class women had rising expectations about the material conditions of their lives. As a result, envy, although greatly disapproved of, was widespread throughout middle-class urban society. The sheer volume and vehemence of the outcry discouraging envy and encouraging contentment is evidence of the great pervasiveness of the emotion. Those who advocated contentment were, by 1890, already on the defensive.

The perception that there was more envy in the 1910s and 1920s may reflect the fact that women felt freer to express their feelings. Envy began to take on a new meaning and to lose its older connotations of sinfulness and immorality. Rather than criticize women for their emotions, fashion writers, economists, social reformers, and journalists spread the revolutionary notion that envy, discontent, and social striving were positive social instincts.[58] And, although a large number of more conservative voices still loudly espoused the doctrine of contentment, it was this new generation whose views would ultimately carry the day. After 1910, their opinions about market behavior became dominant and helped to redefine women's roles in economic and commercial life.

There are a number of reasons why this new view of envy emerged and why traditional strictures on the emotion relaxed. First, there was the sheer abundance of relatively inexpensive goods that Americans were daily encountering. It was difficult to convince consumers that dire consequences would follow should they choose to purchase the machine-made frocks they so desired. Proscriptions on envy and emulation might have carried more weight had such goods been less accessible, for then individuals would have been scrambling and competing for a limited supply of stockings, furs, or dresses, and someone's gain would have meant someone else's direct loss. In such cases, envy might cause hostility and confrontation. With the new efficiency of mass production, however, there was little need to squabble over scarce items, for there were sufficient luxury and imitation luxury goods for all to enjoy.

Many came to believe that, rather than representing moral peril, such abundance might be the key to social progress. Certainly it seemed apparent that cheaper and more accessible goods meant that an ever greater number of people could enjoy a higher standard of living. If envy was a sign of desire for this higher standard, could it really be so bad? Wasn't it instead a force for progress and advancement?[59]

The influence of a new cohort of advisors also abetted the changing emotional code. During the 1910s and 1920s, an eclectic group of secular advisors gained prominence and influence, while traditional religious writers were accorded less cultural authority than in earlier years. Generally college educated, and in most cases born after the Civil War, the new generation of advisors, which included doctors, economists, psychologists, and advertisers, had grown up along with the consumer society and the expanding urban industrial order.[60] Accustomed to material abundance in a way that previous generations were not, many believed that the moral problems traditionally associated with envy and emulation were overstated.

Their perspective on the morality of consumption was often shaped by their social and vocational positions. Most advisors were members of the new middle class who worked for large corporations and institutions like department stores, advertising agencies, universities, and publishing houses. Their positions within these new institutions often disposed them to promote commercial values and also made them willing to support the industrial and modernizing social order.

These factors combined with and to some extent depended upon the gradual weakening of the moralistic Victorian tradition. As historian Peter Stearns points out, Darwinian theory first challenged conventional religious notions about the possibility or desirability of perfect self-control and restraint. If humans were descended from animals, perhaps they too were subject to sometimes ungovernable emotions and instincts. The rise of new academic disciplines, including sociology (with its focus on the effects of larger social and environmental forces in individual life) and psychology (with its interest in how the unconscious worked and how it might be manipulated) also drew attention to the idea that self-restraint was not always possible, nor even always desirable.

Darwinian theory also undermined the idea of a static, providentially ordered universe where people's positions and fortunes could not and should not be altered. Evolutionary theory seemed to endorse the idea that struggle, competition, and change were natural, an idea which many who defended envy and discontent eagerly seized upon. World War I was the final nail in the coffin of the Victorian emotional code. The devastation of the war affected a large group of European intellectuals and a smaller group of

Americans. To the extent that the war undermined religious belief, it also undermined the rationale for controlling envy. As belief in a divinely and beneficently designed universe waned, so too did the idea that God had chosen individuals' stations in life specifically for them and that they should therefore be content with their particular lot.[61]

These social forces and cultural developments resulted in a new and less moralistic approach to the problem of envy in general and women's envy in particular. Many of the traditional moral concerns and dire predictions about envious women's ultimate fate seemed to fade during the 1910s and 1920s.

The new perspective on envy was perhaps most visible in the words Americans chose to describe the emotion. Those who envied were no longer seen as sinfully questioning divine providence. Instead, they were merely "keeping up with the Joneses." Drawn from the title of a popular comic strip of the 1910s, the phrase "keeping up with the Joneses" had come to enjoy great currency by the 1920s. Devoid of any moral overtones, it portrayed envy and emulation as innocuous, ordinary, and expected social instincts.[62]

But the change went far beyond language. Underlying assumptions about the meaning and implications of envy changed fundamentally during the 1910s and 1920s. For instance, conventional wisdom of the nineteenth century held that women who dressed above their station were insincere, imprudent, and immoral. In contrast, this new generation of advisors condoned and even encouraged "dressing up." An early advocate was Dr. Woods Hutchinson, a physician and public health reformer. In 1911, in a column in the *Saturday Evening Post*, he wrote:

Every woman ought to be dressed just as beautifully as she can possibly afford to be, without risking bankrupting her husband—and she need not worry too much about this latter consideration. The number of men, with the right kind of brains, whose business was in sound condition, that have been bankrupted by their wives' extravagance is about as great as the number of those who die in poverty from having given too much to the poor. "Ruined by his wife's extravagance" is chiefly a belated echo of the old whine in the Garden of Eden.[63]

Hutchinson departed from the orthodoxy which said that women's envy imperiled the household's financial security. Instead of seeing emulative spending as dangerous, he considered it to be a woman's duty. Those who were as well dressed as possible merited commendation, and those who were not deserved condemnation.

In 1913 economist Simon Patten, one of the early celebrants of consumerism, assailed another myth about female envy, countering claims that it led to sexual immorality. Dismissing the traditional virtue of saving as mere "folly," he wrote, "It is no evidence of loose morality when a stenographer, earning eight or ten dollars a week, appears dressed in clothing that takes nearly all of her earnings to buy. It is a sign of her growing moral development."[64] The idea that a woman could improve herself morally by improving her wardrobe flew in the face of nineteenth-century advice and indicated the direction that future discussions of consumerism would take.

By 1923 the once conservative editorial staff of the *Ladies' Home Journal* was in fact congratulating American women for dressing so well. "Whatever their background," the editors wrote, women in the United States "seem all to be inspired with what we are told is a typical and standardized American desire to 'look like a million dollars.' " The editors admitted that "some of it may be stupid vanity, some of it may be decadent or degenerate vanity," but "justly weighed and charitably considered, isn't most of it innocent vanity—wholesale ambition to look one's best, to achieve beauty and distinction, to assert good taste and cultivated selection in clothes?"[65] To try to look "like a million dollars" regardless of one's actual bank balance was a goal the previous generation of moralists had roundly condemned. In this new era, however, women no longer had to wear clothes that matched their incomes. Striving to look like a fashionable neighbor was acceptable and, to some, even admirable.

The social commentators of the 1910s and 1920s also contended that married women's consumer spending habits, rather than being at best irrelevant and at worst frivolous and profligate, might instead play an important role in social advancement. Breaking with the conventional wisdom, which held that women who spent on clothes and home decor were imperiling the entire household's security, this new generation recognized that a husband's business success was related to his domestic life and his wife's social talents. Perhaps the most notable of the essays on the subject was the three-part "Confessions of a Businessman's Wife," which appeared in 1930 in the *American Magazine.* An anonymous wife told how she had acquired the correct status symbols, changed her husband's image, and engineered his rise through the ranks. As she charted her course for social success, she made a list of prestige goods that she must acquire. "Two maids I knew I must have, new household equipment of every description—furniture, china, glass, silver. Win [her husband] must get new evening clothes and I at least one beautiful evening dress." This extravagant and unrestrained spending would have earned condemnation a few decades earlier; by 1930 such purchases were considered savvy, practical, and beneficial to the whole family.[66]

Advisors of the 1910s and 1920s also seemed less concerned about the increasingly public role that women were pursuing. Rather than chastising women for wanting to participate in the fashion parade and worrying that such involvement would take them away from their family responsibilities, many columnists and commentators seemed to indicate that it was now part of women's wifely duties to take an active role in clubs, leisure activities, and social gatherings. Envy might lead women to compete with others and seek higher status, but by joining the competition they were helping to establish their families' position. Women need not worry if their envy and competitive instincts took them out into the larger world. This was now their natural place.

Magazine columnists, economists, and social commentators endorsed this new vision of envy and social striving, but it was powerful voices in advertising and other new forms of commercial culture who were the most vocal and persuasive advocates of the emotion. The expanded means of mass communication that developed during the 1910s and 1920s spread the latest tastes and touted their desirability across the country. As Robert and Helen Lynd noted, "The rise of large-scale advertising, popular magazines, movies, radio, and other channels of increased cultural diffusion from without are rapidly changing habits of thought as to what things are essential to living and multiplying optional occasions for spending money." These new forms of communication, particularly movies, which allowed all classes "into the intimacy of Fifth Avenue drawing rooms and English country houses," and advertisements, which endeavored to make "the reader emotionally uneasy," were extremely effective in "reconditioning the habits" of the people of Middletown.[67]

Movies played a vital role in spreading compelling images of happy rich people sporting new clothes, reclining amid opulent furnishings, or driving about in shiny cars. Movies introduced styles of consumption that middle-class urbanites eagerly adopted. Surveys conducted in the late 1920s and early 1930s indicated that moviegoers were far more likely to assign great importance to appearances and "smart" clothing than those who did not regularly attend the cinema. In other studies that historian Kathy Peiss has unearthed, young women reported that movies had shaped their tastes. One woman claimed that at the cinema she found herself "reveling in pictures where beautiful clothes are displayed." Another woman, after seeing a film starring actress Vilma Banky, confided, "I sure wish I could look like her! I've tried, but it's impossible."[68]

Such anecdotes suggest that movie stars became role models for envious young women in the 1920s, rivaling the upper-class society women who had been the nation's most visible trendsetters in previous decades. Social scientists also provided evidence that movie images were influencing women. In 1934, sociologist Francis E. Merrill and colleague Mabel Elliott discussed how movies prompted girls' delinquent behavior. "In their efforts to enjoy clothes, cars, penthouses, and trips to the Riviera, as did the leaders of the screen," 18 percent of the girls surveyed had "lived with a man and accepted his bed and board." Twelve percent "attempted to satisfy an artificially stimulated craze for this sort of life by other acts of an equally disorganizing nature," while 49 percent contended that movies had fostered their "desire to lead a gay and reckless life."[69] Although relatively few women reacted to their envy of movie stars in this extreme manner, many nevertheless left the theater with newly vivid images of the elegance, wealth, and possessions that their own lives lacked.

Another important development was the increasing opportunity for installment buying. When stores began to offer installment plans, they made it easier for those who desired upper-class possessions to act on their emotions. Installment plans only gradually gained legitimacy in a society which had long condemned debt. They became widely accepted around 1920, when the desire to sell cars made dealers more accommodating. Over 60 percent of the cars, radios, and furniture sold in the late 1920s were purchased on the installment plan. The acceptance and rapid spread of installment plans had important financial and moral repercussions for people in moderate circumstances. The merchants who devised these payment plans were allowing consumers with expensive tastes but little money to fulfill their desires.

It was also in these years that advertising gained new prominence in American culture. Advertising began to take on its modern form just after World War I. Whereas earlier ads had been small, black-and-white, text-heavy notices that focused on the objective traits of the product itself, in the late 1910s and 1920s their look and substance began to change in ways important to the history of envy. Through their increased presence and size, their new color, and what Roland Marchand called their "modernistic style," advertisements became a more prominent and visible feature of American magazines and newspapers. According to Marchand, the total national advertising volume increased from $682 million in 1914 to $2,987 million in 1929.[70]

Even more important was the changing tenor of the ads. Earlier advertisements had merely sold the product; ads after the war came to focus increasingly on the attendant social and psychic benefits of the item. Envious women had already long believed what this new generation of ads emphatically told them: Material things had a social significance that existed quite apart from their objective traits. Advertisers sought to capitalize on this popular understanding of the meaning of goods. In 1922 Albert Leffingwell, a Thompson employee, explained this perspective to his colleagues, noting, " 'You're not selling the ticket, you're selling the end of the journey.' And the end of the journey must be somewhere we all want to go." Leffingwell advised his coworkers to focus on the social and subjective meanings of a product, for it was these attributes which made a thing desirable.[71]

In order to sell the "end of the journey" rather than just the ticket, advertisers tried to make consumers feel particular emotions when they contemplated products. One emotion they repeatedly tried to provoke was envy. To this end, many seized on psychologist Alfred Adler's idea of the inferiority complex and incorporated it into their campaigns. Thompson employees created countless ads that promised to elevate the consumer to the level of the "the discriminating hostess," "the particular woman," or "persons of the most fastidious taste." Frances Maule, a Thompson employee in the New York office, explained why such ads seemed to influence consumer decisions:

We all suffer from an eating sense of our unimportance, insignificance, inadequacy, whether we know it or not. And, whether we know it or not, a large part of our energies are directed to making ourselves feel important, significant, equal to anything. When we wear the garments of that cosmopolitan great lady who "assembles, tries, and admits finally to a place in her life only the choicest"—when we drink the coffee "chosen for his own use by the greatest coffee merchants"—we identify ourselves with these exalted personages.

Maule maintained that by buying the products presented in such ads, "we are made to feel that they have 'nothing on us.' And this is what we all want, really, more than anything else in the world. This is the 'grand and glorious feeling' which we are all seeking all the time."[72]

The profit-making potential of the inferiority complex was not lost on any Thompson employee. Stanley Resor, the president of the firm, claimed that among "the masses" there was "a sense of inferiority and an instinctive veneration for 'their betters.' " These feelings led many consumers to try to emulate "their betters" in the hopes of equaling them. Resor maintained that this desire to overcome inferiority had particular power over women's shopping decisions. "The desire to emulate is stronger in women than in men. . . . Woman's ability to excite her imagination with external objects . . . enables her to become princess or movie queen by using the cold cream or toilet soap they recommend."[73]

To spur such emulative spending, advertisers used what they called the "snob appeal," a technique they believed to be well suited to the female psyche. They produced ads containing information about upper-class consumer tastes. They hoped that by publicizing elite preferences, they might persuade the middle classes that there was a national elite culture with clear standards and tastes. Although they might not be a part of it, middle-class consumers could nevertheless emulate those who belonged to it.

A campaign for Woodbury's soap illustrated this approach. Beginning in 1922, Thompson employees interviewed upper-class women about their soap preferences. They questioned students and faculty at elite colleges and universities, debutantes, guests at expensive hotels and resorts, and members of exclusive social clubs and found that a significant number of these women used Woodbury's soap. Consequently, their ad campaign discussed the "strong preference shown for Woodbury's Facial Soap among women of taste and intelligence throughout the country." As the ads appeared in magazines month after month, featuring one elite group after another, with headlines such as "Sixty Two percent of Washington and Baltimore debutantes are regular users of Woodbury's," consumers might be convinced that there was a national consensus about what was best.

In addition to invoking the nation's putative trendsetters in the aggregate, advertisers also secured endorsements from prominent individuals. Various ads claimed that Mrs. Reginald Vanderbilt, Mrs. Nicholas Longworth, Mrs. Franklin Roosevelt, Mrs. O. H. P. Belmont, Mrs. Cordelia Biddle Duke, Mrs. Marshall Field, and several others were the ladies whose habits and styles should serve as models for the consuming public. If these elite American women were not convincing enough, the advertisers might also add testimony from the Princess Norina Matchabelli, Lady Diana Manners, Queen Marie of Romania, and other royals and nobles.

Advertisers concluded that campaigns which used the snob appeal to provoke envy and spur on consumer spending were quite successful. For instance, Frances Maule reported that after one coffee company began to advertise their product as "the coffee that the greatest coffee merchants offer their own guests," and provided illustrations with "the most correct of butlers serving coffee from the most approved of coffee services in rooms of baronial splendor," sales quickly outstripped those of other brands. When Pond's began to use the endorsements of beautiful society women, that company also experienced a surge in sales.[74]

These ads offered a new set of secular guidelines about correct market behavior. They told consumers that there was no longer a moral problem with straining after what one lacked, no modern-day sumptuary law constricting the range of purchases. Envy, according to the advertising pages, was an acceptable and natural motivation for consumer spending. The ads' message was that now all could possess—and indeed should possess—what had formerly been the luxuries of the fortunate elite.

This new message was widely evident in advertising copy of the 1910s. An ad for Pompeian face cream proclaimed, "Don't Envy a Good Complexion—Use Pompeian and Have One." It suggested that the way to cope with envy was not to cultivate contentment and repress one's feelings but to act on one's desires. The ad questioned readers: "Why cast envious eyes at another when all you need to do to have an equally enviable complexion is to use Pompeian MASSAGE Cream yourself?"[75] Innumerable ads would repeat this message indicating that all could have the advantages and pleasures which in the past had been enjoyed by only a lucky few. A 1919 Resinol ad told women:

Don't Watch Others Enjoy Life—enter in! To be deprived of your rightful social standing among your friends through a poor complexion,—to watch others enjoy themselves while you are left out and neglected, is discouraging to the bravest heart,—depressing to the liveliest nature. The question is, how can you, too, enter in? . . . . If your only barrier between popularity and social success be a faulty complexion—now is the time to use Resinol Soap.[76]

Such ads preached that society was open to those with the right possessions and appearances and that good looks and good things were now available to all who longed for them. Envy need not be repressed, nor go unassuaged.

Ads not only told women that it was acceptable for them to feel and act on envy; they also encouraged women to make their possessions and their appearances enviable and to thus provoke the emotion in other women.

Figure 3. Envy need not be endured if one purchased Pompeian. Used with permission of Colgate-Palmolive.

There was no trace of the old fear that inciting envy might lead others to moral or financial ruin. If a women was envied, she was successful. "The Envied Girl—Are you one? Or are you still seeking the secret of charm?" asked Palmolive. Another ad queried, "Do Other Women Envy You? Or do you envy them? The woman who gets what she wants out of life—the woman other women envy and copy—never depends on youth alone, or a pretty face, or brains." Such a woman has "charm," "poise," and Houbigant Perfume.[77]

The ads of the 1920s not only conferred legitimacy on envy; they also offered a new definition of contentment. Whereas once Americans had heard that they could develop a contented spirit by learning to accept their deprivations, by the 1920s women were hearing that true contentment could be gained only by having everything one longed for. A 1924 Cadillac ad perfectly summed up this new philosophy: " 'Contentment'—Absolute contentment in her motor car choice is reserved for the woman who owns a New V-63 Cadillac. . . . It is the car she desires, and the car she possesses, and therein lies the secret of her enviable motoring contentment."[78] The older understanding of the virtue, which had emphasized the importance of accepting one's deprivations, was being obscured by a newer logic, which seemed to argue that it was impossible to be happy without things and that real contentment came from having exactly what one coveted.

These new types of advertisements legitimated the envy that many women had long felt; they tried, however, to do even more than this. They attempted to direct women's desires toward new products by promising social prestige with the purchase of practically everything. It is clear that women already envied a wide range of material goods—dresses, stockings, carpets—before the advent of modern advertising. What is less clear is the degree to which advertisements shaped women's emotions and created new wants and more envy. While it is difficult to gauge the effects of prescriptive literature on its readers, market research offers some information on how women reacted to ads that tried to provoke envy. Investigations of the 1920s assessed whether the claims that ads made seemed credible to consumers and the degree to which they succeeded in provoking women's envy and spurred them to spend. These studies indicate that the ads persuaded some, but certainly not all, women that particular products and particular brands were enviable and socially necessary.[79]

In the surveys conducted by the Thompson agency, a significant number of women remained unconvinced by the rhetoric of ads and believed their promises were hollow. When asked whether the Woodbury ads influenced her, a Boston housewife, described as a "humorous, well-bred person," replied that "no soap will make you beautiful, and any soap will keep you clean." A female chemistry student from Minnesota scolded the Thomp-

The Girl Women Envy and Men Admire

Some girls seem to have all the good times while others look on and wonder how they do it. Yet these popular girls are often not especially endowed with beauty. Why do they inspire so much masculine admiration?

The principal attraction is often the alluring fresh smoothness of skin which all men admire. Did you ever see a girl with a poor complexion receive much attention?

Be the envied girl yourself

There is no reason why you should be content with anything less than a perfect skin. You can make your complexion smooth and fresh—you can free it from blemishes. You can keep it fine in texture and develop a charming natural color.

How necessary it is to wash your face is proved by the statements of leading skin specialists. You risk serious skin disorders when you fail to protect your skin by daily cleansing. Your one big problem is the choice of soap.

Select the mildest

If you feel afraid of soap it is because you have been using the wrong kind. You will have no further anxiety after you try Palmolive. The formula has been perfected to give the women the mildest, balmiest facial soap it is possible to produce. *Palm and Olive oils—nothing else—give nature's green color to Palmolive Soap*

Blended from the palm and olive oils Cleopatra used as cleansers, its smooth, bland, creamy lather cleanses without the slightest hint of harshness.

What Palmolive does

Softly massaged into your skin with your two hands, the fragrant lather enters every tiny pore and skin cell, dissolving the accumulations of dirt, oil secretions and perspiration which otherwise clog and enlarge them. (When this dirt carries infection, blemishes result.)

This thorough cleansing keeps your skin clear and fine in texture. Healthful stimulation of circulation gives you that inimitable and becoming natural color.

After thorough rinsing apply a touch of cold cream. If your skin is unusually dry, rub in cold cream before washing.

10 cents—and the reason

While palm and olive oils are the most expensive soap ingredients, the enormous demand for Palmolive allows us to import them in such enormous quantity that it reduces cost.

This same demand keeps the Palmolive factories working day and night. This is another price-reducing factor which gives you this luxurious cleanser at the price of ordinary soap.

Mail the coupon for free trial cake and let the creamy Palmolive lather tell its own story.

THE PALMOLIVE COMPANY, Milwaukee, U.S.A.

The Palmolive Company of Canada, Limited, Toronto, Ont.

Also makers of Palmolive Shaving Cream and Palmolive Shampoo

Volume and efficiency produce 25-cent quality for

10c

Copyright 1922—The Palmolive Co. 1304

A queen's cosmetics

Palm and olive oils were reserved for royalty and riches in ancient Egypt. Cleopatra used them both as cleanser and cosmetics. And whatever elaborate aids to beauty she employed, her toilet began with ceremonial bathing. To this the ruins of her elaborate marble baths are silent testimony. Now we employ her favorite beautifiers in a toilet luxury all can enjoy at a price all can afford.

Figure 4. A 1922 ad for Palmolive encouraged women to "be the envied girl yourself." Used with permission of Colgate-Palmolive. Courtesy of the John W. Hartman Center for Sales, Advertising, and Marketing History, Duke University.

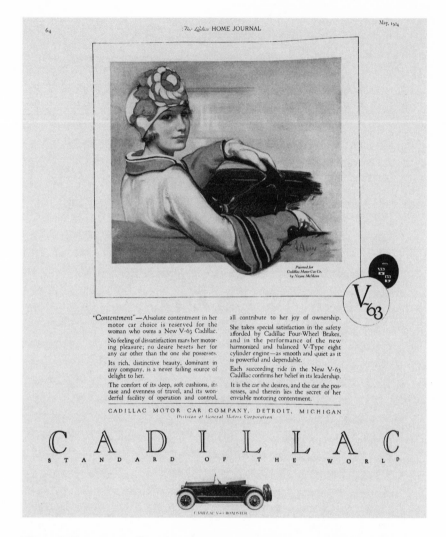

Figure 5. The new meaning of contentment was having everything that one desired. 2001 General Motors Corporation. Used with permission of GM Media Archives.

son staff about the Woodbury ads: "You people get more money because you advertise and your claims are extravagant."[80]

In other studies, Thompson investigators found a degree of skepticism about celebrity endorsements. While consumers may have envied some of the women making the endorsements, that did not mean they automatically would purchase the products to which these women lent their names. Some consumers wondered if the society ladies and European nobility featured in ads actually used the things they endorsed, while others found these elite women's recommendations irrelevant to the more modest circumstances of their own lives. Investigators questioned women in Pennsylvania, Rhode Island, and Ohio about their perceptions of testimonial advertising in general and Pond's cold cream ads in particular. A woman in Columbus, Ohio, told investigators that she "thinks a lot of people would be influenced by testimonials—she wouldn't." An upper-class Providence, Rhode Island, woman "wonder[ed] if they do really use the cream. Not convinced that they use Pond's. Thinks they do not know what they use. Their maids would attend to all this. Doubts sincerity because creams so inexpensive—sure these women would use more costly products."

Still other consumers thought that the particular women pictured in the ads were irrelevant to their lives and would have preferred instead to learn about the tastes and consumer habits of everyday people. Thompson staff reported that a Columbus woman "thinks if names of less prominent women were used the advertising would be more effective and be more convincing to the middle classes." A middle-class woman from Chester, Pennsylvania, echoed this view. She questioned Queen Marie's relevance to her own life, believing that the queen's complexion was probably naturally superior to her own. She said the ads were

interesting in a way, although would be more interested if my next-door neighbor told me what good results she had had. Some of the wealthy women probably don't have as bad skins to care for as people who come from large families with small incomes where doctors were too expensive to be called in always, and skins sometimes suffered because diseases were inadequately cared for. So what Queen Marie does for her skin which is probably very smooth to begin with, would not help me as much as what my next-door neighbor uses.

Other women did not believe the advertisers' contentions that these women, merely by dint of their lineage, were natural role models. A middle-class Providence woman indicated that she would not emulate these celebrities, telling interviewers that she "does not see why she should use them just because these women do." A woman from Circleville, Ohio, told investigators that the ads were "interesting to read, but we can't all use the same things."[81] It was this very idea—that "we can't all use the same things"— which nineteenth-century moralists had tried so hard to implant and which twentieth-century advertisers were trying to overturn.

A substantial number of women, however, wanted to use the same things as the elites and were more willing to believe the ads' claims that various products—and particular brands—could lend prestige to their purchasers. When asked why she used Woodbury's soap, a student at the University of Minnesota declared that it appealed to her because "it seems like a 'refined' soap, if a soap can be called that." A student at the University of Wisconsin purchased the soap "because of its popularity and supposedly prestige in the toilet article world. Advertisement has done it—3/4 of it." Students at the University of Chicago were even more enthusiastic about the soap. One student contended, "The name WOODBURY'S has a prestige that no other soap can equal. It suggests daintiness. . . . I feel perfectly *regal* when using it." Another Chicago coed claimed, "It has a psychological effect. I always feel myself *radiant*—like the pink-cheeked girl in the advertisement—after I use it." At least in the case of soap, then, many women seemed satisfied with their purchase. They felt they had gained what had been promised them in the advertisement. Some in fact used the very terms of the advertisement to describe themselves. They boasted of now having "velvety" and "smooth" skin that "everybody loved to touch." These women found that emulating the women portrayed in ads yielded psychological rewards and made them feel that they had attained the results they longed for.

Significantly, some women told investigators that they were motivated to buy a product not because they wanted to emulate the women portrayed in advertisements but because they longed for the attributes of their real-life friends and relatives. The ads had not created envy; instead, everyday social interactions had. A coed at McGill reported that she had started using the soap "because Mother uses it and I envied her soft skin. I have a friend who would not use anything else as a shampoo and she certainly has lovely hair." Another student confided that she followed her friends' examples: "Because I have seen the successful results of my friends."[82] These women relied on the soap to help them gain parity with their friends, relatives, and acquaintances rather than with the celebrities featured in the ads.

Such findings suggest that advertisers did not invent envy, did not create it out of whole cloth, but instead embroidered upon women's existing desires for a sophisticated appearance and the prestige that it symbolized.[83] Advertisers tried to capitalize on women's long-standing desire for elevated status by promising social advancement with the purchase of goods ranging from soap to automobiles. To be sure, ads were not always successful in directing women's desires toward the specific goods they sold; not all women automatically accepted Queen Marie as a role model. Nevertheless, these ads contributed to a climate of opinion that considered women's envy a legitimate emotion and that encouraged women to act on their longings. They helped to sanction and spread an emotional style that privileged pleasure and indulgence over repression and restraint.[84]

The changing valuation of women's envy and contentment, which advertisers, economists, movies, merchants, and women themselves helped to bring about, illustrates not only the shifting meaning of an emotion but larger transformations in gender roles as well. Until the 1910s, moralists denied that women had or should have desires. In doing so, they upheld women's exclusion from the liberal capitalist marketplace. Market activity required individuals to be competitive, acquisitive, and, indeed, envious. In contrast, women were perceived to be naturally religious, self-sacrificing, without desire or envy, and therefore contented. They were to be unchanging and unchangeable. Accordingly, they had no need to participate in the market economy. Without desires or drive, they had no impetus for the restless, struggling behavior endemic to capitalism.

By 1930, journalists, social commentators, merchants, advertisers, and consumers had redefined the boundaries of acceptable female behavior. The new behavioral model affirmed women's right to consume, to handle money (if not to earn it), and to pursue the objects they desired. They had the right to try to transform themselves and fashion their social image. Businessmen, writers, and advertisers admitted what women themselves had long known: Women had longings and instincts that might lead them to participate in the economy. As cultural leaders and entrepreneurs began to acknowledge, accept, and sometimes literally capitalize on women's envy, bourgeois women found new acceptance and greater opportunities for participation in the consumer economy. Once viewed as a moral failing and the first step down an even more sinful path, women's envy came to be viewed as a valuable economic stimulant and a "natural" part of modern American femininity.

This view of envy as a legitimate and potentially profitable emotion has continued to influence the emotional lives of women as they confront the enticements of consumer society. Since the 1920s, women have become less circumspect in articulating and acting on their envy, and they have encountered little disapproval when they have done so. Many have come to believe the exact opposite of what nineteenth-century moralists preached. Contentment can be gained not by resisting envy and making do with what one has but by giving in to envy and buying what one longs for.

Bourgeois Americans today accept envy as a natural response to the unequal distribution of consumer goods, and they believe that in a market full of mass-produced imitations, emulation is a sensible and harmless way to resolve these feelings. The emotion that nineteenth and early twentieth-century moralists condemned in women as destructive of the social order, contemporary Americans now accept as a central pillar of the consumer society.

2. Envy in the Office

In the 1890s, as he was struggling to establish himself on Wall Street, Bernard Baruch observed around him men who had amassed greater fortunes and secured better positions than he had. He longed to join these men and felt uncomfortable with his relatively modest circumstances. He recalled, "another battle I had to fight out within myself as a young man . . . [was] to prevent feelings of envy from driving me to rash decisions or to be corroded with jealousy of those who were more successful than I was." Baruch eventually surpassed most of the men he had once envied, becoming a fabulously wealthy financier and a celebrated public official, but years later he still remembered his struggle to control his envy. Baruch's battle was one which many bourgeois men of the period faced. They struggled to understand how they should express their ambitions and envy in the business world. When were such feelings constructive, and when were they destructive? How envious and competitive could a man actually afford to be in the early twentieth century?[1]

Journalist Mark Sullivan, a contemporary of Baruch's, offered a broader perspective on the issue. Born in 1874, Sullivan had witnessed a revolution in the way that men thought about their careers. In the late nineteenth century, America was a place "in which every youth felt it his business to seek opportunity and make use of it, to 'get ahead in the world.' "

Americans' attitudes about men's ambitions had changed, however, and Sullivan claimed that by the 1930s many had come to regard "getting ahead" as "passé" and even "sinister." "To 'get ahead' came to be looked upon in a way described by another phrase . . . it became 'anti-social.' "[2]

By the 1930s many Americans shared Sullivan's perceptions. Nevertheless, bourgeois men clung to their dreams of advancement, but learned a new emotional code and developed new ways to demonstrate their ambitions. Part and parcel of this evolving emotional style was a new way of handling and sometimes hiding rankling feelings of envy and competitiveness.

Between 1890 and 1930, the changing circumstances of the economy influenced the way that men expressed their envy and displayed their desire for success. The full rise of corporate capitalism put pressure on men to practice emotional repression in the business world. Workers were expected to subordinate their individual desires to the greater goals of the company. The expansion of consumer society, on the other hand, pointed men in another direction completely. There they were encouraged to assuage their feelings of envy through consumption. Historian T. J. Jackson Lears has noted that Americans were "encouraged to 'express themselves' . . . not through independent accomplishment but through the ownership of things. It was a far different and in many ways diminished sense of selfhood from that embodied in the image of the headstrong self-made man."[3] Men learned new ways to express themselves in the corporate and consumer economy, and they also learned very specific lessons about the proper way to manage their feelings of envy, lessons which continue to hold sway today. Middle-class men tried to get ahead in the nineteenth century, and they continue to do so in contemporary America. What has changed is the manner in which they broadcast their ambitions and respond to their envy.

Success Provokes Envy

Between 1890 and 1930, a growing proportion of middle-class men who aspired to be successful businessmen found positions in the emerging white-collar sector of the economy. In the last quarter of the nineteenth century, the demand for white-collar workers increased dramatically. Between 1870 and 1920, the number of clerical workers expanded ninefold, while the total labor force only doubled. Some scholars, most notably C. Wright Mills, have argued that these white-collar workers formed the core of the "new middle class." Those in the "old middle class" had owned their own property and had worked primarily as farmers, businessmen, and self-employed professionals. In contrast, members of the "new middle class" were managers, "salaried professionals," salespeople, and office workers, who, rather than running their own businesses, held positions within expanding corporate hierarchies.[4]

The men who took white-collar jobs had hopes for advancement. Most longed to live up to the ideal of the self-made, independent businessman that American culture celebrated. Innumerable business leaders of earlier generations had started off as clerks or in other lowly positions and found this to be a reliable route to independent proprietorship. Between 1890 and 1930, however, the men who worked as clerks, accountants, or bookkeepers, or who filled other white-collar jobs, found that their chances of actually advancing beyond these positions and becoming independent businessmen were greatly diminished. The increasing number and size of corporations altered the landscape of opportunity for white-collar workers. A clerk described the dissonance between the celebration of success and the realities of work in a large corporation. "When a male child of respectable, middle-class parents is born into the world he little realizes what he is up against." As a child, his "indulgent parents" encourage him to think "that he amounts to a little something. And when he finds that he has to get down on his knees for a chance to stick pins in a cushion at eighty cents a day, it's a great, sad surprise."[5]

Many other men made the same unhappy discovery that positions of leadership, independence, and responsibility were out of their reach. As Carole Srole showed in her study of clerical workers in Boston, by 1885, 20.0 percent of the men who had been clerks in 1870 owned their own businesses, but only 7.3 percent of men who had been clerks in 1900 owned businesses by 1915. Instead of running their own businesses, this later generation of clerks was more likely to become managers, accountants, bookkeepers, and "commercial travelers."[6] A journalist offered poignant testimony to this new occupational reality in 1901:

A bookkeeper said to me the other day: "I made the mistake of my life when I learned to keep books. I was a good bookkeeper at 25 and was proud of it. I am a good bookkeeper now at 50 and am ashamed to tell anybody that I am a bookkeeper." Draftsmen talk the same way, and stenographers; and yet the railroad presidents and corporation presidents and the great captains of industry today were almost without exceptions bookkeepers or draftsmen or stenographers at some time in their careers.[7]

Traditional avenues to success were becoming dead-end streets. This altered landscape of opportunity frustrated many men. Their own dreams often went unfulfilled, yet they could see around them men who had managed to gain success. As a result, the world of white-collar workers was a breeding ground for envy.

Men who occupied lowly positions in the corporate hierarchy felt envy and anxiety about their status and longed for the day when they could occupy a position of leadership. Isaac F. Marcosson, a reporter who gained considerable fame as a writer for the *Saturday Evening Post*, recalled how as a young man his desire for success had been intertwined with envy. In the 1890s, when he was in his late teens, Marcosson began to work for the *Louisville Times*. He started on the lowest rung of the office ladder, a position he longed to leave. "My initial tasks were far from thrilling," he recalled. "I carried copy from political conventions, envying the man who was reporting them, answered the telephone, and rehashed . . . items in the morning paper. I yearned for more important work."[8] Marcosson eventually received more demanding and fulfilling assignments and became a respected reporter, but his feelings of envy did not entirely abate.

Marcosson came into contact and conflict with another aspiring southern journalist, Louis Brownlow. Brownlow had started out his career as a clerk in a cigar shop in a Nashville hotel. From his shop he watched important politicians and reporters walk by, and he longed to have their jobs. "Almost every day in the Tulane lobby I would see someone else who stirred me deeply. It might be Tom Halley of the *Nashville Banner*, or it might be Bob Moorman of the *Nashville American*; but in any event it would be the political reporter of a daily newspaper. Him I envied, him I was determined to imitate." And Brownlow did. He became a successful reporter and then an editor.

In 1903, Isaac Marcosson and Louis Brownlow met. Brownlow was brought in to be the city editor of the *Louisville Times*, a job which Marcosson, a longtime employee, had expected to be his own. The two men, with their similar ambitions to rise to the top of the *Times* hierarchy, soon came into conflict. Marcosson refused to do some of the work that Brownlow assigned to him, believing it was beneath him. In response, Brownlow fired Marcosson.[9] Brownlow and Marcosson's envy and ambition had motivated them in their struggles for success and had propelled them upward. Their emotions, however, had also led to conflict and confrontation and interfered with the smooth production of the newspaper. Envy motivated men; it also produced tension and resentment. It was the emotion's dual nature which made it so difficult to manage.

As Brownlow and Marcosson's stories illustrate, men's ambitions for professional advancement were often intimately tied to their envy of those with more important duties or higher incomes. Frequently, envy was left out of the inspirational accounts of men's struggles, and discussions instead centered on the more socially acceptable motivation of ambition. The fact remained, however, that envy was prompting many men to press forward in their search for success. Some turn-of-the-century writers were willing to admit that the emotion was prevalent. A writer in the *Saturday Evening Post* lamented, "We see too frequently the spirit of bitterness and envy displayed where nothing but harmonious feelings should exist." He continued, "We see this unfortunate spirit of envy rampant in all classes." He then singled out "the business man who cultivates the spirit of meanness and envy," describing him as a nuisance to himself and to others. Another writer claimed that signs of discontent were visible in "the countenances of most men" and in "the eager haste of the busy throngs, pushing their way through the crowded streets of our great cities."[10]

Such chronicles of envy continued through subsequent decades. In the late 1910s and 1920s, the editors of the *American Magazine* believed that the white-collar world was rife with envy, and they addressed the subject repeatedly. In 1919, in "The Sin That Everybody Commits and How I Cured Myself of It," an anonymous businessman described his experience with envy, an experience he believed to be fairly typical for men of his class and age. "The disease . . . has caused me more bitter hours than I like to think about. Whether you term it envy, as some do, or jealousy, or covetousness, makes little difference: it is the commonest sin in the world." In 1926 another writer in the *American Magazine* recounted how he and other men he knew had based their careers on envy. Envy was such a serious problem that he titled his piece "I Nearly Died of Envy," saying, "You have heard folks say, 'I almost died of envy.' In my case that was true. Envy cost me my job, it cost me my health, it would have cost me my life."[11]

The testimony that envy could ruin a man's health offers another way to trace the history of envy. From the late nineteenth century to the Depression, concerns about the nervous condition of the American people were widespread. As T. J. Jackson Lears points out, whether or not the actual incidence of nervous illness increased during this period is unknowable and, to some degree, irrelevant; what is significant is that observers believed that "neurasthenia," as it was called, was spreading.[12] Social commentators and medical experts spent considerable energy trying to identify its causes. Much of the literature generated on the topic explicitly linked nervousness to the strife and struggle borne of restless ambition and emulation, and envy was often implicated. Dr. George Beard, author of *American Nervousness*, was one of the first to contend that there was a connection between aspiration and neurasthenia. In 1881 he argued that nervousness came with modern civilization and the American social order. "A factor in producing American nervousness is, beyond dispute, the liberty allowed, and the stimulus given, to Americans to rise out of the position in which they were born, whatever that may be, and to aspire to the highest possibilities of fortune and glory. . . . [In Europe] there is a spirit of routine and spontaneous contentment and repose which in America is only found among the extremely unambitious."[13]

Doctors and social commentators believed that it was this social fluidity which caused envy, and envy, in turn, caused neurasthenia. An editorial in the *Saturday Evening Post* proclaimed "Nerves a National Ailment" and then stated, "No other disease known to man is so characteristically national as nerves. . . . The one cure is fresh air, and less of the cause, whatever it may be—less drink, or moneymaking, or ambition, or love of filth." Perhaps even more telling was the testimony of a recovered neurasthenic who told his readers how they might avoid a nervous breakdown: "Never again will I let myself be tempted to go to the limit of my strength. Never again will I listen to the promptings of the miserable fever of emulation that drives so many American men to sickness, despair, and madness."[14]

The author of "I Nearly Died of Envy" recounted the course of his disease. Envy had been with him since youth. "My own boyish spirit was further distorted by a driving, ingrowing ambition. . . . measuring myself constantly against other folks, I determined that the world *must* give me position and money." As an adult in the business world he was constantly haunted by the idea that others made more money and were more celebrated than he. Even at ball games he was envious of the applause that the players received. His health began to deteriorate. First he developed insomnia. At night he could not stop thinking about how he would surpass his rivals and gain fame and glory. Such inner turmoil took its toll. "One hot summer day as I sat down to luncheon in a country hotel, my head fell forward suddenly and I collapsed on the table. When I came to I was in a nice white bed, in a bare white room and it was several days before I took enough interest in things to learn that the place was a sanitarium."[15] While relatively few men ended up in sanitariums, probably many could identify with the author's predicament. The quest for success could take a psychological toll. Bourgeois men's nervous exhaustion may have been a sign of their anxiety. They were pursuing the socially acceptable goal of success, yet the pursuit of wealth and position was often based on invidious comparisons and accompanied by feelings of competitiveness and aggression—emotions that were less socially acceptable and less comfortable to experience.

Despite the discomfort and the widely perceived health risks that envy might bring, ambitious men continued to act on the emotion. They eagerly sought advancement and the chance to change themselves and their condition. They showed this desire in their interactions at work; they also revealed their envy and aspirations when they presented themselves in public.

Suits and Status

In 1895, after having been made a junior partner in a small New York brokerage house, Bernard Baruch invested in new clothes. "I acquired a Prince Albert coat, a silk hat, and all the accessories that went with them." Baruch was eager to show off his new attire and recalled that "on Sundays, I would array myself in all my finery, my shoes polished with more than usual care, take my cane, and sally forth" on Fifth Avenue. Despite the newly purchased apparel, however, Baruch was not happy. The promenades were not "entirely enjoyable" for him, because he would often observe acquaintances who seemed more stylish. "In their splendid traps, behind spanking teams of horses, they would dash by me as I walked along the Avenue. Often I felt envious."[16] Like Baruch, middle-class men envied not just the success, income, and fame of other men but also the rich material goods that bespoke high status. Just as the growth and attenuated social ties of the city made appearance more important as a means of establishing status for women, so it was for men in the white-collar world. In an environment where so many were trying to advance and where individual character was harder to know, men's appearances and use of status-marked items became increasingly significant.

Well-tailored suits were one clear sign of occupational status. They helped middle-class men differentiate themselves from those engaged in manual labor. Thorstein Veblen argued that "gentlemen's" apparel had high status precisely because such attire made it evident that the wearer did not perform any heavy labor. "Much of the charm that invests the patent-leather shoe, the stainless linen, the lustrous cylindrical hat, and the walking stick, which so greatly enhance the native dignity of a gentleman, comes of their pointedly suggesting that the wearer cannot when so attired bear a hand in any employment that is directly and immediately of any human use." Middle-class men's insistence on wearing suits testified to their status anxiety. They wanted to signal to the world that they were not members of the lower classes, who often went without collars or suit coats.[17]

Suits served a dual social purpose. They distinguished bourgeois men from the manual laborers who occupied a place below them on the status ladder. They also communicated middle-class men's desires to join those above them in the social and occupational world. Bourgeois men were very aware, therefore, of how their own clothes compared with those of more prosperous men. Journalist Walter Creedmoor wrote of the struggling young man of small means trying to succeed in business, noting, "He will envy the well dressed, prosperous looking men whom he sees entering the great doors that seem to swing so easily for any one who can pay the price."[18]

Twenty-three-year-old William Allen White fulfilled Creedmoor's predictions perfectly. In 1891, White left his hometown of Eldorado, Kansas, for a job on the *Kansas City Star*. When he arrived, he quickly learned that his clothes, although fashionable in his small community, did not match the attire of well-dressed city men. He was staying at the Midland Hotel, where he rubbed shoulders with "traveling salesmen and visiting capitalists." It was there, White remembered, that "I also learned about clothes. For I had the quick eye of youth in looking at well-dressed men." White came to long for the accoutrements of status, and though he lacked the funds, he was able to find a way to buy his first hand-tailored business suit. "I ordered a suit of clothes on tick by taking the managing editor to the tailor to vouch for my credit. And when I was fitted for this first tailored suit, the tailor showed me a gorgeous suit of evening clothes which had been left unpaid for by a customer of somewhat my figure—taller, but the coat and vest fitted with a few alterations. So I blazed out in evening clothes before I had any place to wear them" or, for that matter, any immediate way to pay for them.[19]

This practice of buying clothes to signal a status one merely hoped to gain was common among young men on the make in the 1890s and became only more so in succeeding decades. In the early 1920s, J. W. Erlich took much the same approach to his wardrobe. A law student who supported himself with a number of part-time jobs, Erlich believed that he needed to broadcast his aspirations through his wardrobe. "All that I earned was going into the project of making me into a high-toned lawyer and making me *look* like a high-toned lawyer." Eager to separate himself from poorer men, Erlich invested in "clothes that would attest I was no boxcar bum (any longer)." He also wanted garments that would display his aspirations, clothes that would help "convince people that I was prosperous," even though he wasn't.[20] Although their incomes did not yet match their tastes, White and Erlich realized that it was important to invest in expensive clothing which reflected not their actual positions but their long-range aspirations.

White, Erlich, and innumerable other ambitious young businessmen quickly realized that not all business suits were equal and that some types and styles carried more prestige than others. Among bourgeois men, tailor-made clothing conferred far greater status than mass-produced or "ready-made" suits. Therefore, the man in the ready-made garment might well envy his colleagues' hand-fitted garments. Journalist Will Irwin described how much these distinctions mattered to middle-class businessmen who were trying to keep pace with their peers. A man newly arrived in New York City "no sooner matches himself with his associates of equal income than he discovers that [his] ready-made clothes rank with overalls in their esteem." As a result, he might begin to have clothes tailor-made for him by an affordably priced tailor, but his problems would not be over. "Perhaps he is contented at first with thirty-five dollar [hand-tailored] suits. That contentment does not last long. Again he compares his garments with those of his associates. . . . It is a matter of keeping the pace—of imitative vanity."[21]

Ambitious white-collar workers did not buy garments that reflected their current positions, but instead purchased garments that resembled those of the men they envied—men who filled the jobs they hoped to one day hold themselves. Bourgeois men's belief that suits were signs of prosperity and high social position was symptomatic of their growing tendency to conceive of success in terms of what they could buy with their salaries and display publicly. Although this material conception of success did not completely replace the more intangible notion of success as high occupational and social position, its power was growing.

The Responses to Envy, 1890–1915

Men's efforts to climb the corporate ladder and attire themselves after the manner of more successful men elicited much comment. Moralists who wrote about middle-class men's envy between 1890 and 1915 took a variety of positions on this behavior. Certainly not all agreed with each other. But there were some similarities that united their diverse responses to the emotion.

First, religious beliefs continued to exert influence over the business culture in a way they would not in succeeding years. Second, what historians have dubbed the "character ethic"—that is, the belief that success might be won through hard work, individual initiative, and moral virtue—although threatened by new consumerist and corporate values, still remained largely intact.[22]

Many social commentators and moralists agreed that middle-class men were envious and discontented, but they could not agree on how to respond to this envy. Envy, after all, could produce various results. It could spur on ambition, but it could also create tension and inefficiency in the office or even foster resentment between different classes of workers. Therefore, while journalists, clergymen, and essayists were united in condemning middle-class women's envy, they met men's envy and discontent with far less consensus. They were unified in criticizing men's envy when it threatened the existing social and economic order, but when men acted on the emotion in subtler ways, more suited to a capitalist economy, their actions elicited multiple responses.

Restraining Envy

Before World War I, commentators occasionally discussed urban men's envy as a catalyst for resentment and strife rather than as a fuel for aspiration and achievement. This type of envy led men to wish misfortune upon those whom they envied, and in the moralists' opinions, this form of the emotion was always base. They believed that those who were envious in this destructive way were fomenting class hatred and threatening the capitalist system. A 1903 editorial in *Harper's Weekly* attacked the "dominant envy" that threatened society. "The envious are with us in all the walks of life," the author noted. "How much is there of envy at the base of the popular fury against the 'coal barons,' the 'captains of industry,' and the 'trusts'? . . . We who make so little of the world's opportunities that the two ends meet with difficulty, are sure that this great accumulation of wealth is the result of an organic economic disease."[23]

At other times commentators implied that men whom envy rendered resentful were not necessarily opponents of capitalism, but that as a result of their envy they became less effective as capitalist actors. Envy weakened and distracted men, making them less efficient. "Covetousness, like a candle ill-made, smothers the splendor of a happy fortune in its own grease," chided the *Saturday Evening Post* in 1897. The *Nation* warned that those who were resentful would certainly end up as economic failures: "The passion is an evil one; twice cursed, injuring him that is envied and him that envies." To preserve social peace and the status quo, the journal warned the poor that their envy would accomplish nothing and would only harm them: "Once let a poor man give himself up to envy, and his lot becomes hopeless."[24]

These turn-of-the-century writers who so roundly condemned men's envy as inimical to economic success sought to defend capitalism in the midst of economic depression, Populist agitation, labor unrest, and a widespread fear of socialism. They opposed the redistributionist impulse that seemed to undergird so many of these protest movements and that appeared to them to spring from envy. In response to those who sought to equalize wealth, these writers argued that if the envious would only cease to be resentful, they too would be able to attain prosperity. Such arguments reinforced capitalist ideology as they emphasized the idea that through hard work all could benefit from the market economy. Resentment and class hatred rather than the inherent inequities of a market economy caused individual economic hardship. Moralists' efforts to combat resentful envy and to proclaim the justice of the market was a sign of their apprehensions about the stability of the social order in turbulent times.

These condemnations of men who envied resentfully and who questioned the justice of capitalism were substantially outnumbered by the assessments of a different type of envy, an envy which encouraged aspiration within the capitalist framework and which reinforced market values. Those who felt aspirational envy hoped to raise themselves to a higher social and economic level rather than lower those who were more affluent to their own level. Among middle-class men, this aspirational envy seems to have been more common than the widely condemned resentful envy. Beneficiaries of the capitalist order, bourgeois men were often property owners, and they commanded salaries that allowed them some comforts. They believed that they might advance further and prosper more if they tried harder. Economist Albert Hirschman has argued that such feelings are typical of developing capitalist economies. He claims that there is a period during economic development when individuals, though not yet advancing themselves, see their peers advancing and therefore become hopeful rather than resentful. They believe that they too may come to prosper as their fellows have.[25] For the most part, between 1890 and the Great Depression, middle-class men shared this hope, believed that the capitalist system worked, and wanted to move up within it. It was this faith in capitalism which fueled their aspirational envy.

While they did not threaten the prevailing economic system, middle-class men who expressed aspirational envy nevertheless encountered mixed reactions to their emotions. There were two contrasting positions on the legitimacy of men's envy and ambitions and the norms of acceptable workplace behavior. Some moralists who believed that contentment was a virtue considered envious businessmen to be hurting themselves as they longed for things they might never attain. Men should learn to embrace who they were and the jobs they held rather than seek to change them. In contrast, other commentators argued that envious and discontented men were socially and morally beneficial, and they consequently encouraged their readers to act on these emotions as they worked.

The moralists who urged men to be content lamented the fact that so many bourgeois men were preoccupied with advancement in business life. They pleaded with their male readers to stop struggling and competing and to start enjoying life by cultivating contentment with what they had. They endorsed hierarchy and inequality and questioned the right of men to rebel against their social and economic circumstances.

These writers looked at the ideology of success as vaguely pathological and somewhat immoral. When men compared themselves to more prosperous men and hoped for comparable salaries and accolades, they destroyed their prospects for contentment. In 1893, a columnist in *Munsey's Magazine* claimed that gradually opportunities for money-making in the United States would disappear. "But is this a prospect to be deplored?" he wondered. Wouldn't American society be improved if men stopped their scrambling and instead lived contentedly? "Is not our national trait one of nervous energy that cannot find time for contentment?" The idea that they might become millionaires "inflames young men and old with a restless fever to get, get, with never a moment to enjoy that which they already have." The problem was that not all who dreamed of fortunes could acquire them, and "those who do not advance, and to whom the prospect of ever advancing grows dimmer instead of brighter, become discouraged and discontented with a competency that would bring them deep content were it not for the unrest engendered by contrasting their condition with that of those who have accumulated more than they can use."[26] The antidote to such unrest, according to the *Christian Advocate*, was to realize that "no one can enjoy his own opportunities for happiness while he is envious of another's. . . . Life has its full measure of happiness for every one of us, if we would only make up our minds to make the very most of every opportunity that comes our way, instead of longing for the things that come our neighbor's way."[27]

Another solution to the problem of envy was to learn to live in the here and now. The obsession with success made men think of the future rather than of the present. Consequently, they overlooked the good things that they possessed and instead contemplated what they desired but did not yet own. These far-off pleasures, when actually attained, never yielded the satisfactions that the envious expected. An editorialist for the *Independent* explained that while a man might legitimately hope "to be more prosperous" or to have a "better position" in the future, such hopes should not distract him from the pleasures at hand. "He should not let that hope interfere with his appreciating the position he has won for himself this year." Instead, he should consider whether his neighbor, with "more servants and a larger house and income," was really better off. After reflection, readers would realize that despite their modest incomes, they were happier than the richest of men.[28]

The numerous paeans to contentment directed toward businessmen are evidence that not all Americans were comfortable with the idea of men struggling to leave their social and economic position. According to the advocates of contentment, some would have to learn to be satisfied with less.

Magazine writers and religious authors offered more than abstract discussions of the value of contentment. They also offered concrete vocational advice. They suggested that men should cultivate feelings of contentment and even love for their jobs. They should see their positions not as stepping-stones to greater things but as ends in themselves. These writers were trying to reinvigorate older intellectual traditions, which endowed work with a transcendent meaning. Renaissance and Protestant philosophies of work—although they differed—both portrayed men's labors as having a higher and nobler meaning and purpose than merely the wages they provided. The Renaissance tradition emphasized the idea of craftsmanship and exalted man's role as creator, while Protestant visions of work tied earthly success to spiritual salvation. Both traditions asked men to feel an abiding and noninstrumental commitment to their labors.[29] It was these conceptions of work which the apostles of contentment believed to be endangered and which they hoped businessmen would once again embrace.

Many moralistic writers lamented the fact that so many men felt little loyalty to their present positions or employers. They decried the widespread restlessness of American men as they ceaselessly searched for new opportunities for promotion and abandoned one enterprise in order to pursue another. In 1897 moralist and career advisor Orison Swett Marden criticized men who envied others' positions, noting that it was "easy to see the thorns in one's own profession or vocation, and only the roses in that of another." This outlook made men switch jobs far too frequently. Marden decried the "fickleness, this disposition to shift about from one occupation to another," which seemed to him to be distinctively American. American men should overcome these tendencies, resist the impulse to glance enviously at the better positions which their peers occupied, and instead learn to be loyal to their work. It was loyalty, purpose, and perseverance, rather than envy, ambition, and restlessness that men should cultivate.[30]

Marden and other moralists encouraged men to "love" their work. "The real secret of happiness is to be in love with your job; to do work that you like to do; that interests you," argued a writer in the *Saturday Evening Post* in 1908. Such affection for one's work would counter the instrumental way in which many were regarding their positions.[31] Essayist Charles Richard Dodge lamented the fact that "too many young men are occupying uncongenial positions, their minds filled with discontent, their hearts with envy of the success of more fortunate acquaintances in other occupations." To redress this situation, he encouraged young men to find "a congenial occupation" that offered enjoyment. It was, after all, "the contented man, the man who finds out what is his proper sphere in life . . . [who] is the truly rich man in this frenzied strenuous age."[32]

The moralists who tried to convince white-collar men to love their jobs were trying to reinvigorate the idea of a personal commitment to work precisely because work was becoming increasingly less personal and pleasant, not merely for manual laborers in factories but for men in the white-collar sector as well. Numerous scholars have described the decreased autonomy, personal contact, and possibility of advancement that white-collar workers encountered in the emerging corporations. Daniel Rodgers maintains that white-collar work came to resemble factory work as it became ever more regimented.[33] Middle-class men's alienation from their work and their ever more manifest desires for advancement and rewards alarmed moral leaders, who saw such feelings as having the power to destabilize the economy and threaten the moral fiber of American manhood.

Those writers who advocated contentment and encouraged men to stay in one position firmly believed that there were naturally occurring divisions and hierarchies which separated men and which should not be dismantled. Many commentators and scholars have maintained that restlessness and the desire for self-transformation have been long-standing and socially accepted characteristics of Americans. While men may indeed have been restless throughout U.S. history, this attribute was far more controversial than prevailing interpretations of American manhood would suggest.[34] Men who envied, who dreamed of advancement and self-transformation, did so in an environment where their dreams were sometimes sharply questioned.

Fanning the Flames of Envy and Ambition

Not all, however, agreed with the ideal of contented manhood, nor were all ready to condemn envy and discontent. "Content," claimed one editorialist, " . . . is a kind of diluted despair. . . . Content makes the trained individual swallow vinegar and try to smack his lips as if it were wine."[35] Contentment, in fact, offered false comfort, quenched desire, and kept men from doing great things, while discontent prompted men to pursue their dreams. As Episcopal bishop Phillips Brooks explained in his address "The Duty of the Business Man," "Dreadful will be the day when the world becomes contented, when one great universal satisfaction spreads itself over the world. Sad will be the day for every man when he becomes absolutely contented with the life that he is living, with the thoughts that he is thinking, with the deeds that he is doing, when there is not forever beating at the doors of his soul some great desire to do something larger."[36]

Brooks and countless other writers opposed the doctrine of contentment and urged bourgeois men to act on their envy. The writers who lauded discontentedness were not merely secular capitalists assailing the fortress of contentment and religious belief. They often were religious writers or ministers whose works were published in the same journals as those essays that urged men to be contented. Those who praised discontent spoke of it in ways resembling the paeans to contentment. They sought to legitimize the emotion by presenting it as rooted in divine will or natural order.

Some writers who praised discontent argued that it was superior to contentment because the latter emotion led men into the sinful states of sloth and indolence. "[A]s a rule, the content that is praised is not a virtue, but a vice full-brother to laziness," warned an editorialist in the *Saturday Evening*

Post.[37] The man who lived contentedly lacked spirit, initiative, and drive. "The man who is satisfied with his daily earnings, who seeks in his business the means of existence and nothing more, is a poor miserable creature, fit only to bear burdens as the ass bears gold, to groan and sweat under the businesses, either led or driven," wrote educator Robert Waters. Rather than seeking contentment, he argued, every man should be struggling to advance.[38] Such struggle was good for the individual and the society as a whole, for as a *Saturday Evening Post* reader claimed in a letter to the editor, "Without discontent there would be no strife, no progress."[39]

If discontent led to progress, then it was a social good. By extension, those circumstances which bred discontented men—the inequalities of condition which caused envy—were also good. An editorialist in the *Saturday Evening Post* claimed that "if there is one man in the community, richer or more powerful than the others, they naturally look up to him, see his position, feel his success as an incentive, and seek to equal it. Then progress begins. In a community where all are exactly equal in wealth or poverty there is no real growth." In sum, "Inequality promotes discontent, and discontent progress."[40]

Commentators who preached that envy and discontent led to progress often invoked the laws of nature to justify their positions. Their arguments showed the influence of Darwinian theory and relied on evolutionary metaphors. The central claim of their position was that discontent had made mankind advance as a species. Man, wrote a columnist in the *Christian Advocate*, "is not content with his possessions, his attainments, or his work. . . . Man is not content with what he is. He has made progress. The highest type of man today is far in advance of the best type of man a thousand years ago." On the other hand, the writer noted, "The lower animals are content with their situation. . . . They eat their food and enjoy their pleasures and never think of anything higher or better."[41] These contented lower animals, according to the Reverend W. F. Tillett, were typified by the oyster and the swine—hardly creatures for men to emulate.[42]

These discussions of struggling and discontented men, although they applied evolutionary concepts to society, stopped short of promising the harsh outcomes that were described by conventional nineteenth-century social Darwinists. The implication of many of these paeans to envy and discontent was that the emotions would enable everyone to strive and increase their possessions. There would be inequalities, but these inequalities, rather than causing the poor to perish, would lead them to struggle for more. Envy and dissatisfaction would inspire ambition in all men and lead to progress and change.

The linked ideas of discontent and evolution contrasted sharply with the doctrine of contentment. Exponents of contentment often invoked the Great Chain of Being and the idea that all creatures had a divinely ordained niche to fill. Both those who advocated contentment and those who advocated discontent used conceptions of nature to justify their doctrines, but they clearly saw different patterns in the natural world. The ideas of discontent and evolution legitimized movement, competition, desire, and a changing self, while the doctrine of contentment preached that God had endowed all people and animals with a fixed and unchanging identity and had assigned them a social position with which they should be contented. More specifically, both apostles of contentment and apostles of discontent used the natural world to justify the inequalities in society but envisioned strikingly different outcomes for those with less in the natural and the social worlds. They attributed different degrees of permanency to these inequalities. The apostles of contentment argued that all must stay where God and Nature had placed them and accept their unequal status while the proponents of discontent believed that these inequalities need not be lasting.

Those social commentators who embraced the evolutionary model and saw discontent as a natural and perhaps beneficent part of the human condition often expressed the linked belief that there were not particular ordained positions for men in society. The English evolutionist T. H. Huxley articulated this idea in his 1894 work, *Evolution and Ethics* which was reprinted several times in America. Huxley wrote, "Among mankind . . . there is no such predestination to a sharply defined place in the social organism. However much men may differ in the quality of their intellects, the intensity of their passions, and the delicacy of their sensations, it cannot be said that one is fitted by his organization to be an agricultural labourer and nothing else, and another to be a landowner and nothing else."[43]

Many American writers whose works appeared in popular magazines offered a version of these ideas as they repudiated the notion that men were designed for a particular job. Instead, they encouraged their readers to act on their envy and discontent and to keep climbing the career ladder. These writers intimated that it might be harmful for men to stay in one position for their entire careers. "[T]hroughout the various situations of life, you will find everybody dreaming of something other than he possesses," wrote Robert Waters. "Let him always strive after the upper stories in his profession, for there is happiness in the very strife. Nor will his duties be less faithfully done for his having this ideal; on the contrary, he will do them all the better; for the man of ideals has a stimulus and a spur which the idealless man lacks."[44]

Men would help themselves and their communities if they constantly tried to gain better things and better positions. To stand still and repress desire was harmful to all. An editorialist in the *Saturday Evening Post* claimed that "no worse blight can fall on any nation or community" than the "passion for the steady job." American men who were constantly looking for new positions should be congratulated. "It is often charged that Americans do their work in slovenly fashion because they work with one eye ever roving in search of something better. But, although it is bad not to put one's whole heart into one's work, and although the quickest way to get something better is to do the task in hand thoroughly, still far worse than lack of thoroughness is lack of enterprise." The editorialist seemed to suggest that what gave meaning to men's lives was not the actual content of their work but their disposition as they carried out their duties.[45] Another *Post* editorialist admitted that the jobs men held might be "worrying" and "tiring," but if a man had hope for the future and "look[ed] forward to some position above him that by effort he may attain," his life and his work would have meaning.[46]

Both those writers who praised dissatisfaction and those who urged men to love their jobs realized that work might not afford the same satisfactions to their generation as it had to previous generations. Many men, wanting more money, greater chances for advancement, and greater satisfaction, and unable to get them in their own work, looked enviously at other people's positions. Some moralists responded to this development by invoking the idea of a calling and encouraging men to adopt a loving outlook toward their work. They hoped that such an attitude would transform even mundane, alienating, inherently unfulfilling tasks into satisfying employment. Other writers assured men that there were better, more satisfying positions higher up and that their ambition was legitimate. Neither response could remedy the root problem, however. Middle-class men's work had changed profoundly, and neither blind love nor driving ambition could make it satisfying or guarantee success and advancement.

Thrift or Emulative Spending

Another debate that raged among business leaders, clergymen, and editorial-ists between 1890 and 1915 centered on the question of spending. Moralists did more than merely consider whether bourgeois men should strive for higher positions. They also considered whether or not men should emulate the habits and fashions of those who had enviable careers. Affluent men often attired themselves with great elegance. Young men, eager for similar prosperity and privilege, sometimes tried to replicate these fashions. Their attempts provoked mixed reactions. Some moralists believed that men should follow the "character ethic" and practice frugality and self-restraint. Others maintained that young men should make strategic purchases that would help them fashion themselves into desirable commodities, spending some money in order to get more.

Those commentators who argued that frugality was the key to success believed that men should gain recognition based on their efforts rather than on their possessions. They encouraged young men to save their money and warned them not to envy and emulate the spending habits of their neighbors and more successful colleagues. Thrift served two purposes. It helped a man save money to finance his future endeavors. It also built character: If a man denied himself what he wanted and did not give in to temptation or envy, he would become stronger and more virtuous.

Self-made men who had first gained wealth and prominence in the mid to late nineteenth century, before the full emergence of the modern con-sumer economy, often praised frugality. John D. Rockefeller instructed men to control their spending and their envy, telling them, "Live within your means and don't think too much of your neighbor's good fortune." Russell Sage advised young men that saving was the surest way to prosperity and happiness and that those who did not practice thrift were on the sure road to failure. "The young man working at a desk wants the most stylish cut of clothing and the most expensive pleasures, simply because his neighbor in-dulges in these extravagant fancies. He is not strong-willed enough to resist, and of course that leads to inevitable ruin." Other voices joined in the cho-rus, admonishing men that if they observed a peer "changing his furniture or new hanging his rooms, because the fashion has changed, do not be fool enough to copy him; but think how much he spent idly and estimate what you saved wisely." Young men should make sure they possessed no more "servants, dogs, or carriages than are necessary or suitable to your fortune or rank in life." The money that young men saved through policing their spending habits would be significant; perhaps even more important, through such underconsumption they would develop a virtuous character.[47]

Many moral and business leaders believed that if young men spent too much money they would lose not just their savings but their virtue as well. Living beyond one's means was a sign of a dishonest and flawed character; it therefore might harm a man's prospects because it bespoke profligacy and insincerity. Orison Swett Marden, who had criticized women who lived beyond their means, also criticized men who engaged in the same practices. He lambasted the "young men who live in attics, in the midst of poverty of surroundings, and deny themselves all but the bare necessaries of life in order that they may appear two or three evenings a week in dress suits in the Waldorf Astoria, or in some other fashionable hotel or restaurant in New York." Marden believed that to dress above one's station was to lie, and "when a man sacrifices his honesty he loses the mainspring of his character." He advised young men to resist the temptations of the "great city" and to avoid being "dazzled or led away by the glitter and show, the false display, and the flaunting of wealth on every hand." A man must have "a well-posed mind and a steady, well-balanced character" in order to "cling to his aim" and gain success.[48]

The success writers, businessmen, and moralists who believed that thrift was necessary for success and that emulative consumption ruined men's chances argued that envying another man's successful career was legitimate, but that envying his possessions was not. They subscribed to an older producer ethic, which held that men's identities depended on the work they performed and the things they made rather than the goods they purchased.

Yet envious men who wished to emulate the fashions of the successful did not find universal condemnation. While many advisors encouraged thrift, there were other writers at the turn of the century who suggested that those with dreams of success would do well to imitate the spending habits of the wealthy. Writers who encouraged strategic spending recognized that in the emerging consumer society, men were constructing a new language of goods. Success was coming to be recognized by its symbols. Wise spending rather than careful saving, therefore, would bring rewards.

In cities, where swelling populations prohibited employers from knowing everything about their potential employees, and where many young businessmen were migrants from farms and villages, some success writers assumed that it was becoming easier for men to make an impression with their appearance—which all could see—than with their reputations—which few might know. Consequently, spending money on items of appearance was a wise career move. In particular, success writers urged young men to spend money on well-cut suits, even if they were expensive and did not accurately reflect their earning power. Men should emulate those whom they hoped to equal. Perriton Maxwell, an advice columnist for young men in the *Saturday Evening Post*, wrote of the "importance of being well dressed." He emphasized that in the business world, people were snobs and judged each other on the basis of appearances. Men who were inattentive to their attire therefore were "not on the main road to success." Dress was a "kind of personal weathervane, showing the direction of man's ideas and ambitions," and it was a powerful signal of self-esteem. For this reason, "the modern Knight, fighting in the tournament of commerce or entered in the jousts of professionalism, can wear no more impregnable armor than a suit of good clothes." Expensive clothing was a badge and a means of entree. It was a way for middle-class men to exhibit their familiarity with the requirements of comportment in business culture.[49]

Good clothing not only allowed men to look the equal of men higher up in the business world; it allowed them to feel equal as well. Walter Creedmoor, a journalist for *Munsey's Magazine*, wrote that after an initial year of frugal living in the city, a young man could legitimately begin to spend money on fine clothing. Charting the progress of a hypothetical young man as he struggled for success in New York, he wrote that after the first year had passed, the young man might be seen promenading on Fifth Avenue, "wearing a silk hat and a long frock coat of the very latest fashion." Creedmoor acknowledged that there were "moralists who would shake the warning forefinger and declare that he was treading a path which would invariably lead him down to death and destruction." Creedmoor, however, would not join in the chorus of condemnation. "For my own part, I cannot see that a desire to appear well in the eyes of the world is a reprehensible one. His high hat and frock coat will give him a certain degree of self-confidence and will undoubtedly tend to increase what is known variously as his 'self respect,' his 'personal vanity,' and his 'good opinion of himself.' " Creedmoor maintained that because elegant clothes would make the young man feel equal to those he envied, he would be more effective in business life. "He will find that he may appear just as well as the most respected and prosperous citizens in the town, and the feeling is bound to encourage him in the struggle in which he is engaged."[50] Clothes offered a veneer of equality, even if men's underlying economic circumstances differed dramatically. This veneer, however thin, could partially and temporarily obscure status differences and ameliorate uncomfortable feelings of envy and inferiority.

Advertisers, naturally more interested in spending than in thrift, also encouraged the perception that emulative dressing might lead to success and resolve social tensions. They nurtured the already widespread belief that appearances mattered and that people were constantly watching and evaluating each other on the basis of their looks. The "parable of the first impression," described by Roland Marchand as a prominent theme in advertisements of the 1920s, was already appearing in ads by 1908. "Young men," warned an advertisement for Strauss Brothers clothing, "the world sizes you up by the clothes you wear." "We are living in an age of impressions. . . . The appearance of a young man nowadays is a great factor in his success," claimed an ad for Society Brand Clothes. "Tailor your way to opportunity," the Royal Tailors cajoled. "Many a man has tailored his way into the confidence of total strangers—has tailored his way through coldness and distrust—has tailored himself into life opportunities through sheer attractiveness of good clothes." According to these advertisements, conforming to certain class-identified fashions would allow a man to enter that class. White-collar men needed to show that they understood the language and the symbols of the successful business class in order to join it. The ads told readers that little mattered besides appearances. Character, moral virtue, and unflagging industry went unmentioned. External qualities decided one's fate, for a man was known not from long association and careful consideration of his qualities but from the image he constructed out of broadcloth and leather.

The ads also explicitly encouraged middle-class men to act on their envy. The Royal Tailors, a national group of tailors who would custom-fit suits for men, took the lead in this strategy. Men might avoid wearing ill-fitting, ready-made suits if they would patronize the affordably priced Royal Tailors. "All Eyes Envy the Tailor-Dressed Man," one of their ads claimed, showing a group of men looking longingly at the apparel of an elegant man (Figure 6). In another appeal they described in detail the causes of and cures for men's envy. They wrote, *"Deep down in your heart,* you have always coveted tailor-made clothes—every man has. Some men may perhaps have smothered Pride and accepted a factory-made substitute because of fancied economy. But envy of the man with a good tailor lies inrooted in the soul of every untailored clothes wearer. That envy need no longer remain ungratified in *you.*"[51] These ads told men both that their envy of other men was un-

All Eyes Envy the
Tailor-Dressed Man

This street-car scene is a snap-shot from everyday life.
Wherever men gather there is always at least one among them

whose appearance stands out — whose clothes have a certain refinement, good taste and style in them that lift them above the commonplace.

And the secret is always the same. A *real tailor* made those clothes — made them to the special order of the man who wears them — and made them to harmonize with every line of his body.

There is a tailor like that waiting to make *your* clothes to your *order* in our great Chicago and New York shops — a tailor who will work with *hand* and *head*, specifically and individually for you, to make your clothes fit and compliment your every body peculiarity.

The Convenient Tailoring System

No man who has not actually tried our system, can begin to realize from mere description, how convenient, how economical, how satisfactory it is to order his clothes tailored to order in our way.

Understand you deal with your own leading merchant, who is as near to you perhaps as your butcher or baker and probably a good deal better known in your town than any of the local tailors.

That merchant, who has been schooled by us for years in measure-taking, sends us a virtual blue-print of your body — and you pick the cloth for your suit or overcoat from over 500 beautiful woolen innovations — the season's newest and best — on display at his store.

Then in our great tailoring studios, in Chicago or New York, where we have the pick of the world's greatest tailors — we build your suit or overcoat to your individual measures — and have it ready to ship to you by the fastest returning express six days after the order reaches us.

But that is not all. This system not only makes it easy for you to get real New York or Chicago tailor-made clothes, but it enables you to get them on the safest clothes-buying plan in the world.

You get a contract-guarantee with your garment when it comes, made out individually to you and signed by our President that warrants your complete and perfect satisfaction or you needn't accept the garment.

In fairness to your wardrobe please call on our local dealer to-day. Let him show you, how $25, $30, and $35 will buy for you the very utmost in a custom-cut, pure wool suit or overcoat. But for your protection — be sure you find a real Royal dealer. If you are not sure write us for his name — or look for our tiger head trade mark on all woolen samples you are shown. And when you get your garment, insist upon getting our written guarantee, made out to you and signed by our President.

This Big Book of Beautiful Cloth Samples — Free

Name

Address

The Royal Tailors

President

Chicago   New York

Figure 6. In the early years of the twentieth century, middle-class men were encouraged to act on their envy and acquire the badges of elite status.

derstandable and that it could be easily resolved and satisfied. They promised men that by purchasing a suit they could also achieve the status that it represented.

Many men already believed in the power of clothes. They found it difficult to put the lessons of thrift into practice in American cities where the pace of spending was quickening and conspicuous display was commonplace. Yet they could not make their purchases with complete serenity because they knew that some social critics condemned emulative spending as profligate and dishonest. It was often difficult to reconcile the reality of daily social life with the cultural prescriptions of the day.

The United States was changing from a face-to-face society and an entrepreneurial economy into an urban industrial nation with a growing corporate economy. The old rules for success in business seemed increasingly outmoded, but a new set of clear guidelines for emotional comportment in the corporation had not yet been agreed upon. Men entering the business world between 1890 and 1915 thus found a culture in transition. Sometimes advisors advocated perseverance, loyalty, and thrift, while at other times the cardinal virtues seemed to be discontent, envy, and emulation. In succeeding years, business leaders would gradually develop a set of cohesive rules to govern men's behavior and emotional style in the office—a set of rules still very much in evidence today.

The Responses to Envy, 1915–1930

Attitudes toward middle-class men's envy did not change abruptly in 1915. Some moralists regarded men's envy much as earlier generations had. But between 1915 and 1930, the cultural and economic transformations accelerated and came to have greater influence on the way in which businessmen and cultural commentators evaluated envy.

During these years it became increasingly apparent that both white-collar men and those who offered them advice regarded business and success in a far more secular light than had their fathers and grandfathers. Men no longer invested their work or their occupational futures with the same religious significance as they formerly had, perhaps because it was ever more difficult to believe that God had actually chosen to create the occupations which the corporate economy offered to workers. Secularized attitudes were evident in many of the articles which discussed careers. Aside from those essayists who wrote only in denominational journals, most writers discussed emotions like envy and contentment in terms of business efficiency or personal fulfillment rather than in moralistic language.

Other transformations had profound effects on white-collar culture as well. First, the size and power of corporations increased. As even more middle-class men came to work for corporations, many commentators and business leaders questioned whether envy and ambition were desirable traits in a corporate environment. Second, expanded advertising campaigns began to influence cultural assumptions about the material objects necessary for a successful career. As a result of these circumstances, envy was gradually channeled out of the world of work and into the world of goods.

Competition or Cordiality: New Problems in the Corporate Office

During the 1910s and 1920s, editorialists, inspirational writers, and business leaders continued to argue about men's commitment to their work and struggled to define the role of the individual in modern corporate life. Some defended individualistic traits and lauded ambition and envy, while others condemned these traits and believed they had no place in the new corporate setting. This latter group of opinion makers increasingly influenced the tone of the corporate workplace.

Some businessmen who headed corporations championed the nineteenth-century vision of success and praised discontent, ambition, and industry. Those who were the most outspoken champions of discontented, ambitious men had themselves gained prosperity and prominence by acting on these emotions and following the advice of nineteenth-century success writers. They had gained affluence and renown through their individual initiative, often working independently of corporations. In their writings, they invoked their own experiences in the nineteenth century as models for young men in the twentieth century. Consequently, the advice which they offered young men frequently seemed more suited to a market where the individual rather than the corporation was the central economic actor. Even in the face of new corporate conditions that limited men's mobility, these self-made men praised individualism, ambition, willpower, and discontent, because, for them, they had borne fruit.

In 1918 Charles P. Steinmetz, a well-known scientist and consulting engineer for General Electric, told readers of the *American Magazine* that "the world belongs to the dissatisfied." Steinmetz, who earned $100,000 per year, argued that those "who were at the front of the pack" knew the power and value of dissatisfaction, whereas those "men in the rear are the ones who are content with little. Such men will always be in the rear until they become unsatisfied and begin to sprint to catch up with the others." Admitting that not all jobs gave men equally good chances for success, Steinmetz warned male readers not to be content with the "blind alley job." "The man who gets into a blind alley job does not have to stay there unless he so wishes. If he has imagination enough to become discontented, he will soon move into a better job." Striking at the very root of the belief that men should love their jobs, Steinmetz argued instead that blind affection for their jobs garnered men few rewards. "The main trouble is that these men are too satisfied with their jobs, or, if they are dissatisfied, they are not discontented enough." Steinmetz, a German emigré, joined General Electric shortly after it was formed in 1892. After two years, he was promoted to consulting engineer, a position he held for the rest of his life. In addition to working for General Electric, he remained active in numerous scientific societies, and his reputation was not dependent merely upon his association with GE. He was able to retain his individuality and gain prominence while working for a large corporation.[52]

Other prominent business leaders agreed with Steinmetz's recommendations. Cyrus H. K. Curtis, founder of Curtis Publishing Company, argued in 1925 that "what young men need most today is ambition. If a lad goes into a sawmill for his first job he should do so with the idea that one day he will own that sawmill. If he's content from the outset to be a worker in the ranks, that's what he'll remain unless blind luck picks him up and puts him elsewhere. . . . A plodder may be reliable, but he's rarely noticeable."[53] Curtis's own life story resembled nineteenth-century fables about success. Born in 1850, he began selling newspapers on street corners in Portland, Maine when he was twelve. At fifteen Curtis published his own paper for young boys, which he sold for two cents. In 1879 he started the *Tribune and Farmer*, which would spawn the *Ladies' Home Journal*. In 1890 he established the Curtis Publishing Company which acquired numerous publications including the *Saturday Evening Post* and the *Philadelphia Inquirer*. Because he ended up at the head of a corporation rather than in a midlevel position as so many others did, Curtis believed that the old formula for success still held true. He did not seem to realize that the level of success which he had attained was exceptional for the new age.[54]

The irascible Henry Ford, after his successful ascension to the top of the corporate ladder, also spoke out in favor of discontented men:

We always keep our eye on a young man who shows signs of being dissatisfied, especially if he thinks he has anything to offer by way of improving things. The chance that a boy or a young man who is content with the way things are done now will develop into a leader is pretty slim. The restless boy, the one who wants to know *why* things are as they are, and why they can't be done better shows signs of possible leadership. At times he may be a nuisance. But no boy ever became a leader without making himself a nuisance to somebody at some time.[55]

Ford, born in 1863, moved from job to job in his early years. He worked first as an apprentice to a machinist, and then set up and repaired Westinghouse machines. From 1891 to 1899 he worked for Edison Illuminating Company, but still found time to build his first automobile. In 1899 he quit Edison and helped to organize the Detroit Automobile Company and then in 1903 established the Ford Motor Company. Unlike many men, Ford was able to advance beyond his entry-level position in other men's companies and establish himself as an independent businessman. Undoubtedly, his ambition, discontent, and restlessness had served him well.[56]

These businessmen spoke from privileged positions within the corporate world. They had gained fame, wealth, and status and managed to ascend the corporate ladder by acting on individualistic ambitions and desires. They argued that their experiences provided models for the rising generation of young men, never recognizing how atypical their situations were becoming. They represented an older generation of entrepreneurs whose experiences and advice were more symptomatic of and suited to the realities of the nineteenth-century economy than to those of the twentieth century.

These businessmen who advocated discontent were opposed by business leaders and business writers who asked workers to repress their dissatisfaction and cultivate an affection for their jobs. They claimed that unfettered envy and ambition might no longer be appropriate for the modern economy. These commentators used the rhetoric of an earlier generation as they entreated men to love their own jobs and to stop looking enviously at others' positions, yet they employed the familiar rhetoric for a different purpose.

The difference was that many implicitly indicated that while such a commitment to work might benefit the individual employee, it would be of even greater use to the company for which he worked.

If men were constantly casting envious eyes at other men's positions, switching jobs in the hope of advancing, and putting their own ambitions ahead of the corporation's fortunes, they might be inefficient workers and neglect the company's interests. Henry Ford admitted that discontented workers could be a "nuisance." Journalist Isaac Marcosson's conflict with editor Louis Brownlow provided a concrete example of how ambition and rivalry within the office could interfere with company goals. Recognizing the problems that envy could create, many business leaders and advisors implied that in the new corporate atmosphere, middle-class men could not function as autonomous actors, for they were now part of a larger system and hierarchy. They needed to make their desires and emotions conform to the company's needs. Somehow, men raised on individualism had to learn how to be part of a team. Business leaders told men that if they learned cooperation and teamwork, both employer and employee would benefit. The corporation would be better served if men had a unity of purpose. The employee would be happier if he did not have false illusions about his future and realized that not all men could rise any longer.[57]

A shining example of this new emotional model was offered by Joseph Appel, the director of advertising for the Wanamaker department stores and later the executive manager of the New York Wanamaker store. In his memoirs, he described how he had gradually learned the corporate emotional style, a style he hoped his readers would cultivate. Appel began to work for Wanamaker in 1899, and in his early years, he was often beset by envy and insecurity about his position in the world. After working at the company for six months, Appel asked for a raise. He believed he should earn twice as much as he did. His request was kindly but firmly denied, and Appel began to think what lessons he might learn from the experience. He decided that he must realize first of all that he was "not independent: no man is. We must live with and for each other." He also concluded, "I am now part of a great organization and I must mold myself to its ways." Finally, he decided that he must learn to accept the fact that "there are others ahead of me who first must be promoted."

Unfortunately, these maxims proved harder to follow than Appel expected. After working for Wanamaker for another year, he began to listen to the complaints of several discontented coworkers. Listening to them made him feel envious and discontented as well. He realized he had gradually allowed the "rank poison" of "suspicion . . . jealousy . . . hate" to enter his "mind and heart." Things came to a head when the men learned that company executives had planned festivities to celebrate the store's anniversary. Part of the celebration included a parade of employees who were supposed to march by the "Head of the House" and salute him as they passed. This idea rankled many of the young male employees, who believed that it smacked of imperial Rome or feudal Europe. Accordingly, they stayed away from the event in protest. They were chastised for their absence by the store owner and put on furlough. Eventually, after long conversations with Wanamaker, Appel was allowed to come back to work. From his conversations and experience, he had gained a new perspective—a perspective which left little room for envy. Appel came to realize, and thereafter preached, that while one's individuality might be a source of strength, it might also be a source of weakness. "Our individuality—our strength—grows only as we merge it with the *Universal*." What was the universal? It was the "Spirit of Business," which was also the "Spirit of Life." True union with this larger corporate spirit meant that one was "pulling together with your fellow-creatures" instead of being a "sour-face, shriveled-up, envious and jealous pull-back." Appel claimed that once he learned to master his emotions and rid himself of excessive individualism, he was able to become enormously successful. Suppressing envy and ambition was the key to his rise.[58]

Middle-class magazines popularized Appel's message with editorials that focused on the importance of controlling one's emotions and limiting one's ambitions. Several *Saturday Evening Post* editorials made this new position clear. In 1923, in an essay entitled "The Value of Stability," an editorialist argued that "the inspirational idea," which encouraged men to be ambitious and try to advance was "being carried to an extreme. . . . Clerk, mechanic and salesman are taught to keep a wide-open eye fixed on the day when they will be ensconced behind a flat-topped desk, operating a battery of push buttons." The writer then discussed the difficulties this ambition caused for the modern corporation. Most notably, it made men resent their middling positions in the company, because they were ambitious for higher employments, which they had little likelihood of attaining. The reality was that "not more than one man in a hundred can become an executive in American business as it is organized today." Unfortunately, few realized this, and consequently "too many of the ninety and nine who must always remain in the ranks become unsettled and lose some of their value as subordinates."

Their "determination to advance" led them to ignore the complexities of their present job and focus instead on the promotions they so keenly desired. "[T]he forward-looker is often likely to gain a contempt for the insignificant job of today because it contrasts so meanly with emoluments of his mental future." With such a contemptuous attitude, the worker performed his job poorly. In the process of pursuing his own ambitions, the envious man was undermining corporate efficiency.[59]

Excessive ambition therefore must be discouraged and a different set of personality traits encouraged. A *Post* editorial argued that to counter the problems that overly ambitious men caused in the corporate environment, American society must temper the ideology of success and begin to value the "routine worker." "Is it not time that we reassess the value of the man who sticks to his job and handles it with steady efficiency?" asked the editorialist. "The tendency has been to regard the go-getters as the only really valuable type." Instead, the nation needed to value the man who found his niche and stayed contentedly at work there. For "there could be no real efficiency in an organization where every man was looking for a job above. Such general clawing and struggling for the next rung would inevitably upset the ladder. The truth of the matter is that the really successful business is one which maintains the proper proportion of go-getters and stay-putters."[60] Some large sector of the working population must reconcile themselves to the idea that they might not attain success. They must control their envy and ambition in order for the corporate structure to remain stable.

Telling men that they should not be ambitious at all, however, might diminish their incentive for industry, so many journalists and commentators told readers that if they could make their envy less obvious, they would be able to gain the object of their desires. In 1923, another *Post* editorial explained this outlook: "With all the recipes given the young man on how to succeed, it is strange that they are not told more often that an essential is willingness, indeed eagerness to be a good soldier, to perform enthusiastically the duties that lie immediately before them, rather than to exhale discontent because the actual summits have not been reached."[61]

First-person testimonials from the formerly envious personalized these same lessons. The authors of "The Sin That Everybody Commits and How I Cured Myself of It," "I Nearly Died of Envy," and "Why I Quit Thinking About Myself," all published in the *American Magazine*, offered similar stories about the effects of envy on business careers. The authors had all been white-collar workers in corporations, desperate to get ahead and envious of their colleagues and superiors. After suffering a crisis caused by envy—a nervous breakdown, the loss of a job—the men learned that they needed to overcome their envy and learn to love their work and their coworkers in order to attain success and happiness.

These authors told their readers how to develop a love for their work. The narrator of "The Sin That Everybody Commits and How I Cured Myself of It" told readers that after he resolved to stop envying others he had drawn up a code for himself so that he would not fall back into his old ways. One of the principles of this code read, "Fortunes have been made in this business and other fortunes will be. They will be made by those who love the business, and stick to it."[62] The author of "I Nearly Died of Envy" confided to readers that he too had discovered ways to avoid envy. The first was to realize that "[t]he greatest illusion in life . . . is that other people are having a better time than we are, that their work is more interesting than ours, their situations more free from dissatisfaction."[63]

In addition to learning to love their jobs, men must learn how to have friendlier interactions with their coworkers. In effect, they must cease to be competitive with others. In "I Nearly Died of Envy," the narrator claimed that the businessman was only in competition "with himself." The author of "The Sin That Everybody Commits" reminded himself that "there are no finer men in the world than those with whom I am associated."

These authors also instructed their readers to celebrate the good fortune of others rather than to envy it. This was another way to diminish competition. A teacher had once advised the author of "The Sin That Everybody Commits" that he should "form the habit of getting pleasure out of other men's success. You can, if you will, be a partner in progress. You can get so much joy out of their achievements that you will yourself be picked up and carried along with them." The man who had "nearly died of envy" also discovered the power of such an approach: "Suppose you train yourself to get pleasure out of the good luck of a hundred friends, or of five hundred, or a thousand. How you have cheated a niggardly old nature! What a millionaire in happiness you have become!"

The authors of these cautionary tales drove this point home by arguing that if men succeeded in repressing their envy and came to regard their coworkers as friends, not competitors, they would reap the very rewards they once had envied. One of the lessons offered in "I Nearly Died of Envy" was that "friendliness that seeks no reward is the most rewarded investment that a human being can make. It puts a thousand constructive forces to work, and their influence bobs up at the most unexpected times and places. I should be willing almost to say that if a man will devote himself to friendship he can forget position and money. For his friendship will win him both." In the essay "Why I Quit Thinking About Myself," an executive advised the narrator that if he would develop genuine friendliness in himself, he would achieve great success. The narrator at first found such friendliness difficult: "I had been so long introspective, self-centered, envious of others' successes, restless for fear I was overlooking some chance, that I found myself repeatedly slipping back into the old ruts." After much effort, however, he finally came to be genuinely friendly and kind in his interactions with others: "There was so much fun in it that I forgot to consider it as a matter of possible profit. And at that point, the real profits began."[64]

Advice like this asked men to hide their motives and passions and at least pretend to abandon the goals of profits and prominence. Only by abandoning these goals might they attain them. In the following decade, such advice would be codified most famously by Dale Carnegie in *How to Win Friends and Influence People*. These articles and Carnegie's book explained to businessmen how to use what seemed to be sincere relationships for instrumental ends. They told men to subtly advance their own cause by pretending not to.[65]

The business writers of the 1920s promised that a love for one's job and an affection for one's competitors would help a man go further in life. They claimed to offer this advice solely for the benefit of the businessman himself. It seems likely, however, that an even greater beneficiary of such attitudes would have been corporate leaders who wanted their employees to have a unity of purpose and a commitment to corporate rather than individual success. Instead of condemning envy and competitiveness on moral grounds, they condemned these emotions because they were not congruent with the needs of the corporation.

What was also revolutionary about this new advice to businessmen was that it flouted traditional gender conventions about men's emotions. The self-made man of the nineteenth century was widely—although not universally—celebrated for his aggressive behavior. The businessmen of the 1910s and 1920s were told to be more passive and friendly. A number of scholars have commented on the changing emotional expectations for men and women in the modernizing economy. Peter Stearns has shown how social expectations about anger and self-expression changed, as men in the twentieth century were instructed to suppress their emotions, particularly at

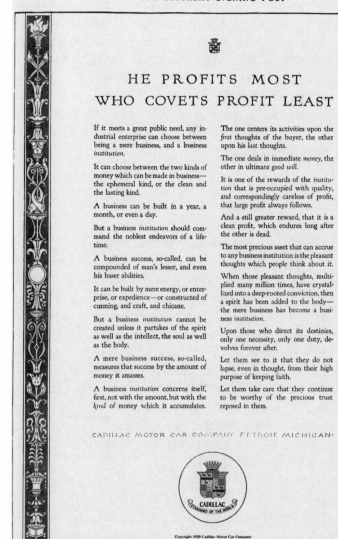

HE PROFITS MOST
WHO COVETS PROFIT LEAST

If it meets a great public need, any industrial enterprise can choose between being a mere business, and a business *institution*.

It can choose between the two kinds of money which can be made in business— the ephemeral kind, or the clean and the lasting kind.

A business can be built in a year, a month, or even a day.

But a business *institution* should command the noblest endeavors of a lifetime.

A business success, so-called, can be compounded of man's lesser, and even his baser abilities.

It can be built by mere energy, or enterprise, or expedience—or constructed of cunning, and craft, and chicane.

But a business *institution* cannot be created unless it partakes of the spirit as well as the intellect, the soul as well as the body.

A mere business success, so-called, measures that success by the amount of money it amasses.

A business *institution* concerns itself, first, not with the amount, but with the *kind* of money which it accumulates.

The one centers its activities upon the *first* thoughts of the buyer, the other upon his *last* thoughts.

The one deals in immediate *money*, the other in ultimate *good will*.

It is one of the rewards of the *institution* that is pre-occupied with quality, and correspondingly careless of profit, that large profit always follows.

And a still greater reward, that it is a clean profit, which endures long after the other is dead.

The most precious asset that can accrue to any business institution is the pleasant thoughts which people think about it.

When those pleasant thoughts, multiplied many million times, have crystallized into a deep-rooted conviction, then a spirit has been added to the body— the mere business has become a business *institution*.

Upon those who direct its destinies, only one necessity, only one duty, devolves forever after.

Let them see to it that they do not lapse, even in thought, from their high purpose of keeping faith.

Let them take care that they continue to be worthy of the precious trust reposed in them.

CADILLAC MOTOR CAR COMPANY DETROIT MICHIGAN

CADILLAC
STANDARD OF THE WORLD

Figure 7. To gain wealth and success, businessmen of the 1920s were expected to follow this motto and suppress their envy. 2001 General Motors Corporation. Used with permission of GM Media Archives.

work. Angel Kwolek-Folland has likewise argued that men in the corporate economy were asked to surrender the aggressive and individualistic traits traditionally associated with "bourgeois manhood" and instead practice many of the more submissive virtues traditionally associated with bourgeois women.[66] Envy too fell into this pattern. By the late 1910s and 1920s, men heard that it was imperative that they repress their desires. In the nineteenth century, such repression had been expected of women and had indicated their relative powerlessness in a patriarchal society. That men had to learn to repress their envy and aggression was an indication of the power they had lost in the corporate economy.

Channeling Envy into the Marketplace

Although corporate leaders asked men to suppress their envy in the workplace, they were encouraged to act on the emotion in the marketplace. As Peter Stearns points out, during the 1920s American men were encouraged to repress their emotions at work, but they were given increasing opportunities for emotional release outside of it.[67] Consumer spending on status goods represented a silent and less aggressive form of competition with coworkers and acquaintances. It gained acceptance because it assuaged envy in a fashion that did not threaten the stability or efficiency of corporate culture, as more overtly competitive actions might have. This new pattern of emotional repression at work and release outside of it benefited not only the corporations in search of office harmony, but also the companies that produced cars, office equipment, furniture, clothing, and countless other items that could be used for purposes of conspicuous display.

The widely held conviction that well-kept business clothes, stylish cars, and well-appointed offices were crucial to higher social status was symptomatic of the growing cultural emphasis on material goods as signals of success. While this concern with consumer goods was apparent before 1915, it gained greater significance. By the late 1910s and 1920s, some commentators claimed that the desire to own class-marked objects was what motivated men to work. Men no longer struggled to win positions for the honor and prestige that they inherently possessed but for the buying power that they would grant. Success was no longer only or primarily evident in the job a man held but in what he owned and displayed. As Edmund Wilson noted in 1932, "Americans have come generally to accept an ideal of personal glory and merit based solely on the possession of things: cars, clothes, electrical appliances."[68]

At the turn of the century, Bernard Baruch, William Allen White, and countless other young men had determined that they must dress above their actual station in order to succeed. At that time, this practice, while not uncommon, was nevertheless controversial. By the time Wilson was writing, however, the controversy had subsided, and the idea of dressing above one's income had gained widespread acceptance. In his 1916 essay "The New Wealth," Walter Weyl observed that men's appearances were becoming ever more crucial to their success. He maintained that earlier generations' enjoinders to practice thrift no longer seemed to fit the conditions of modern society. "It is not economy to save overmuch on clothes, which are the poor young man's advertisement. We must dress up to our jobs, even to the jobs we merely hope to get."[69] In *Middletown*, Robert and Helen Lynd described why many followed this logic as they repeated the words of a "leading citizen" of the town. He sought to explain "the almost universal local custom of 'placing' newcomers in terms of where they live, how they live, the kind of car they drive, and similar externals: 'It's perfectly natural. You see, they know money, and they don't know you.' " This understanding of the power of clothes and other material goods which the citizens of Middletown had internalized was reinforced by writers in their daily newspapers. The Lynds quoted columnist Dorothy Dix, who reminded her readers that "the world judges us largely by appearance. If we wish to be successful we have got to look successful."[70]

Advertisements fostered this belief with their claims that clothes might help a man elevate himself socially and economically. Hoffman Presses promised men that they could overcome their feelings of shame and insecurity and could equal those who were above them if they would only dress as prosperous men did. In their 1929 ad (Figure 8), a wistful man proclaimed:

I wish people liked me as much as I like them. . . .

The men I admire! I'd give an arm to look like them—easy, successful, sure in their work. They have the trim, unruffled look of success. The clothes of success. The laugh of success.

I sometimes think that if I looked like these prosperous men, there'd be no reserve in their welcome of me.

The trim, unwrinkled look of success! At least that's one thing I can get.

Figure 8. In this 1929 ad, Hoffman Presses suggested that men might acquire the "look of success" even if they could not acquire success itself. Courtesy Hoffman–New Yorker Corporation.

With a well-pressed suit, one could acquire the "look of success" even if actual success and prosperity proved more elusive.[71] In addition to emphasizing the importance of personal appearance, advertisers encouraged men to think about their larger surroundings and the image that these surroundings projected. Advertisements reminded consumers that offices and homes also helped to construct personal and business identities. These settings were filled with consumer goods and could increase or diminish a man's status. The Sikes Chair Company, for instance, reminded men that the appearance of their offices might influence the course of their careers:

Human Nature Is So Awfully Human! . . . The world backs winners and worships success. . . . All of which is but another way of saying: "Appearances *do* count." . . .
But what about the appearance of your *office*? Does it *look* like the home of a flourishing, prosperous business? Or does it place you at a disadvantage among those of your competitors who realize the dollars and cents value of "better offices"?[72]

By making office chairs an object of envy, advertisers suggested that even the most mundane object, if it had the correct class status, could bring a man success. All personal possessions might be read as statements about a man's identity and aspirations. Even the paint on his house might determine a man's career path. Devoe Paint and Varnish asked, "Failure or Success . . . Which does your home reflect? The world believes what it reads in the outward appearance of your home. . . . To win the respect and admiration of your friends and neighbors—beautify and protect your home with Devoe Paint."[73] In all aspects of life, a man must emulate and replicate the consumption practices of the wealthy. Emulation would help him construct the image of prosperity, even if this image did not accurately reflect his real financial condition.

Other products claimed to give men different advantages that they might need in the business world. Chevrolet, for instance, promised men increased efficiency, which would allow them to equal the truly successful. They might stop envying others if they would only buy an automobile (Figure 9). "What is the man in the picture doing? *Watching others go by him,* just like thousands of other men, who let the procession of live ones pass them by. Perhaps he is wondering why these other men of no greater physical strength or mental ability can own automobiles and *ride* toward success while he plods along, year after year, not only not making progress, but actually falling behind." Such a problem could be solved, however, through the purchase of a Chevrolet, which would allow a man to "move twice as fast" as "some other chap."[74]

By the 1920s, middle-class men wanted the class-marked things that

Figure 9. According to Chevrolet, men needed automobiles to be on equal footing with others in the business world. 2001 General Motors Corporation. Used with permission of GM Media Archives.

accompanied success as much as they wanted success itself. The Lynds noticed this pattern among the breadwinners of Middletown. Men worked in order to have money to buy the things that successful men owned. The Lynds observed, "For both the working and business class no other accompaniment of getting a living approaches in importance the money received for their work. It is more this future, instrumental aspect of work, rather than the intrinsic satisfactions involved, that keeps Middletown working so hard as more and more of the activities of living are coming to be strained through the bars of the dollar sign."[75]

Between 1890 and 1930, success gradually became associated with what a job allowed a man to buy rather than what a job allowed him to do. Consequently, many men came to envy possessions more than they envied occupational status. Corporate leaders and advertisers abetted this transformation. Business executives attempted to suppress envy in the workplace while advertisers tried to excite envy in the marketplace. Men learned to limit and restrain their feelings of competition and discontent in the office, because such emotions did not suit the corporate environment. On the other hand, they discovered that these feelings were welcomed and in fact encouraged in the consumer world because such emotions so precisely met corporate needs by fueling consumer spending.

The emotional prescriptions for men that emerged in the 1910s and 1920s are, in large part, still in place today. Men continue to experience envy in the office, but they have been conditioned not to show it. Their ambition for success is still strong, but they have learned the rhetoric—and perhaps even the instrumental value—of teamwork, cooperation, and (at least some) loyalty to the company. They have also learned that their success and social standing will be judged not merely on the basis of their position but on the richness of their possessions. The nineteenth-century ideal of middle-class masculinity—an aggressive and individualistic creature, who was all the more manly and commendable because of the simplicity of his attire—has been largely eclipsed by the amiable and well-dressed office worker surreptitiously eyeing the adjoining cubicle.

3. "The Prizes of Life Lie Away from the Farm"

When urban women and men felt twinges of envy as they looked at more affluent people on streets and in stores, they could try to assuage their envy through emulation. They could attempt to recast themselves into what they longed to be. America's rural population had little opportunity to do the same. While envy was at least as prevalent among country folk as city folk, country dwellers encountered a number of difficulties when they tried to actively address their sense of deprivation.

Those rural Americans who envied and were eager to alter their circumstances faced a daunting task. The social environment of rural areas made it difficult for dissatisfied men and women to change their lives. In part, this was because individual identity was more anchored and less fluid on farms and in small towns. Who one was depended on where and to whom one was born. Neighbors and fellow townsmen often had a collective memory of each other's childhood days and deeds, finances, histories, and prospects. These memories frustrated the efforts of individuals intent on changing themselves and their circumstances. In consequence, a new wardrobe or car was ineffectual in altering long-standing perceptions of one's social status. In stark contrast to this social environment stood cities, where the accidents of birth and family history mattered less. In an anonymous bustling city, ambitious individuals could try to shake off their old identities and assume new ones by changing their clothes, their addresses, their acquaintances, and their work. In cities they could also avail themselves of the many stores and specialty shops that offered material goods which might serve to alter their identities.

These fundamental differences between the urban and

rural environments shaped the emotional experiences of country people. Increasingly aware of the possibilities for self-transformation that the urban commercial culture touted, yet unable to effect these changes in their own lives, many rural dwellers became convinced that the modern world was passing them by. As Theodore Roosevelt noted in a 1908 letter, there was a widespread belief among rural people "that the prizes of life lie away from the farm."[1]

Rural people were discontented because their expectations and desires had changed but the daily reality of farm life had not. As Herbert Quick, an Iowa-born chronicler of the rural migration noted in 1913, the nation had shifted its priorities and interests away from rural life and toward urban life. He conjectured that the rural migration was "the outward evidence of something which has taken place inside the people." What had taken place "inside" the people was the dawning realization that their style of life and life chances in the isolated country, far from the economic opportunities, conveniences, pleasures, and excitement of the city, were inferior to those of city dwellers. Young men and young women growing up on the farm or in small country towns (here defined as having populations of fewer than 2,500 people) were newly aware of the pleasures and possibilities of urban life and felt entitled to them. They manifested their envy and discontent in a number of ways. Some rural men and women merely felt inadequate, some tried to imitate city modes and lifestyles in the country, and others left the country for the city in late adolescence or young adulthood.[2]

The number who chose to migrate was substantial. During this period there were great changes in both the profile and the prevailing conceptions of country life. The nation's population shifted from being primarily rural to increasingly urban. In 1880, country dwellers made up 71.4 percent of the nation's population, in 1890, 64.6 percent. By 1900 rural inhabitants constituted 60.0 percent of the population; by 1920, 48.6 percent, and by 1930, only 43.8 percent. Between 1920 and 1930 alone, rural migrants to cities numbered 5,734,200—11.1 percent of the total number of residents who had been living in the countryside at the beginning of the decade.

A substantial portion of those who migrated to the city were members of the rural middle class. Sociologists and historians have argued that at the end of the nineteenth century, farm families represented a shrinking "old middle class," which was being challenged in numbers and in status by the "new middle class," employed in cities by large corporations, the government, and universities. This new middle class was growing in power, influence, and size, and was fast supplanting the farmer middle class as the economic keystone of the nation. The rising status and centrality of this urban white-collar class was a further source of discontent for rural dwellers who increasingly felt displaced and undervalued.

The falling status of farming motivated country dwellers to take action; it was the young, however, rather than the middle-aged or elderly who acted most decisively and abandoned farming altogether. The effects of the mass migration of rural youth were plainly visible in census reports. By 1920, 48 percent of farmers were forty-five or older; by 1930 the figure was almost 53 percent. More than 75 percent of the migrants who set off for cities between 1920 and 1930 had been under twenty-five at the start of the decade. During the 1920s, 41 percent of the rural population aged fifteen to nineteen and 29 percent of the rural population aged twenty to twenty-four had migrated.[3] Young people were less invested in farming as a career than their parents, more mobile, and more susceptible to the charms of consumer culture. And while not all of those who left the countryside were driven by envy, it is quite clear that the emotion was widespread among young migrants.

The Consumer Ethic in the Countryside

In the late nineteenth century, information about urban life was flowing into the countryside. The postal service carried letters, magazines, newspapers, and catalogs that described the latest trends and styles, while railroads transported both passengers and goods from city to farm. By the 1910s and 1920s, rural dwellers could find out even more information about tantalizing urban amusements and lifestyles by watching movies, listening to the radio, or driving to the city. Regardless of how they received the information, however, many rural young women and men found news of the city tempting and ultimately frustrating—for they realized that much of what they heard and read about they could never acquire in the country.

Until World War I, the main sources of information about the city came from mail-order catalogs, magazines, society pages, and relatives and acquaintances who returned to the country bearing news of urban modes and manners or even modeling the latest fashions. Freight and passenger cars also carried urban mass-produced goods and news of city styles over the rails and into countless small towns and farming settlements. "I did not know that the smell of coal smoke, which first greeted my nostrils with the railroad engine, was to be the sign and signal of the decay of a town and indeed of pioneer times, when men made things where they used them—all the things necessary to a rather competent civilization," wrote editor William Allen White of the railroad's advent into his small Kansas town in the 1870s. White added that the arrival of the railroad led to the decline of homemade goods and the importation of products from afar.[4] The changes White witnessed in Kansas were occurring throughout the nation, as Sears, Montgomery Ward, and other retailers began to distribute their catalogs and their wares across the rural United States. In addition to dresses, suits, bonnets, farm implements, pianos, phonographs, fans, musical instruments, and other miscellany, railroads transported travelers. Small-town men and women of some means would frequently return from a trip to the city sporting new clothes, describing new plays, and flaunting new tastes.

To those who could not travel to far-off cities, periodicals and papers carried news of the excitement of metropolitan life. Magazines like the *Ladies' Home Journal*, *Women's Home Companion*, *Munsey's*, and the *Saturday Evening Post* enjoyed large circulations among the middle class in both urban and rural regions. Across the United States, country and city readers saw the same new styles touted in articles on fashion, entertainment, and home decor and read the copy of advertisements for national brands of goods. Through such reading, bourgeois Americans separated by vast distances developed similar tastes and longings. Essayist Joel Benton, writing in *Harper's Weekly* in 1895, described the effects of such periodicals, noting that "when the daily paper and the issues of the pictorial press are to be had each morning or before noon on far-off farms, telling of human activities in great towns, of fortunes rapidly made, and of multiplied schemes and entertainments, dazzling to the imagination," young and energetic people would be "stirred" to join in the excitement.[5]

These older channels of transmission continued to carry information about urban styles, while newer channels developed alongside them in the early twentieth century. Advertisements, while included in publications of the nineteenth century, were accorded more space and prominence in magazines published during the 1910s and 1920s. During the 1920s, for instance, White noticed that national advertisers were spending unprecedented amounts of money to place ads in the small-town newspaper he published. He recalled that "from the east came thousands of dollars in advertising calling attention to national products—automobiles, radios, phonographs, tobacco, oil, transportation."[6]

From such ads, farm families and small-town dwellers could learn of new products and styles and develop new tastes, even when the actual goods were not yet available in their areas. Market researcher Mary Hoffman of the Ferry-Hanly Advertising Company studied the consumer habits of shoppers who lived in small midwestern towns, and discovered that by the 1920s many women relied upon national advertising to learn about the latest consumer trends and product lines. Of the 394 women she surveyed, 249 reported that they paid either a good deal or a great deal of attention to advertisements. One respondent reported, "It's only through advertising that you can learn about some products, as jewelry and silverware." Another woman concurred, noting, "Get so many new ideas—on clothing, house, interior decorations, household appliances and cooking."[7] Such new ideas often brought with them feelings of disgruntlement. Ernest Groves, a sociology professor at New Hampshire State College, maintained that "advertising has forced rural people to contrast their manner of life with urban conditions, and often with the result of discontent."[8]

By the mid-1910s, movies were beginning to have at least a limited impact on rural mores, and by the 1920s, films were offering rural men and women important information about the outside world, particularly the world of fashion. Movie censor Will Hays noted the role that films had in spreading city tastes: "More and more is the motion picture being recognized as a stimulant to trade. No longer does the girl in Sullivan, Indiana, guess what the styles are going to be in three months. She knows because she sees them on the screen."[9]

Sociologist Albert Blumenthal noted the same phenomenon in Mineville, the small Montana town he studied in the late 1920s and early 1930s. The movies, he wrote, brought "a steady flow of insight into life in a large city since so many pictures have their settings in that background." During the 1920s, country dwellers also learned of urban ways through automobile rides to cities. The car increased contact between city and country dwellers. As Blumenthal noted, "As fast as automobiles, railways, and the radio can operate, the little town is brought the latest mechanical devices, books, papers, song hits, and wisecracks." Bobbed hair and short skirts also became popular throughout Mineville after news of such urban styles spread to town.[10]

There were other routes of transmission as well. Many of the writers who sought to improve rural life, to assuage country dwellers' envy and dissatisfaction, and to stop the rural exodus were themselves carrying news of city standards and styles. Columnists who railed against envy often wrote for magazines that published articles on fashions and home decor. Sociologists, home economists, demonstration and county extension agents, dedicated to improving rural life, often brought urban technologies, fashions, and decorating schemes with them. They also brought novel outlooks with them. They were members of the new middle class, whose lifestyle contrasted so sharply with the experiences of farm people. Consequently, despite their strenuous efforts to assuage the discontent of the country population, these writers and reformers frequently imported new tastes into farming communities, which excited envy and sometimes altered the existing rural culture.

Some historians, including Hal Barron and Mary Neth, have maintained that while rural men and women were increasingly exposed to urban culture, this exposure, at least initially, did not fundamentally alter their lifestyles or their outlooks. They claim that rather than country residents becoming urbanized in their tastes and preoccupations, farming folk used new goods to reinforce older patterns of living and sociability. Both qualify these claims, noting that rural young people seemed most susceptible to the charms of cosmopolitan culture. I think they understate the case. While rural culture had never been free of capitalist or consumerist influences, it was dramatically transformed by the greater knowledge that farm folk and small-town dwellers acquired of urban life at the turn of the century. Suddenly there was an external standard to compare oneself against. Farm families read of Paris fashions, heard of the latest New York entertainments, studied pictures of the latest parlor suites, and measured their own lives and experiences against such models. While young people were more likely to engage in such comparisons and take decisive action to attain urban amenities, their parents were not unaffected by their new and more intimate knowledge of metropolitan life.[11]

As they traveled by car or train, read magazines, advertisements, and newspapers, watched the silver screen, listened to the crackling airwaves, or even attended extension classes, rural women and men came to share many of the same tastes that their city sisters and brothers held. The widely disseminated consumer culture standardized tastes: It led middle-class men and women, separated by vast geographical distances, to measure themselves against the same ideals, and it prompted them to long for similar goods and lifestyles. A new culture was being knitted together.

Authentic Paris Chic is Easy to Achieve

Redfern—1135

THE year 1929 will be remembered by countless grateful women as the year when a great difference between good and indifferent dressing ceased to exist. This difference was the availability to the American woman of authentic last-minute Paris fashions, were used to be—so short a time ago that we all remember—the woman who could afford to in Paris, or in the smartest shops at home, could always pick her out at parties, in the ier, on the street. Her dresses had, somehow, ir about them. It might be only the way a -waisted tie contrasted with a cleverly cut blouse, or the cut of a skirt, or the drapery going down to the ankles from an evening frock. Whatever the reason, there she was, smart and as distinguishable as the creative and inspiration of great dressmakers could her. And she stood out among an eddy of others who dressed in moderately expensive ready-made clothes, almost—but not quite—perfect, with compromises in color and pattern and cut, perhaps, which were occasioned by the that the "Moderately Priced Dress Section" had quite what they were looking for. as well dressed were the women whose were made for them by dressmakers, although certain sameness in general pattern and a certain of originality were distinctly evident in their clothes. They were the top of a very rapidly sliding which reached its lowest ebb with the woman "ran up" her own dresses at home, and naturally something very ..., which, though it met such pitfalls as beset the amateur maker, also lacked ...

BUT in 1929—nary of 1929, to be —these hard and lines began to fade women with fashion ism, whether they Rue de la Paix or gain-basement methbooks, realized the introduction of designs from which could select their ies was of importance to them. We do mean that the difference is absolutely indispensable now. But details, the clever combinations, the ing cuffs, the new —sufficiently of the mode to be ssing, but not so far as to be bizarre conspicuous—are ible for anyone. at, comes the objection. In the first place, do we really know those dresses are made in Paris? And, ed—a very important second—aren't original, Paris-signed dresses too

complicated and difficult for anyone but the most professional couturier to attempt to make?

We would like to send out with every dress design an autographed letter from the head of the house where it is designed, saying that it is as authentically a true Parisian *grande couture* frock as though it were purchased between the four gray or mauve or modernistic walls where its creator works. Obviously, this is impossible. But the statement is nevertheless true—a sketch, a complete dress in muslin, gives us the working model for each design, and details are not tampered with. The dress as it was designed in Paris is there for your selection. Seeing is believing. Hence we are publishing the very smart photographs which you see on this page. The young women who are wearing the dresses—every stitch of which, every operation, from cutting to finishing, they did themselves—are not professional seamstresses. They are college students.

The Bryn Mawr student at the top of the page is also a New York debutante. She makes many of her own clothes, and chose for a summer wardrobe a Redfern dress, Design No. 1135.

The photographs at the bottom of the page show you a Pratt Institute student, photographed in the Philippe et Gaston dress, Design No. 1022, which she made for this fall.

She chose this particular model because the loose bolero back with its unexpected buttons, the belt with its "tricky" interlace fastening, were unusual and amusing—but she found it easy to make even in the angora in which you see it photographed. And angora isn't so easy to work with, after all.

Philippe et Gaston—1022

ACTUALLY designed in France—in Paris, more exactly—these designs are made in this country, cut to American-figure proportions and measurements in American standard sizes. They are cut, moreover, accurately and carefully. And the charts and directions that accompany them are clearly written for American readers to follow. They are as simple as it is possible to make them.

Some of the most interesting "tricks of the trade" hints on draping, putting a dress together on a dress form, how to manipulate it so that it will have the graceful and correct hang of a custom-made frock, have been incorporated in an interesting booklet by Miss Rose Baird, which we will be glad to send you if you will address your request, with a two-cent stamp, to the Fashion Editor, LADIES' HOME JOURNAL, Philadelphia, Pennsylvania.

... may be obtained from any store selling Paris Patterns, or by mail, postage prepaid, from Paris Patterns Bureau, French Building, 551 Fifth Avenue, New York City. Price, 65 cents; Canada, 65 cents.

Figure 10. Features such as this 1929 article in *Ladies' Home Journal* exposed women on farms and in cities to high fashion. Copyright © September 1929, Meredith Corporation. All rights reserved. Used with permission of *Ladies' Home Journal*.

Deprivations and Desires

Country dwellers came to realize, however, that while they might share the tastes and aspirations of city folk, they did not have the same opportunities to fulfill their desires for new consumer goods and experiences. While the promotional vehicles of the consumer society—ads, movies, magazines, radios, and word-of-mouth—infiltrated even the most remote parts of the nation, the actual retail establishments did not spread as rapidly or as far. Because of the uneven distribution of consumer outlets and modern conveniences, it was much more difficult for rural people to attain the urban lifestyle and standard of living so celebrated in the emerging mass culture.

Surveys indicated that by the early twentieth century, many of the conveniences, institutions, and entertainments which had become available to urban dwellers had not yet spread to America's farms. For instance, by 1935, while 70 percent of urban homes had electricity, less than 10 percent of farm homes had electric power. Such a disparity resulted in widely divergent lifestyles, particularly for women. City women were far more able and likely to use labor-saving appliances like vacuum cleaners, which according to another study could be found in 44 percent of urban households and only 17 percent of rural ones.

Women and men living in cities also enjoyed access to department stores and specialty shops, which sold a wide range of goods priced for a variety of pocketbooks. The bounty of consumer society was in easy reach. In addition, city residents had their choice of glittering entertainments, including vaudeville shows, movies, museums, and amusement parks. In contrast, the material circumstances of rural life lagged far behind city conditions. Residents of farming communities faced substantially fewer consumer choices. General stores were often overpriced and understocked, and the wares they did offer were frequently outmoded. Mail-order houses brought some relief, yet their goods were generally less elegant than what was available in urban stores and their delivery was far slower. Rural amusements were less commercialized and more communal; many rural residents also believed that they were far too scarce.

Not surprisingly, then, rural dwellers often appeared less fashionably dressed than urbanites and generally possessed fewer luxuries like radios, phonographs, and pianos. In surveys conducted in the early 1920s, the J. Walter Thompson Agency found that while 49 percent of residents in large towns owned pianos, only 38 percent of farm residents had the status-marked instrument in their houses. Similarly, while 57 percent of large-town dwellers possessed phonographs, only 50 percent of farm families did. Radios were even scarcer in farmhouses: 19 percent of large-town dwellers could tune in, whereas only 7 percent of farm residents could.[12]

The lack of comfort and material pleasures was further compounded by the nature and limitations of social interactions in rural communities. The siren call of consumer society was that one could turn oneself into a new person by purchasing new things. This message was commonplace in the advertising copy, the magazine features, and even the movie plots to which rural people were increasingly exposed. While the promise of transformation through purchases often may have been an empty promise, it was an attractive one. And many men and women, both urban and rural, put their faith in it. However, to the extent that material goods offered their owners social power, they seemed to work best in urban environments. Envious urbanites eager to raise their status often sought to create new social identities for themselves through emulative purchases. By purchasing the same goods as the wealthy (or at least similar ones) they would be able to appear more affluent than they truly were. Because cities were bustling and anonymous, with a constant stream of newcomers, there was the possibility that such a bluff might be carried off, for one's social and financial background was often unknown to casual acquaintances. While some might decry these anonymous conditions of city life, many men and women found its promise liberating. In urban settings they would have the freedom to fashion a new image and to attempt to become what they envied.

In contrast, in rural communities, the oft-heard complaint was that "everybody knows your business." Young women and men with hopes and aspirations found the intimacy of rural social relations cloying. Many expressed frustration over the lack of privacy in their farming communities and country villages. Ambitious individuals could not easily transform themselves in small towns, where identities were fixed in the common mind and one's status was not something one created through action and display but what one acquired through long acquaintance. Albert Blumenthal described social intercourse in the town of Mineville. He reported that all people knew one another, and when one town resident encountered fellow residents, "he pigeonholes them more or less accurately with reference to the parts they play in the community life, and he is aware that they are rating him with the same thoroughness."[13]

Given the familiarity rural people had with each other's circumstances, conspicuous consumption, a useful strategy for urban aspirants, served little purpose in the country. Thorstein Veblen claimed that showy display was most successful and serviceable in those places where "the human contact of the individual is widest and the mobility of the population is greatest." Such conditions were to be found in urban centers, not in rural ones, for among people living on farms in small villages, "everybody's affairs, especially everyone's pecuniary status, are known to everybody else."[14]

For rural young people eager to make themselves fashionable and sophisticated, such circumstances proved difficult. To emulate upper-class urban styles might invite mockery, for the falsity of one's image would be apparent to all. As Albert Blumenthal noted, "He who would indulge in pretense in Mineville must be very cautious lest he be wasting his time or be making himself a target for scorn, ridicule, or amusement." While Blumenthal noted that "a certain amount of bluffing can be done," he warned that "this bluffing must not be of a sort that easily can be uncovered, for the people have little patience with pretenders. Persons long in the community know that there is scant use for them to 'put on a front' of the more obvious sort such as by the wearing of fine clothes or the purchasing of a costly automobile."[15] Other observers of small-town life came to similar conclusions. In *Hoosier Village: A Sociological Study with Special Reference to Social Causation*, sociologist Newell LeRoy Sims noted that in his field site, "Aton," in northeastern Indiana, "those who 'put on airs' are objects of ridicule. 'Swell dressing' is odious and rarely seen."[16]

In such an atmosphere there was limited utility in displaying one's wealth and ambitions through conspicuous display, and consequently many farm fathers limited their families' spending on consumer goods. In both urban and rural middle-class families, men controlled the finances; however, urban bourgeois men often believed there to be a social value in domestic expenditures, for in societies with more attenuated social ties they could use their family's clothing, carriages, and houses to broadcast their position or their aspirations. In contrast, because rural families could see how other farms were faring and could judge whether the crops were flourishing, it proved less useful to spend money on furnishings or fashions. Farmers could not pull the wool over each other's eyes through the display of consumer goods. Farm fathers therefore were less likely to share money with wives or children, or to encourage them to adorn themselves or their houses, because there was little social or economic benefit in doing so. A frequently heard adage among Iowa farm families in the early twentieth century illustrated this outlook: Farm people often remarked that the sign of a well-run and wisely managed farm was a barn that looked better than the house did.

In addition to having different attitudes about consumption, farmers also faced a perennial shortage of cash. The currency shortage which so many farmers of the period complained of meant that even had they been disposed to spend, many farmers would have had difficulty doing so. The lack of cash affected not just the heads of households but the whole family. Young people in farming communities found that there were few opportunities to earn the money necessary to support consumer spending. A 1911 article estimated that perhaps as many as 90 percent of farm boys in their late teens received no wages or profits from their work, while a study of rural young women's economic prospects in the country described the similarly limited nature of paid employment for country girls: they might gather holly for wreaths, tend cows, sell vegetables, grow fruit, or do a host of similarly sporadic and unremunerative tasks. Other studies from the period indicate that in 1920 only 16 percent of farm women were able to keep for themselves the money they earned from egg or butter sales. In most cases profits were turned over to husbands or fathers.[17] Given their own inability to pay for desired goods, and given their fathers' and husbands' unwillingness to do so, the practice of advertising one's position through material symbols was less frequent in rural districts than in urban ones.

Yet despite their scarcity and limited utility, consumer goods exerted considerable power over the imaginations of rural young people. Many therefore felt sharp pangs of envy and harbored deep feelings of deprivation as they contemplated their lot in life. In his 1895 *Harper's* essay, Joel Benton explained that "the bucolic days went when the locomotive and telegraph came." He cited as "their later allies, the telephone and the trolley, with other devices for extinguishing time and quietude," which had the effect of "drawing active spirits into the whirl, and causing discontent with slow and ancient ways." Despite the passage of time and the gradual rise in the rural standard of living, such dissatisfaction was still evident some three decades later. In 1929, Professors Wilson Gee and William Henry Stauffer of the University of Virginia explained that the "standard of living set by the city dwellers . . . and the social and recreational values have overflowed from the city to the country, and the . . . influence of such . . . intangible factors is now widespread, and deeply effective in producing rural dissatisfaction."[18]

As they contrasted the many constraints on their own lives with the possibilities available in cities, young women and men living in the American countryside must have found it frustrating to contemplate the future. There was no escaping one's fixed identity in the town mind, no point to aspiring or working toward self-transformation. These young people were watching film stars take on a multitude of personae, reading about the transformative power of consumer goods in the advertising pages, and studying magazines that touted new fashions and conveniences. Every day, however, they were confronted with the reality that in their small insular communities, these tantalizing offerings of consumer culture were rarely available and could do little for them when they were available.

Longing for the "Town Sense"

A number of sociologists, politicians, extension workers, and rural reformers believed that while both sexes experienced such feelings of discontent, young women were particularly prone to feel a sense of deprivation, to long for city life, and consequently to leave the farm. In a 1913 essay in *Good Housekeeping*, Herbert Quick confided that both his own research and his observation of his "mother, sisters, aunts, cousins, and women neighbors' lives" had persuaded him that the " 'drift to the cities' has been largely a woman movement. I have found the men on farms much more contented and happy than the women. . . . I have found the men and boys filled with the traditional joy of open spaces and the freedom of spirit which goes with it; but in many many cases, their women were pining for neighbors, for domestic help, for pretty clothes, for schools, music, art, and the things tasted when the magazines came in." Statistical surveys confirmed Quick's impression. A 1927 study published by the Missouri Agricultural Experiment Station indicated that while 44 percent of farm boys preferred to live on a farm, only 34 percent of girls did. Such differing preferences translated into different rates of migration as well. According to U.S. government studies, between 1920 and 1930, 55 percent of all migrants were female.[19]

In seeking to resolve the "country problem" and to stem the migration, many social observers worked to identify the specific causes of rural women's discontent. In 1913, Juliet Virginia Strauss, an Indiana writer who sometimes used the byline "The Country Contributor," wrote in the *Ladies' Home Journal* that too many rural residents suffered from the "common delusion" that socialites in cities and towns were inherently superior. She observed that this belief "causes considerable envy and unrest among them, and it often leads a good farmer to move to town and join the profitless ranks of the 'retired'—those men who sit in innocuous desuetude for twenty years or so before they die. This is because the wife and daughters kept hankering after that sophisticated town sense which they imagined they could absorb."

The "town sense" was both an attitude and a particular lifestyle that rural women hoped to gain for themselves. They thought that in a larger, more anonymous setting, they might have sufficient liberty and opportunity to change their identities and become more like the people whom they envied. Part and parcel of their hopes for self-transformation was a change in their material circumstances. Rural women of all ages longed for a higher standard of living. They wanted more conveniences, less drudgery, shorter working days, and more opportunities for relaxation and refinement. As a farm woman put it, "After a visit to her sisters in the city where you can push a button and get plenty of good lights instantly . . . the farm woman comes back dissatisfied with her lot."

Such women wanted a standard of living equal to that enjoyed by urban middle-class women. Historian Allan Kulikoff has argued that rural women had been pushing their husbands and fathers for greater marketplace involvement since at least the early nineteenth century. Their desire for more amenities and comforts had in many cases spurred their husbands to pursue more commercial forms of agriculture. Yet despite the fact that by the late nineteenth century most American farms were integrated into the commercial economy, many farm women continued to feel discontented with their standard of living and envy of urban styles of life. Indeed, during the late nineteenth century and early twentieth century, the problem of rural women's desire remained unsolved and in many ways was worse than it had been in preceding years because farm women had even greater knowledge of what they were missing. In the words of one journalist writing in 1912, "farm women find themselves in a new civilization, but not of it." What they saw in this new civilization, and what they believed to be lacking from their own lives, was summed up in 1930 by the manager of a girls' club in Richmond, Virginia. Rural young women believed that farm work was hard. In contrast, the city offered "easier work, more to see, less loneliness and more money to buy pretty clothes."[20]

Rural women expressed their envy particularly clearly when they compared their clothing with that of city women. As they studied the images of sophisticated, well-dressed women that were circulating in magazines, ads, and films, country women realized that it would be difficult to effectively emulate these models. Although many farm families considered themselves to be members of the middle class, studies indicated that they generally spent less money on clothing than did urban working-class families. This was in part because they had less cash to invest in clothing. They were also stymied by a dearth of retail establishments. In a 1927 study of women's sewing habits, 14 percent of the seven hundred farm women surveyed indicated that they often sewed because "good stores for ready-made goods [were] inaccessible."[21] Rural women had less money to spend and fewer places to spend it. Their home sewing, however, could not always satisfactorily fill the gap, because certain urban styles were difficult to replicate by hand, and necessary materials were often unavailable or else prohibitively expensive. Therefore, country girls often had to make do with unstylish dresses or with poor imitations of city styles.

Lulu Rutenber Bartz, born in 1901 in Tacoma, New York, described how it felt to be unfashionably attired. She recalled her envy of other girls' skirts and her frustration at her inability to dress similarly. Like many country girls, she relied on her mother's handiwork for clothes, and these garments often proved unstylish. "When I went to school, Mother made all our clothes, and I had but one dress to wear. That was kinda hard for me. We were from the farm, and some of those village kids wore those broomstick skirts that were so pretty."[22] Lulu's unfashionable clothing made her feel excluded and inferior.

Unfashionable clothing led Mary King to feel inferior to her girlhood friends as well. Born in Idaho in 1905, King and her family moved to the very small farming town of Cedarview, Utah, in 1912. There King became friends with a girl named Clea. Clea and her family eventually moved to the larger town of Price, but when the girls were in their teens, Clea came back to visit Mary and her family. As she contemplated her friend's impending visit, Mary worried that she would not measure up to Clea's urban standards. She recalled, "all of a sudden a worried fear almost weakened me. 'What if Clea will be so changed, she won't even remember our childhood days, or will have outgrown our friendship. Perhaps all she would see in me would be a "graceful damsel of the soil" with skin browned by wind and summer sun. Hands calloused and hardened by the grip on a hoe handle. . . . Would my dresses, fashioned by Myrtle's expert hands, stand comparison with Clea's ready-made ones bought from the best shops?' "[23]

Although Mary and Clea had a joyful reunion, Mary's fears were not unwarranted, for many urban dwellers did indeed regard farm folk with some disdain. Annie Pike, born into a prosperous family in 1879, recalled her youthful contempt for country people's way of life. "I recall the cold revulsion with which, seated, as I often was, in our fringed-top phaeton, I observed the jangling, rattling, bumping farm wagons that came into town."

As she looked down on the world from her high perch, her strongest feelings of derision were reserved for farm women, whom she considered graceless and almost brutish: "The farmer's wife was particularly the object of my contempt." She remembered watching as a farm woman awkwardly lowered herself from a wagon, placing "one red, raw, coarse hand over the other. Her foot, encased in its heavy, hideous shoe, hovered for safe purchase over the hub of the wheel. The things she wore were of different style-periods—to my superior taste, ugly in the extreme."

Little did Annie Pike suspect that as an adult she would live in the country, envy the clothes of city women, and encounter their disdain as they scrutinized her appearance. In 1905, she married Charles Greenwood, and the couple moved to southern Idaho. There they homesteaded. So scarce was good clothing in their community that during World War I, Annie lent her best white dress to a hired girl in the neighborhood. The hired girl was plump and burst the seams of the dress. Annie vowed to buy herself a new one and consulted the Best and Company catalog. Ultimately, however, she decided that she should not waste scarce money on such frivolous goods and instead invested in a Liberty Bond. A sense of duty made her restrain her spending and content herself with her old patched dress.

She was not able to restrain her desire to appear well dressed in public, however, and she decided to remodel her old ripped dress with "some scraps of organdie and some dainty old embroidery." She wore the dress to a Grange picnic, where she encountered the wife of a successful Boise lawyer and rancher. The lawyer's wife "was wearing an exquisite frock of peach-colored organdie, with an ashes-of-roses pattern [with] blossoms running over it, and it was lined with soft, peach colored taffeta. She was a brunette, pretty enough, with mountains of assurance. I felt that shrinking inferiority engendered by my old, patched, Liberty Bond white dress." Annie Greenwood made apologies for her dress, noting that it was several years old. The lawyer's wife then "stared in contempt at my pitiful dress and remarked, turning her cold eyes away, 'Ah couldn't stand to wear a frock mo' than one season.'" Greenwood wrote, "I deserved that blow, that terrible, cruel, blow, for my foolish effort at toadying to a city woman. It was like a dash of cold water."[24]

The rudeness of the lawyer's wife cured Annie Greenwood of her envy, at least temporarily. Yet her feelings of envy and inferiority, and those of Lulu Bartz and Mary King, while they may have been fleeting, were not at all rare. Countless other rural women who came of age during the period felt just such twinges of envy, insecurity, and consumer desire in the course of their interactions with urban women.[25]

Rural women envied broomstick skirts, organdie dresses, and other fashions so popular and accessible in cities and towns. Their longings for urban styles and their distaste for their own handiwork were indicative of the power of the national, homogenizing culture that was sprawling across the United States. Country women looked to women from large cities and towns rather than to their own communities to discover what was fashionable and current. Urban tastes and styles had become national tastes.

Rural young women also longed for the more exciting recreations that were available to young people in America's cities. As sociologist John Gillette noted, the lack of appealing amusements was a significant problem, one that young men and young women shared alike. "There are many factors in cities that appeal to the young men and women of the country which seem to them worth attainment." He described the "confusing number and kinds of attractions in cities," which included "theaters, dance halls, museums, parks, bathing beaches, contests in baseball and other sports, conventions and pageants; an incessant flow of cars and vehicles; the magnetic contact with crowds, tumult, hustle and bustle—always something going on, something new or novel." To rural youth, "the city appears to be the worthwhile place. . . . It is the place where something is always happening and where it is possible to avoid the monotony and the hard physical drudgery of the farm."[26] In contrast, country life afforded few recreations. In a survey of country residents conducted in 1908, investigators found that 20 percent of the rural population reported few or no recreations. They noted that country youth participated in some of the existing adult amusements, but also observed that many of the old-time pastimes were fading.[27]

More intensive studies of rural culture indicated that there were indeed pastimes in the country but that the recreations available were not always what rural young people wanted. As O. Latham Hatcher's research illustrates, as late as 1930 amusements for country girls still remained vastly different from those enjoyed by city girls. Hatcher, an educator and reformer concerned with rural girls' welfare and the founder of the Alliance for the Guidance of Rural Youth, surveyed one hundred country girls and found that reading was the most popular amusement, followed by sewing things for themselves, visiting, and hiking. A few listed fishing and swimming, three reported driving, and "three played on the piano and one on the ukulele. Two considered it recreation to 'fix up the house,' five to sleep, two to 'fix up' their clothes and rooms, two to work in flowers, one to do gardening of another sort, two to raise poultry and one to 'plunder about the house.' " Young women with only these mundane diversions no doubt shared the sentiments of a high-school girl who confided to sociologist Albert Blumenthal, "I'll go mad if I don't get out of this town this summer. I'm in an awful fix. I hate to go to school, and, when school is out I will hate things because I will have nothing to do—not even school."[28]

Such rural girls, bored with their lives and frustrated with their circumstances, had very definite ideas about what they would like to do, given the opportunity. When social scientists studying conditions in rural Missouri asked young women what they would do if they had a chance, 47 percent responded that they would join an organization, 30 percent wanted to attend concerts, 22 percent wanted to visit people in the city, and 19 percent wanted to attend movies.[29]

During the late 1910s and early 1920s, more commercial recreations spread to rural regions. Yet while movie theaters gradually opened in country towns, farm families could not visit them as frequently as city people did, for the distance from farm to town was often prohibitive. According to surveys conducted in the 1920s, a third of all farm families studied in Minnesota spent no money on commercial amusements such as movies or theater productions. And while the spread of automobiles gave rural dwellers increased access to some of these new amusements, not all could take advantage equally of the mobility offered by the car. While entire families complained of the lack of recreation, young women seem to have suffered most acutely. Historian Mary Neth points out that rural young women had the fewest opportunities to go to town and enjoy those recreations which did exist or which they could afford, because they were the family members who were least likely to know how to drive. Studies of Missouri youth indicated that while 81 percent of country boys drove cars, only 46 percent of rural girls did.[30]

In an essay they wrote together, six country girls summed up the problems they faced as they sought recreation in their small rural communities. "Without some social interest, few young people could be expected to be contented. On the farm or in the average rural community there is rarely any amusement. To lounge around the village store every afternoon in the week is not the sole ambition of an enterprising boy; and the girl, having no clubs and perhaps not inclined to church societies, naturally turns her steps cityward in search of amusement."[31]

To young women, country life was filled with frustrations. They were keenly aware of and entranced by the urban consumer culture, which touted the value of modernity, fashionability, amusement, and novelty, yet their own lives seemed to be old-fashioned, their dress out of fashion, their recreation paltry or nonexistent, and their opportunities to change themselves extremely limited.

The Doctrine of Contentment in Rural Life

Rural women made their longings and dissatisfactions known, most visibly by migrating to larger towns and cities. Their actions caused academics, politicians, members of the clergy, and rural leaders great alarm. Between 1890 and 1930, this diverse group generated a substantial literature concerned with halting, or at least slowing, the "funeral procession of the nation cityward." During the 1890s and early 1900s a fairly eclectic group of ministers, editors, and journalists decried the rural exodus. They viewed the problem of envy through the lens of sin and believed that rural people should steadfastly resist urban influences. They should instead cling to their divinely ordained position and accept their circumstances.

With Theodore Roosevelt's appointment of the Commission on Country Life in 1908, a more organized movement began to develop—the "Country Life Movement"—which sought to improve and glorify country living. Made up of highly educated professionals, social scientists, and editors, many—but not all—Country Life activists came to see modern technology and consumer goods as the solution to rural discontent.[32] The contrast between the advice of moralists at the turn of the century and that of Country Life activists and other rural reformers in succeeding decades illustrates the changing cultural assumptions about both the nature of rural life and the nature of womanhood.

Between 1890 and 1910, moralists concerned about the rural migration strongly condemned country women's consumer desire because it contradicted so many fundamental assumptions about the virtue and purity of both women and the American countryside. Many writers believed that of all members of the middle class, rural women were the creatures for whom consumer involvement was least appropriate. Like their urban sisters they were presumed to be endowed with an unchanging and unchangeable identity and expected to be without desire or longings. Their feminine nature, therefore, made them unsuited for market activity. Rural women's location added to the perception that they were unfit for participation in the commercial economy. Moralists, reformers, social critics, and politicians often idealized the countryside as free of commercial influences or materialistic desires. Luxury goods, and those who longed for them, were supposedly found in cities, not in farmhouses. According to prevailing gender ideals, rural women were therefore doubly unsuited for consumer participation.

Moralists tried to persuade rural women, infected with rising expectations, to accept their divinely sanctioned roles. They invoked the flexible doctrine of contentment, so useful for teaching people in all sorts of situations to reconcile themselves to their circumstances. They told women that they must embrace their conditions, control their envy, and remain on the farm.

Rural young women who tried to dress like urban sophisticates received sharp reminders about the need for a contented spirit. In an article entitled "The Country Girl," *Ladies' Home Journal* columnist Ruth Ashmore warned that visits from city cousins bearing details of city fashions and mores should not be occasions for envy. The country girl might legitimately ask about city ways but should be careful not to become discontented with her own life in doing so: "Talk about frocks if you like, there is no harm in that; hear pretty ones described, they are a pleasure and a delight to the eyes; but if you feel the little demon of envy biting at your heartstrings, change the subject right away." Further, Ashmore lectured, to translate one's envy into action and to try to look like a city girl was inappropriate. A young woman's dress should correspond to her class and location in society. Country girls should therefore not try to resemble city girls, for imitations of urban modes would look silly and be unsuccessful:

That country girl is wise who, remembering that the blue of the skies and the green of the trees form her background, elects that during the summer she wears pretty cottons daintily made, and wide-brimmed, somewhat fantastic straw hats. She would be entirely out of place in stuffy woolens or elaborate silks. . . . She is unwise in imitating her city cousin, who nine times out of ten looks overdressed. I know it is in the heart of every girl to long for pretty gowns, and a much-betrimmed lace silk frock may look very charming to the girl who has not one, while to the unprejudiced observer it seems absolutely out of place.[33]

Ashmore tried to console country girls who felt inferior to city girls. In another essay, "The Girl in the Small Community," she wrote that when city girls came to visit, "it seems to you as if your gowns were shabby and as if you knew nothing." True, the country girl's gowns might not "have the hallmark of the latest style" as did her city cousin's, but they suited her well. The envious girl should not try to make herself over in her city cousin's image. "Any attempt on your part to make your gown look like hers will result in a failure, for undoubtedly a dressmaker, knowing her trade well, designed and made that one you so admire."[34]

As they preached contentment, editorialists, rural reformers, and ministers were also reminding rural women of the importance of sincerity. A country woman should not wear city clothes, for they were inappropriate and misrepresented her true station in life. In a tale published in the *American Magazine* in 1890, Helen Burgess told of one young woman's misleading actions. Alice, a country girl in town to visit her cousin, had spent all of her clothing money on one beautifully tailored dress rather than on a full wardrobe of less expensive clothes, as her mother had intended. The good fit and graceful lines of her one new outfit implied wealth, and Alice hoped her cousin and her friends would conclude that she possessed many such gowns and had brought just one because of the brevity of her visit. Her underlying hope was to look as fashionable as the city girls she was visiting. Her ruse succeeded, but then Alice returned home and was beset with guilt. She told her mother of her actions and lamented that she was "a sham and had been sailing about under false colors . . . I have deceived everybody, and made Grace's friends believe that that dress expresses my condition of life." Alice eventually told some of her city acquaintances of her artifice and, having been forthright about her actual condition, became happily engaged to one of the most eligible bachelors in New York.[35]

Significantly, Alice had been able to sustain her deception in the city, where her financial circumstances were unknown. It was upon returning to her small town that she realized that she must embrace her true condition. By contrasting the urban milieu, where individuals could and did deceive one another, with the rural community filled with family and friends who dealt honestly with one another, Burgess was pointing out that urban life encouraged envy, bluffing, falsity, and self-transformation. Rural young women should resist such temptations and embrace, rather than rebel against, their circumstances. They should realize both the futility and the immorality of attempting to change themselves.

Those who preached contentment to the country girl also addressed the question of rural recreations. In their eyes, not only was envy of city recreations wrong but it was also unfounded. Following in a long tradition of agrarian writers, journalists and reformers preached that rural communities offered abundant natural amusements, while city life was corrupt and artificial. They believed that the commercial recreations were meaningless and spiritually unredeeming. Amusements like vaudeville shows and movies offered no lofty message or noble ideals; instead, they had been created merely for profit and offered only empty pleasures. In contrast, the recreations available to rural people in their own communities were virtuous, wholesome, and meaningful. Rural girls could turn to their churches, homes, and families for sociability. Then, too, nature provided abundant opportunities for renewal and enrichment. The problem was that the glitter and allure of cities sometimes blinded country girls to these grand opportunities available in their own communities. Editorialists therefore hoped to help the country girl see the advantages of rural life. Ruth Ashmore wrote that she hoped the country girl might learn to appreciate

the restful charm that there is in her simplicity, and I wish I could make her content. . . . You think the city girl as she talks about her amusements and admirers must have a very good time in life. It is not as good as yours, for she does not have plenty of fresh air, she does not know the joys of singing birds, she cannot tell the flowers or the blooms of the tree. . . . her world is curiously enough, a smaller one than yours.[36]

In 1895 another *Journal* commentator joined in the chorus. She argued that those who believed a happy social life depended on "artificial accessories" were wrong. Country women, with fewer cultural amenities, had greater and deeper joys. She maintained that more women actually wanted a "hammock under the trees" than "luxurious upholstery." While the country did not have opera, it did have birds and "country sounds," which were the "sweetest music." Although there were no art galleries in the country, there were "woods full of ferns and other treasures, blossoming orchards and hay fields."[37] Mrs. James Speers, a columnist writing in the YMCA journal

*

Rural Manhood, added to the list of artistic and cultural treasures to be found in the country. She reminded girls that "there isn't a gallery in the world that can compete with the landscape paintings to which you have free access." Likewise, while city girls had to settle for "cheap perfumery," farmers' daughters might enjoy "the scent of the warm earth after a summer shower, of new-mown hay, of a field of clover, of the pine woods—sweet perfumes that money cannot buy."[38] These natural attractions, the writers implied, surpassed the value of city amusements, which were tawdry, commercial, and morally suspect. Just as earlier generations of Americans had invoked the nation's natural splendor to respond to charges that the United States lacked culture, so late nineteenth- and early twentieth-century writers and moralists defended the rural lifestyle against charges that it could not compare with the city. Nature was simple, beautiful, spiritual, and superior to culture, while culture—at least city culture like cosmopolitan fashions, vaudeville, and movies—was corrupt and had the potential to undermine country life.[39]

Whether they wrote about clothes or entertainment, these turn-of-the-century reformers emphasized the value of the known and the familiar. They tried to counteract girls' discontent and make them immune to the temptations of commercial culture. Girls might long for the opportunity to change themselves. Rural reformers ceaselessly reminded them of the value of staying put and lowering their expectations. These reformers seemed to be fighting not just envy but consumer society as a whole. The consumer goods and commercial attractions flowing into rural districts were the tokens of a new economy and the bearers of a new set of values. They promised and encouraged pleasure, indulgence, and self-transformation. It was these values which moralists at the turn of the century so strenuously fought as they tried to preserve country life from the immoral taint of commercial culture.

These writers, however, were fighting an uphill battle. They could not stop the flood of goods and new tastes from reaching farms. What started out as a trickle of information flowing from city to country soon became a strong current. Indeed, many moralists became swept up in it themselves. They relied on the *Ladies' Home Journal*, *Good Housekeeping*, *Munsey's*, and other mass-circulation magazines which were so instrumental in spreading consumer values to publicize their anticonsumerist message. Their belief that rural people could and should be kept separate from commercial influences came to seem increasingly naive. Reformers in succeeding generations would regard such views as counterproductive, for they did not ame-liorate discontent or bring an end to the rural migration. A new approach to rural women's envy would have to be found.

Bringing the City to the Country

Carl C. Taylor, the dean of the graduate school of the North Carolina Col-lege of Agriculture, outlined this new approach in 1927. He wrote, "city de-sires must be satisfied even in country people. The only legitimate grounds upon which such satisfactions can properly be denied to country people is when they lead to recognized evil, degradation, or degeneracy." In the past, he noted, "Farm people have been criticized for wanting to use goods which are a part of the habits of consumption of the higher income families of city life." Rather that criticize them, Taylor argued that it was "natural" for rural folk to want urbanites' belongings, "now that they come constantly in con-tact with city people and observe city modes of life." After all, it was only "by the urge obtained by such conscious observation or through conscious education that all standards of living have been raised. . . . Sooner or later the luxuries of all classes who live in contact with one another must ap-proach equality or discontent will become perpetual."[40]

During the second decade of the twentieth century, as rural youth con-tinued to migrate despite the sermons they heard and read, many rural sociologists and Country Life activists began to offer this new message. While some writers continued to preach the old message of contentment, a significant portion of these rural reformers came to admit that the charms of country life could not compensate for all of the shortcomings of rural exis-tence. They therefore urged rural people to become more like city dwellers and to raise their standard of living. As part of this effort, they encouraged farm people to develop the desires and emotional habits that would make them better consumers.

Drawn from the ranks of the new urban middle class, the rural reform-ers of the 1910s and 1920s seem to have felt a certain satisfaction about their own way of life. They believed the education and comforts that they them-selves enjoyed represented progress. They were eager to share these break-throughs with the benighted country folk. Sometimes they did so with tact, but on occasion their advice was tinged with condescension. In their efforts to redress envy, they often excited other emotions in the rural population, like hostility and resentment.[41]

Because the new generation of rural reformers wanted to change rural culture and increase rural consumerism, they encouraged country women to be discontented, believing this emotion would spur them to action and spending. They maintained that it was contented people who represented a threat to rural society, for only the placid and dull would contentedly accept the substandard conditions of country life. As Martha Foote Crow, an English professor and an agricultural reformer, put it, "The only failure is to cease trying, to stop aspiring, and to let the vision fade away from the face of the unresponding clouds. . . . We wish every Country Girl in the remotest stronghold of conservatism to be touched with that divine discontent that will stir her to an upward struggle."[42]

Most of the rural reformers of the 1910s and 1920s came to believe that country people's "upward struggle" ideally should lead them to a higher standard of living. In contrast to the preceding generation of writers who had worried that material enrichment exacted a heavy moral price, the reformers of the 1910s and 1920s believed that a higher standard of living was a sign of lofty ideals and a benefit to all of society. If the desires of rural women could be met, if more creature comforts could be brought to farming communities, women might be able to live a richer life and enjoy the fruits of civilization to which they were entitled. As rural sociologist John Gillette declared in 1922, "New wants must be created among the masses of the rural people. It should be evident that no society . . . ever attains or moves toward achievement who are not spurred on by new wants."[43]

The revolutionary outlook that country people should develop more wants and become modern consumers led to the creation of new programs designed to improve specific aspects of rural life. For instance, instead of dismissing country women's perennial complaints about their attire and condemning their envy, rural reformers of the 1910s and 1920s began to encourage emulative dressing and offered farm women assistance in their efforts to keep up with city styles. Sometimes, rather than merely responding to existing desires, they even worked to create new ones.

In 1926, Laura Amos, a rural student, presented the new perspective on farm fashions at the National Country Life Conference. In her speech she celebrated the fact that she dressed just as city girls did. And her audience—full of Country Life reformers—praised her speech and her recommendations.

It is very difficult to recognize a country girl from a city girl. One used to be able to say, 'There is a country girl or boy,' but you can no longer. My hair isn't bobbed now but it was two years ago. My skirt is the new length and I even confess that I help nature a wee bit to put color into my cheeks. . . . And nine-tenths of the girls on the farm would stand before you tonight just as I do. They color their cheeks and shorten their dresses and bob their hair as the city girls do. They want to do it and why shouldn't they?[44]

Amos asked the crucial question. Rural girls dressed and acted like city girls, "and why shouldn't they?" Country Life advisors and rural girls themselves no longer thought it necessary to choose their dress according to their geographical location and social station. Indeed, many reformers encouraged young women to do just the opposite and to keep up with city trends.

Some reformers even claimed that it was a social necessity for farm women to improve their appearances. One woman who articulated this new position was Mary Meek Atkeson, a self-proclaimed farm wife and a member of the Grange who also happened to hold a Ph.D., taught at a number of universities, and published several books. Although she wrote her 1924 book, *The Woman on the Farm,* from her own farm in West Virginia, Atkeson was not living as most rural women did. She offered what was essentially an urban perspective on the way clothing shaped women's social identity. She maintained that the typical country woman wanted to "dress so much like her city sisters that she can mingle in the city crowds without an added glance in her direction." The way to accomplish this was to send away for clothes from "the shops on Fifth Avenue" and to avoid the "general mail-order [catalogs] which cater particularly to the country trade." It was necessary to do this because "the only way to look exactly like the city woman is to wear exactly the same kind of clothes."

Atkeson emphasized to farm women how important it was that they dress well, reminding them that "the people you meet take your clothes as an expression of your individuality. They cannot see the real 'you' inside. . . . the 'you' they are seeing is the outside. . . . For most of us it is almost impossible to be ourselves unless we are arrayed in a fairly becoming garment." Unlike past generations of reformers and advisors, Atkeson seemed to be arguing that a woman's self was at least partially constructed by her material possessions and adornments. The self was changeable, and what one wore could make all the difference in determining who one was. Country women therefore should strive to wear the best dresses they could find and should consciously craft their social image. They should respond to their desires for finer apparel so that they could become the people they longed to be.[45]

This new leniency toward women's desires for fine fashions certainly encouraged women in their quest for stylish clothes; equally important to their efforts were the new technologies and institutions which gave them greater access to urban attire. The spread of the automobile made it easier for farm women to acquire the latest modes. By 1930 rural inhabitants traveled greater distances to buy their clothing than they did for other goods. In a study of 1,328 midwestern farm families, rural sociologists J. H. Kolb and Edmund deS. Brunner found that farmers traveled approximately six to eight miles to buy hardware, groceries, car parts, and farm implements. They traveled fourteen miles to buy furniture and approximately twenty miles to buy women's ready-to-wear. Forty-seven percent of all dress purchases were made in towns or cities ranging in population from 2,500 to 10,000. Sixteen percent of all dress purchases were made in cities of over 10,000. Women, therefore, made roughly two-thirds of all clothing purchases out of their country environs. In 1925, the J. Walter Thompson Agency noted similar trends among the readers of the *People's Home Journal*. Of those surveyed in rural New York State, 11 percent bought most of their clothes from local country stores, 12 percent bought from mail-order, 46 percent bought their clothes in town, and 41 percent bought their clothes in the city.[46] Such statistics point to a strong, widespread, and accepted desire to dress according to urban norms. With the help of the automobile, country women could act on their discontent and match the urban women whose clothes they envied.

By the 1910s and 1920s, rural women also found that state and community institutions stood ready to help them in their search for style. Some farm girls and their mothers were lucky to have agricultural extension programs as they sought to copy city fashions. For instance, Cornell University sent out bulletins and lessons for farmers' wives. As federal funding for extension work increased with the passage of the Smith-Lever Act in 1914, these bulletins and programs became increasingly diversified, and some explicitly addressed the clothing needs and wants of the young woman in the country. For instance, the December 1918 *Cornell Junior Extension Bulletin* was entitled "Elementary Garment Making." It showed junior extension workers how to teach girls to make their own kimonos, chemises, bloomers, middy blouses, shirtwaists, and dresses. The Cornell Extension Program also offered lectures and demonstrations to county or district groups. The most popular of all lectures given in 1924 (the only year for which there are records) was entitled "The Well Dressed Woman." Twenty-nine counties participated in the program, and total statewide attendance for the demonstrations was 4,597 women. Other programs, somewhat less popular, included "How to Buy Ready-Mades" (attendance: 1,479), "Accessories— Their Use and Abuse" (attendance: 1,209), and "Successful Homemade Clothes" (attendance: 996). Many other states had similar programs. In Kansas, farm women might learn about dressing well, with special lessons on jewelry and stockings. While some Kansas women were offended that anyone at the extension agency believed that they needed instruction on how to dress well, they attended the course and, at its conclusion, dressed more modishly. While their pride may have been injured, their envy was also to some extent assuaged.[47]

As was the case with Kansas, some reformers and extension workers, rather than merely responding to country women's desires, actively worked to create them. They hoped that by introducing farm women to urban standards of living they would incite discontent and dissatisfaction with old habits and lead women to pursue more modern modes and ways of life. By teaching classes on dressing well, extension workers were implicitly denigrating rural styles and trends and elevating urban ones. The extension agents in Kansas and New York were not alone. Throughout the 1910s and 1920s, rural reformers repeatedly celebrated urban modes of life. Mary Meek Atkeson, for instance, suggested to farm women that they adopt the beauty products of urban women. Each night they should brush their teeth with a dentifrice, rub some Vaseline between their toes, dab astringent on their faces, and apply glycerine to their hands. Atkeson and advisors like her were bringing not just new products but new standards of beauty and skin care to rural women. By introducing farm women to these standards, they were also creating new desires and occasions for consumer spending.[48]

Reformers tried to increase farm women's consumption across the board. In 1929, Ellis Lore Kirkpatrick, an agricultural economist for the U.S. Department of Agriculture, described an extension worker's efforts to teach farm women urban standards of home decor. The extension agent was frustrated because she encountered too many farm women

who for some reason or other cannot be led to refinish, set aside or discard certain "out-of-harmony" pieces of furniture or equipment. In a number of homes she has solved this problem by having the family set aside one room for a sort of "sentimental store room," usually in the attic. Thus, the way has been cleared for a new living-room or dining-room suite, a new separate article of furniture or a more convenient and cozy arrangement of those pieces which are at hand.[49]

The anecdote illustrates the complexity of the relationship between some farm families and their local extension workers. The new goods and furnishings that extension agents promoted might be welcomed as an improvement and taken as a token of a higher standard of living. On the other hand, they might be viewed with some hostility and resistance. If farm women felt pride in their way of life and were contented with their present belongings, they no doubt resented the intrusion of the agents. Rural dwellers also realized that much of the support for the ideology of rural progress came from town merchants who would benefit financially if farm families increased their consumer spending. Country people then were aware of the mixed motives of the reformers and their merchant supporters. Yet while they may have had reservations about the new programs to improve country life, certainly some sector of the rural population, particularly the young who often longed for the very goods the agents were promoting, welcomed these efforts.[50]

Reformers of the 1910s and 1920s took a similar approach to the shortcomings of recreation and preached that city amusements offered more glamour and excitement than country ones. In the last decades of the nineteenth century and the first decade of the twentieth, editorialists exhorted envious and restless youth to find wholesome, traditional, and spiritually improving amusements for themselves and to take joy in birdsongs, ferns in the woods, blossoming orchards, and the like. In the 1910s, reformers, scholars, and politicians began to fully acknowledge that country communities needed to improve recreation for young people. They believed that rural girls' discontent and envy were warranted given the limited nature of rural amusements. Country girls would only become contented once they were given access to the pleasures and attractions of city life. "The thing to be done," wrote Martha Foote Crow, "is to cut off this thread of inevitable sequence at the beginning; to give the girl in the small town the movies and other varied amusements that will make it impossible for her to think of going away."[51]

While bringing more movies and commercial recreations into rural communities may not seem revolutionary to contemporary Americans, to many in the 1910s and 1920s it represented a significant development. The issue of amusements brought into focus the question of whether pleasure for its own sake was legitimate. This question lay at the heart of debates over the morality of consumerism. On one side of the debate stood the elders of the community, who condemned many of the desires and activities of modern youth as worldly, commercial, and in some cases immoral. They argued that rural youth should be contented with the morally improving and wholesome activities that country living afforded. On the other side stood youth, who wanted to participate in commercial culture merely for the sake of pleasure, just as their urban peers did. In his article "Why the Young People Leave the Farm," Chester T. Crowell described the attitudes of older rural residents. He maintained that many of them viewed young people who wanted to go to movies and dances as "wicked or selfish or half-witted." Crowell argued that this older generation in the country, with its "Puritanical" outlook, dominated country culture. Their control of the culture meant that "restrictions" had been "thrown around pleasure in the country." But the younger generation chafed against such constraints. "Rural youth today reads the modern magazines, hears the music of the day, is caught in the national craze for pretty clothes, considers the automobile a pleasure vehicle, loves to dance and is at least on speaking terms with the boys and girls of New York City." Crowell chastised rural communities for their overly moralistic attitudes and argued that young people should be allowed to have the same pleasures which city youth so enjoyed. The pursuit of pleasure was not sinful, he insisted, and all were entitled to join in it.[52]

In 1927, social scientists E. L. Morgan and Henry J. Burt examined the social life of several rural communities in order to better understand the debate over recreations and pleasure. Like Crowell, they discovered that the desires of the old and the young in rural communities were often at odds. After conducting extensive surveys in rural communities, they concluded, "The older people are providing a maximum of religious expression and a minimum of recreational expression for the young people. The young people, on the other hand, are demanding a greatly expanded recreational expression and are seeking practically nothing further in the way of religious expressions." Added to the problem of these incongruent priorities was the fact that recreational organizations seemed to be losing influence and membership while religious groups were growing. Given that fact, there were few places for rural youth to turn for fun. Morgan and Burt concluded that "farmers appreciate the church most and play and recreation for young people least. Young people appreciate the church least and play and recreation for young people most." Rather than fault young people, Burt and Morgan considered their wishes for greater recreational activity to be as legitimate as other people's religious or educational needs.[53] These reformers and social scientists seemed to recognize that the much touted virtues of nature and country living were insufficient to satisfy the very secular hunger that young people had for commercial amusements.

While there continued to be some resistance in rural communities to young people participating in commercial amusements as city folk did, increasingly the perspective of social scientists, Country Life activists, and urbanites held sway. Even if they seemed spiritually unredeeming, movies and dance halls might keep youth down on the farm. Consensus seemed to form around a larger principle as well: The pursuit of pleasure should be acknowledged as legitimate and meaningful, and all people, not just city dwellers, were entitled to seek it. If youths were allowed to fulfill their desires and had no reason to envy their city peers, they might be content to remain in their rural communities.

Yet while these more liberal attitudes were a first step in dealing with discontent, they ultimately were insufficient to solve the problem of rural recreation. The country, because of its conservative culture, low population density, and decentralized social life, would never be able to support commercial entertainments on any large scale. Rural leaders could try to make the country environment more attractive socially, but it would never be able to compete effectively with the city. In the face of such attitudes, little could be done to stop the rural exodus. O. Latham Hatcher noted in 1930 that despite decades of effort, country life still lacked adequate amusements. She concluded that girls' envy was completely understandable. "Nothing would be more natural than that the surge of dissatisfaction with country life should grow, as recreations, conveniences and opportunities of every sort multiply for young people in the city."[54] In the eyes of many commentators of the 1910s and 1920s, rural girls' discontent with country recreations was legitimate. Yet they also recognized that it might be impossible to ever remedy these glaring inadequacies. Reformers might discuss the need for more recreation in the country, yet little resulted in the way of improvement. Making envy and discontent legitimate did not make the feelings go away.

Rural young women's envy was a sign of their rising expectations and their inability to meet them. Girls in the country joined the growing commercial culture when they subscribed to the *Ladies' Home Journal*, when their families purchased radios, and when they began to see movies. From these sources they learned many of the values and developed many of the emotional habits of modern consumers. They felt envy and longed to change their identities. They believed that with the right material goods they might resolve their envy and transform themselves. But rural girls' membership in this new consumer community and culture was not complete, much to their chagrin. They wanted to be full-fledged participants in modern commercial society, but their circumstances limited them. Living in rural America, they were deprived of both the specific elements of urban culture for which they longed—clothes and commercial entertainment—and the larger environment that made self-transformation possible. By 1930 their feelings of deprivation and their desires for more and better material goods were viewed as justified and even laudable. Yet while their problems and desires were now recognized as legitimate, short of moving to the city there was often little rural women could do to actually resolve their feelings of envy. Consequently, many young women on farms and in small towns continued to believe that the world was passing them by.

4. From "Sturdy Yeoman" to "Hayseed"

Day after day, Edgar Lee Masters gazed out the window of his father's second-floor office in the small town of Lewiston, Illinois, and watched the farmers and townspeople go about their business. As he contemplated the scene before him, and thought about his own future in the town, Masters became deeply pessimistic. "I was accumulating a soul fatigue which would in a few years drive me to the city. There was a loneliness in this town and the surrounding country which could not be borne many years longer. It was this loneliness and an introspection produced by the country that gave me melancholy."[1]

Like Masters, many young men found their rural circumstances stifling and longed to be somewhere else. These young men lived in an age when the national economy, society, and culture were undergoing radical transformations, yet they had little access to the new social world being created. Aware of promising white-collar professions, recreations, and conveniences, rural young men nevertheless felt excluded from them.

Young men growing up in the country learned of city norms and standards in the same manner that their sisters did. Mass-circulation magazines and newspapers spread news of the city, and Rural Free Delivery expanded these periodicals' influence as it increased their accessibility. Railroads and, later, automobiles allowed trade and travel between the country and the city, and such travels and visits exposed rural dwellers to the opportunities, fashions, and air of refinement that urban life offered. Eventually, movies and radios would bring the sights and sounds of city life into rural communities. As sociologists Pitirim Sorokin and Carle C. Zimmerman noted in their 1929 book, *Principles of Rural-Urban*

Sociology, "in the dynamics of cultural phenomena, whether they are good or bad, there always exists a powerful stream flowing from the city to the country."[2]

The stream that carried city culture to the country was powerful. It inspired another stream—a human stream—which flowed in the opposite direction. Many young men left farms and small country towns in search of the promise of urban life. Others, while envying those who left for the city, nevertheless remained in the country. They continued to feel discontent and envy, but they may have also experienced a sense of resignation. They settled for life on the farm, but were continually haunted by a feeling that their lives did not quite measure up.

Fortune and Fame

In 1889, Theodore Cuyler, a Presbyterian minister and revivalist, worried that "country life, brought closer to the cities by railways and the press, catches the infection" of urban materialism. He worried specifically about the effects of this urban culture on young men. Writing in the *Christian Advocate*, he complained that

the rage for sudden wealth is not confined to Wall Street; it infects the stores and shops and counting-rooms everywhere; it starts a host of bright boys from country farms and villages into the great cities to try their chances in what they regard as the lottery of life. I fear that the country blood does not come up to town as pure and strong as it formerly did; for the taint of mammon is increasing and church-going is decreasing in the rural districts.[3]

"The rage for . . . wealth" had long been present in rural America, as a number of historians have demonstrated. For decades, and according to some, for centuries, farmers had been oriented toward national markets and longed to increase their profits and comforts. At the turn of the century, however, a greater number of men than ever before were exhibiting a strong desire for increased wealth and opportunity.[4]

Farmers' discontent with their financial prospects set in at an early age and often stayed with them throughout their lives. Many young men complained that although they worked hard on the family farm they received little recompense for their efforts from their fathers. In the short term, they wanted spending money and were perturbed that their labors gave them no immediate rewards. Their lack of pay limited their ability to participate in rural consumer society. These young men also worried about the future. Raised on the same success stories and literature as urban boys, rural males longed to become rich. They believed, however, that rural life would not afford them sufficient opportunities to realize these financial dreams.

Farm fathers withheld money not merely from their wives and daughters but from their sons as well. Many young men complained that their fathers would not compensate them for work they did on the farm and that consequently they would never have the resources to start a life of their own. A farm boy expressed this fear in 1909, telling a journalist, " 'I reared two calves. . . . When they were old enough to sell, father sold them and kept the money. They'd always been my calves. Father doesn't allow me any money, although I've been to school and have been graduated, and must begin to think of life. I'm going to Chicago or New York, if I have to walk.' "[5] Journalist Truman S. Vance, writing in the *Independent* in 1911, argued that such complaints were commonplace, and he offered an informal estimate that in 90 percent of farm households, boys received no remuneration and were without spending money well into their late teens.[6] The problem of pay for farm boys continued. A 1927 study indicated that although 75 percent of the young men surveyed worked for their fathers, only 45 percent of them earned money (and those who did were not necessarily earning it on their family's farm).[7]

Even those youths who were untroubled by the lack of immediate remuneration on the farm still believed that as adults in the country their opportunities for reaching the much celebrated financial heights of successful men were few and far between. Writer after writer charged that the countryside did not afford opportunities for men to become wealthy. Popular culture held up the successful, monied man as a model for young men to emulate, yet farming and small-town economies did not allow rural men to realize this ideal. While farm men of the middle class could support themselves through agriculture, their discontent came from the fact that they were not keeping even with city men. Magazines, newspapers, telegraphs, and trains had enabled them to gain a clearer sense of how others were doing in the economy, and they began to compare themselves with bourgeois men from across the nation. They saw that their relative standing was inferior to that of city men, and they concluded that so long as they remained on the farm this would always be the case.

Indeed, no matter how much the economic conditions of agriculture changed between 1890 and 1930, the belief in the relative unprofitability of agriculture persisted. The decade of the 1890s, with its long periods of economic depression, was a difficult one for farmers, whereas the years 1900–1914 represented one of the most prosperous periods ever for Americans on the farm and have been called the "golden age of American agriculture." Yet during both decades of depression and decades of prosperity, the rhetoric about the unprofitability of farming remained virtually the same. Over and over one heard the same refrain: Although farming offered some rewards, one could never become rich or even receive incomes equal to those in the city by staying in the country.

In the 1890s some commentators believed that farmers' envy of urban men's profits was merely a transient condition, brought on by the depression. An author in the *Atlantic* claimed that "we must consider . . . the existence of a widespread discontent. . . . These malcontents are not as prosperous as they think they ought to be, and they think that there is some artificial barrier to their prosperity. . . . One important cause of discontent is the shrinking of agricultural profit."[8]

But it was not merely this temporary condition of shrinking profits which left farmers discontented; it was the enduring fact that no matter how good a harvest a farmer might have, chances were slim that he would ever be rich. In 1906, in the midst of widespread agricultural prosperity, Professor Liberty Hyde Bailey conducted a study of farm boys enrolled at Cornell University. Among other questions, he asked whether they planned to return to farming after graduation. Of those respondents who had decided against returning to the farm, "the predominant reason is that farming does not pay in money." One student said he was abandoning farming because "it is unprofitable." Another said he was leaving because there is "no money in farming." Yet another stated, "I do not care to be a farmer because, first, I do not like farm-work, second, I do not think there is the chance for advancement on a farm that there is in other lines, either social or financial." In the study at Cornell, 155 students responded to the question "Why do boys leave the farm?" Forty percent of those surveyed indicated that boys left because "farming does not pay; there is no money in it."[9]

Income statistics confirmed these young men's perceptions that they could amass fortunes with far greater ease in the city than on the farm or in small towns. John Bookwalter, an industrialist who took up the cause of agricultural reform, pointed out that of the nation's total wealth in 1900, "the urban or lesser element of the nation succeeded in amassing over three quarters of it, leaving less than one quarter of the whole as a reward for the labors of the far more numerous agricultural classes." A 1916 study illustrated the persistence of this disparity as it examined rural and urban salaries. The cash income of farmers was estimated at $200 per year; in addition, it was estimated that farmers earned $400 worth of supplies, food, and fuel from the farm itself. In contrast, nonsalaried city workers on street railways earned an estimated $674 per year, laborers in iron and steel works earned $610, city patrolmen took home $1,052 per year, and federal employees pocketed $948 per year. By 1928, the average income of farmers was one-quarter of the average income of nonagricultural workers. While young men on farms did not have access to these statistics, their own experiences and their contact with the outside world offered them compelling evidence of the financial limitations of farming and the enviable size of urban incomes.[10]

Charles Seabrook, who grew up to be a prosperous truck farmer, explained how he had felt when he realized the significant gap between urban and rural incomes. As a young man in rural New Jersey, he had despaired of his future. As a magazine article noted, "When he was twenty-five he was still drudging along on the wages of a farm hand, hating the job and wanting to do almost anything else." Seabrook himself recalled:

Other men, who were boys with me, struck out for the city, because there was no chance on the farm. They used to come back sometimes, prosperous and well-dressed, and look on us with a sort of good-natured pity. A man could make twenty-five dollars a week in the city; maybe fifty dollars a week; maybe even a hundred dollars! And we were plugging along, showing a little profit one year and losing it the next. Sometimes at night when I got to thinking, it seemed as if everyone else in the world had a better job than I had.[11]

The farm environment was also frustrating to young men who dreamed not just of being rich but of becoming great and important, who longed for acclaim and renown. The drive for accomplishment and distinction, part and parcel of the liberal preoccupation with the individual, seemed to many to be out of place in the countryside. "Ambition has a wider field" in the city, proclaimed Henry Fletcher in 1895. In *The Rural Mind and Social Welfare*, sociology and psychology professor Ernest Groves concurred, arguing that cities were the location where men could make their mark in politics or commerce. "It is reasonable to suppose that men and women who love struggle, who covet self-assertion, whether it be expressed in individual or group form, will find the city increasingly satisfactory, and the country place an impossible environment."[12]

Even young men who lived in small towns rather than on farms felt that their opportunities would remain limited if they lived outside of America's big cities. Although they were perhaps better situated than farm boys, they nevertheless questioned their chances if they stayed in their small communities. As sociologist Albert Blumenthal noted of his Montana field site, Mineville, "a paucity of cherished objectives toward which their workaday labors promise to lead them are matters of lamentation. Youth and their elders alike say: 'If you stay in Mineville long enough you are almost bound to fall into a rut. Minevillers who amount to anything have to leave town for their opportunities.' " Residents of Mineville, in fact, sometimes talked of the "Mineville Sleeping Sickness," a malaise which affected those who remained in the town and did not venture off in search of fame and fortune. Given the constraining atmosphere of Mineville, most young men shared the sentiments of a boy who confided to Blumenthal, "A fellow has no future here. There is nothing to aspire to. There are about a half-dozen good jobs in town and the chances that a fellow would have one of those twenty years from now are very slim. A fellow might not get anywhere by leaving town but at least he has a chance."[13]

Young men across the nation rebelled against the constraints that the country environment placed on their futures. As Walter Chrysler wrote of his life in small-town Kansas, "I just knew that any other town was better than Ellis; any time I met a stranger, no matter where he came from, he knew things that were unknown in Ellis." Although his parents objected to his plans to leave the town (which had a population of just a few hundred), he would not be deterred. "To my parents, my defense was that I had ambition and wanted to get ahead." And though his mother shed many tears, he nevertheless left Kansas and got ahead.[14] Young men's ambitions for success, combined with their feelings of inadequacy and envy, hastened their removal from the countryside.

Standards and Status

It was not just a high income and occupational prominence that eluded young men on farms; other things proved elusive as well. At the end of the nineteenth century, farm boys recognized that they enjoyed a much lower standard of living than city dwellers. By 1890, farmers and their families had far more creature comforts than their parents and grandparents had enjoyed, yet this improvement was not satisfying. Their homes were more comfortable than earlier generations, their clothes perhaps more stylish, yet rural residents knew that they fell far short of contemporary urban standards. While some improvements spread to the countryside during the first quarter of the twentieth century, the country standard of living continued to lag behind that of the city. In 1930 Florence Elizabeth Ward, a USDA official who coordinated agricultural extension work, argued that the farmer's "condition should not be compared with the farmer of 25 or 50 years ago, but with that of the man living in the city, with equivalent intelligence and thrift. Does he have more or less comfort in his home? . . . The living standards held by the modern farm family are the 'motivating force' which determines eventually whether or not they will remain on the farm."[15] Many young men, after looking cityward, concluded that their living standard was inferior, and they came to long for what editor Henry Wallace described as the "fine houses, nice lawns, lighted and paved streets, people well dressed, working in shady offices, crowds on the streets, bands of music, pretty girls, churches, theatres, games, society, [and] comfort" of city life.[16]

Men who had grown up on the farm testified to their discontent with their standard of life. Hamlin Garland, the turn-of-the-century author of *Main Traveled Roads* and *A Son of the Middle Border*, recalled in his works of fiction and his memoirs the envy and discontent he had felt as he compared farm life with town life. He was also conscious of the envy and discontent he caused when he returned from eastern cities, well dressed and worldly wise, to his boyhood home in rural Iowa. In his 1891 short story "Up the Coule," Garland wrote emotionally of the contrast between city standards and farm standards. The main character, Howard, had migrated to the city and returned to visit his family in the country after a long absence. His brother, Grant, left behind on the farm, angrily contrasted his life with Howard's:

Singular we fellers here are discontented and mulish ain't it? . . . Singular we think the country's going to hell, we fellers, in a two-dollar suit, wadin' around in the mud or sweatin' around in the hay-field, while you fellers lay around New York and smoke and wear good clothes and toady to millionaires?[17]

These were not merely the sentiments of a fictitious character, for Garland had felt much the same discontent with his own life in rural Iowa. First he became aware that some young men dressed with a cosmopolitan flair which he was hard pressed to equal. The garments he longed for were not appropriate or necessary for a farmer's lifestyle; indeed, perhaps it was the very fact of their sophistication and urbanity which made them so attractive: "a long, yellow, linen robe called a 'duster' was in fashion among the smart dressers. John Gammons, who was somewhat of a dandy in matters of toilet, was among the first of my circle to purchase one of these very ultra garments, and Burton [Hamlin's best friend] soon followed his lead, and then my own discontent began. I, too, desired a duster." Garland, like many farm boys his age, worked for his father, but received little money from him. He could not afford the duster himself, and his father believed it to be unnecessary and unsuitable, so he was forced to do without.

When he entered his late teens, Hamlin Garland's discontent grew. In 1876 and 1877, Garland and his family lived away from the farm, occupying a house in the small town of Osage, Iowa. During those years, Garland was enrolled in the Osage Seminary. Although he now lived in town, he experienced the disadvantages of his more modest farm background and felt inferior in his attire. As he studied his new classmates, Garland came to believe that his clothing was a social handicap and revealed all too clearly his rural origins. "Two or three boys wore real tailor-made suits, and the easy flow of their trouser legs and the set of their linen collars rendered me at once envious and discontented. 'Some day,' I said to myself, 'I too, will have a suit that will not gape at the neck and crawl at the ankle.' "

When the Garland family returned to the farm in 1877, Hamlin found that he had been infected with other cosmopolitan tastes. From life in the town "we had gained our first set of comparative ideas, and with them an unrest which was to carry us very far away." To Garland and his brother, the return to the farm was a step backward:

Over against these comforts [of the town], we now set our ugly little farmhouse, with its rag carpets, its battered furniture, its barren attic, and its hard rude beds.— All that we possessed seemed very cheap and deplorably commonplace. . . . [My brother] too resented the curry-comb and the dung-fork. We both loathed the smell of manure and hated the greasy clothing which our tasks made necessary. Secretly we vowed that when we were twenty-one we would leave the farm, never to return to it.

In 1884 Garland left the countryside and traveled east to Boston, where, after some struggling, he gained recognition for his literary talent. In the late

1880s he returned to the Midwest to visit his family and found that his contact with eastern urban mores rendered him enviable in the eyes of his old friends: "My presence stimulated their discontent. I was one of them, one who having escaped had returned as from some far-off glorious land of achievement. My improved dress, my changed manner of speech, everything I said, roused in them a kind of rebellious rage. . . . Their mood was no doubt transitory, but it was as real as my own."[18]

While not all who compared their lot with that of city folk felt such a rage, they nevertheless had to cope with the knowledge that their standard of living was far below that of city people. Iowa farm boy H. E. Wilkinson, born in 1892 in Cerro Gordo County, recalled how traveling to cities and towns alerted him to the contrast between farm and town life. Even when he traveled only a few miles from the family farm to go to nearby Mason City, he felt he was "transported into another world of bright lights, soft carpets, music, and gay handsomely dressed men and women." When he was about sixteen, he and his cousin ventured farther away and visited their aunt in Madison, Wisconsin. In their city relatives' home they saw with even greater clarity the contrast between rural and urban life. "We saw moving pictures . . . went bobsledding on the hills that overlooked lovely Lake Mendota, and I had my first drink of brandy. . . . The ten days we spent at Aunt Amelia's home were glorious. There were no cows to milk, no cream separators to turn, no skim milk to carry to the pigs, and we were entertained like young princes." As he matured, Wilkinson sought out greater contact with the modern world he had glimpsed in Madison. Although he continued to farm for at least part of his adult life, he also attended Iowa State College and eventually worked for the Iowa Mutual Insurance Company.[19]

Adding to the sense of deprivation and discontent that drove many young men to leave the farm was a conviction, partly based on fact, that many urban Americans viewed country people with disdain and considered them coarse and backward. In the modernizing economy, the occupational status of farming was eroding. Whereas Thomas Jefferson, J. Hector St. John Crèvecoeur, and other early writers of the Republic had discussed the farmer as the center and strength of the body politic, by the late nineteenth and early twentieth centuries, farmers' social position had changed. They had become less central to the identity and health of the nation, as cities gained in stature and influence. As a contributor to the *Atlantic* pithily put it in 1896, "the 'sturdy yeoman' has become the 'hayseed.' " He claimed that farmers were discontented in part because they had suffered "a certain loss of dignity" and that their "relative social standing has been lost."[20]

Farmers, exemplars of the old middle class, had lost standing, while white-collar workers in modern corporate offices increasingly seemed to be at the center of national social and economic life. One cause of this decline in status arose from the nature of farm work. Rural labor was unspecialized in an age that valued specialization. As one journalist put it, "In these days of the expert, the farmer is inexpert, and therefore lonesome." This lack of specialization, combined with the fact that farmers performed manual labor, wore work clothes rather than business suits, and received relatively little remuneration for their labors, led many Americans to consider them old-fashioned and out of step with the new economy. Rural sociologist John Gillette noted that "the farmer has not been rated as the equal of city residents. He is backwards as a social class." Proof of his lowered status might be found in "the caricatures of 'country Rheubes' which have appeared in the press and comic papers of the nation. He is represented as uncouth and primitive in his dress, as slow and stolid like the ox, as a gawk, and as generally inferior to city dwellers. He has been caricatured and depicted also in the names which have been applied to him, such as 'Reuben' or 'Reube,' 'hayseed,' 'spinach,' 'clod-hopper.' "[21]

Such insults and stereotypes were pervasive. Wilkinson remembered driving his father's wagon into school in Mason City. Twice a week he dropped off cream from the farm on the way to school. "I detested having to carry that cream can in my buggy, not realizing, of course, that the income from it was probably keeping me in school. The town kids laughed at me and yelled derisively, 'Look at the old farmer and his milk can!' . . . I was thoroughly ashamed of that old cream can. I tried to hide it by throwing the lap robe over it, but it still looked like a cream can."[22] Such taunts reinforced the idea that farming was a low-status profession.

Country school teachers sometimes strengthened these impressions as they pointed their students toward the urban, white-collar jobs of the new middle class. John Bell, writing in the *Outlook* in 1909, complained that all too often, "when the teacher of the farmer's boy wishes to incite him to study and effort, wishes to create an ambition, he tells the boy that if he studies hard and learns well he may some day be a clerk in a store, or a bookkeeper, and tells the girl that she may become a stenographer and typewriter." Even parents sometimes urged their children to search for occupations that enjoyed higher status than farming. At the 1926 Country Life

Conference, panelists discussed the pressure some parents put on their children to leave the farm. One speaker noted that farm parents "want the boys to be looked up to. They want the boys to be in a business of which they may brag just a bit. They want them to be dressed well from morning until night."

The education that farm boys received both in the classroom and from popular culture stiffened the resolve of many to become city dwellers and hold white-collar jobs. In *Rural Sociology*, John Gillette described young men's emotions, writing, "conscious that he is different in clothes and calling, and feeling at a disadvantage, the country boy comes to partly accept his assigned position to a lower class and to resent the situation and want to 'get even.' " A survey published in 1927 substantiated this observation. Of 2,100 high school boys from rural communities, only 20 percent planned to farm after graduation, while the remaining 80 percent of boys planned on being engineers or members of the "business and learned professions." To such country boys, urban life and white-collar professions had become synonymous with refinement, modernity, and bourgeois status. In contrast, even some farmers themselves believed that agricultural work signified rudeness, backwardness, and low social status.[23]

Keeping the Boys Down on the Farm

Because feelings of envy and deprivation motivated many who migrated to the city, reformers, editorialists, and moralists worked vigorously to combat the emotion. Country people's envy was worrisome because it contradicted the popular vision of contented and virtuous farmers as the backbone of the nation, a vision most famously articulated by Thomas Jefferson and further elaborated on by succeeding generations. Even if the general society no longer accorded farmers great significance in daily life, they occupied an important place in the national mythology. That many farmers were envious of city life seemed to undermine these cherished national ideals. For that reason, moralists and editorialists tried to quench desire, halt the migration, and safeguard the idealized, if mythical, order of the nation.

In 1912, *Rural Manhood,* a publication of the YMCA, printed "The Country Boy's Creed." The Creed contained a number of the themes that reformers used to discourage envy. It declared:

I believe that the Country which God made is more beautiful than the city which man made; that life out-of-doors and in touch with the earth is the natural life of man. I believe that work is work wherever we find it, but that work with nature is more inspiring than work with the most intricate machinery. I believe that the dignity of labor depends not on what you do, but on how you do it; that opportunity comes to a boy on the farm as often as to the boy in the city, that life is larger and freer and happier on the farm than in the town, that my success depends not upon my location, but upon myself, not upon my dreams, but upon what I actually do, not upon luck, but upon pluck.[24]

The Creed incorporated several defenses of country life. First, it asserted that rural life was purer and more consecrated in the eyes of God. Consequently, rural residents were more virtuous than city people. Second, it claimed that young men might be able to gain success even if they remained in the country. Finally, the Creed sought to convince readers of the social value and benefits of their work. With its focus on the noncommercial advantages of rural life, the Creed encapsulated the major strains of the message that envious country boys would hear in the last years of the nineteenth century and the first years of the twentieth.

Editorialists tried to convince rural young men of the beauty and blessedness of nature. They used much the same rhetoric that they had employed in their appeals to young women. They maintained that nature was superior to the culture of the city; nature was spiritual whereas city life was base and materialistic. If young men could be convinced of the superiority of nature, they might not envy the amenities of the city. Writing in the *Forum* in 1895, Henry Fletcher queried, "Is it not possible that the fierceness of the rage for wealth will one day abate, and the people begin to look above them for the sweetness and serenity which human nature longs for in its highest moments, and which are best found under a pure sky, amid the quietness of nature?"[25]

Some commentators, aware that purity and beauty alone would not cure a young man's envy, took the argument further, claiming that the rural environment would give country boys an advantage over city boys. The conditions of farm life, away from the softness and ease of city life, produced strong and able men. Orison Swett Marden, in his 1897 work, *Architects of Fate or Steps to Success and Power,* argued that if you took two boys "as nearly alike as possible" and placed one in the country and one in the midst of the wealthy and cosmopolitan Vanderbilt family, there would be striking differences between them as youths, but these would not foretell the order of the future. Marden asked his reader to suppose that as boys, "the two meet":

The city lad is ashamed of his country brother. The plain, threadbare clothes, hard hands, tawny face, and awkward manner of the country boy make sorry contrast with the genteel appearance of the other. The poor boy bemoans his hard lot, regrets that he has "no chance in life," and envies the city youth. He thinks that it is a cruel Providence that places such a wide gulf between them.

But in the next line, Marden showed how mistaken this envy was:

They meet again as men, but how changed! It is as easy to distinguish the sturdy, self-made man from the one who has been propped up all his life by wealth, position, and family influence, as it is for the shipbuilder to tell the difference between the plank from the rugged mountain oak and one from the sapling of the forest.

Marden was trying to placate the country boy who "often bemoans his lack of a chance as did Clay, Webster, and thousands of others, and thinks his youth among the rocks, the mountains, the forests has been almost thrown away; and he longs for the time when he can shake off his farm fetters, and flee to the city where there is opportunity." He argued that despite the country boy's misgivings about his career and future, when crucial moments came that demanded forceful leadership, the country-bred youth always proved superior. Invoking the principles of agrarian republicanism, Marden warned the boy not to turn his back too quickly on country life and the advantages that it might confer. Rural culture, sheltered from the ostentatious, indulgent, and materialistic influences of the city, produced a superior type of man.[26]

Boys raised on the farm might not want to stay there permanently, but many reformers suggested that they stay as long as possible so that they would be able to absorb the virtues that accompanied country life. Farm journal editor Henry Wallace claimed that young men could develop character and integrity "easier on the farm than you can anywhere else; therefore do not be in a hurry about choosing your profession." As he discussed the dearth of upright men, he explained to his readers that such men "are wanted in every store, factory, and bank, and it is this kind of men that in the end lead in all the professions. A farm is the best place in the world to grow this kind of boys and men; therefore, do not be in a hurry to leave the farm, and do not make a final choice of your profession . . . until you are sure you are doing the right thing."[27] Marden, Wallace, and others endeavored to convince country boys that what they considered to be the deprivations of country life were actually advantages which would benefit them in the future. Young men need not long for the high salaries, fine clothing, or modern amenities so easily acquired in America's cities. Farmers' virtue, in fact, depended on their underconsumption and their modest income and way of life. In the end, these hardships would pay off.

Many writers tried to convince restless young men that farming, in addition to having great spiritual and moral value, had great social importance as well. Countless authors stressed the centrality of farming to the health of the polity and the economy, echoing republican and Physiocratic arguments of earlier centuries. An author in *Munsey's Magazine* wrote, "To see the real Americans, the backbone of the country, the material from which the motive power of our cities is drawn, the visitor must go to the interior—the smaller towns, the wide rural regions. Here he will find the men who have time to think; the women who have time to bring up their children."[28] Reprising Physiocratic arguments that the wealth of a nation was based on its agriculture, journalist Isaac F. Marcosson wrote an article entitled "Why the American Farmer Is Rich." In it he posited that "the bulk of all its [the nation's] bigness is agriculture. Without this there would be no 'tallest buildings,' no 'queen cities,' no 'fastest trains in the world.' . . . In short, our real progress is rooted in the ground."[29] These journalists and editorialists attempted to placate young men who felt that farming was backward and superfluous in the modern economy and who believed that other careers were much more modern, exciting, and central to national life. They told farm boys who longed to be involved in the great economic concerns of the day that they need look no farther than their own fields for the true source of the nation's wealth.

Despite their high-flung prose, these celebrations of rural life did not succeed in assuaging the sense of deprivation that envious young men felt so very keenly. Many refused to believe that the abstract virtues of rural life could equal the far more tangible charms of city life. It brought boys little satisfaction to hear that their fields were the source of the nation's wealth when they themselves received little income from them. Similarly, celebrations of the simplicity of rural life ignored the fact that simplicity often meant hardship and struggle. Judging by their continued and, in fact, increasing migration, envious young men seem to have taken very little solace from these sermons on the joys of country living.

Making the Farmer Modern

During the 1910s and 1920s, the discussions of rural young men's envy shifted in focus. While in the late nineteenth and early twentieth centuries young men had been encouraged to ignore urban culture and turn a blind eye to its many temptations, in succeeding years, they were told to immerse themselves in city culture and to increase their involvement in the national economy. Rural sociologists, extension agents, government officials, and many—although not all—Country Life activists encouraged farmers to modernize their farms and their lives in much the same way that they had encouraged farm wives and daughters to update their homes and their appearances. They suggested that farmers change their methods of farming in order to equal the efficiency and profitability of urban businesses and raise their standard of living so that they would equal city modes of life.[30]

These reformers and advisors validated men's desires and discontents, assuring them that they were entitled to the same profits and privileges as city men. In the vision of modern agriculture that they promoted, however, young men did not need to flock to the city and become white-collar workers in order to get wealth, respect, and comforts; instead, they could become the managers of their own farms, specialists in their own fields. If farmers transformed their agricultural practices, their work lives and home lives would become roughly comparable to those of urban men. They could live in modern and comfortable houses, wear city clothes, and gaze in admiration at their stylishly dressed wives. In contrast to earlier generations of rural reformers, most of those active in the 1910s and 1920s generally expressed few concerns about the moral costs of these material improvements, and they appeared unworried about the way that imported urban tastes and goods would affect rural life and values. Instead, they considered the benefits of such an approach to be quite substantial. By modernizing farming and raising the farmer's status and standard of living, reformers believed that they might put the agricultural economy on firmer footing, respond to the status anxieties of farmers, and address the destabilizing discontent that seemed to be sweeping the countryside.

Farm men greeted these efforts at farm modernization with much the same mix of emotions as did their sisters and wives. Many farmers, particularly older and more experienced ones, resented the advice and arrogance of upstart city folk who took it upon themselves to instruct them on the intricacies of farm management and good living. While farm families may have felt a sense of deprivation and envy, they also had pride. It was one thing to envy and long for things that city folk had; it was another for outsiders to imperiously declare that farmers were backward and inferior because they lacked these amenities. Additionally, farmers often saw the efforts to modernize farming as an attempt by self-interested urbanites to increase farm production and thereby lower prices for urban consumers. The goal of increased production was regarded with some suspicion because many farmers feared that it would ultimately lower farm profits and decrease the amount of money which they could pocket or direct toward consumer spending.[31] Those who interpreted farm reform in this skeptical light may have also concluded that the reformers' agenda reflected the ever growing power of urban civilization. In this new vision, America's farming communities, once considered the moral center of the nation, now seemed to be the mere handmaidens of the cities.

Yet while the idea of modernizing and industrializing agricultural production upset some farmers, the (sometimes illusory) promise of more cash and more consumer goods was certainly welcomed by others.[32] Then too, while many of the reformers had mixed motives, they nevertheless legitimated and tried to assuage the very real feelings of envy that many rural young men felt.

The first step in the process of assuaging envy was to make farmers the social and economic equals of the urban middle class. This required that farmers receive incomes that were comparable to those of white-collar workers. Accordingly, the new model for young men was not the humble yeoman of Jeffersonian America but the man who, in the words of one early advocate, Charles Dillon, "ran a farm as a man should run his business."[33] Unlike previous generations, these reformers no longer idealized farming as a pure and noncommercial activity but instead contended that it was no different than urban commerce. Rural sociologist John Gillette explained that "Agricultural production is a business just as is retailing goods, manufacturing, or banking." Elsewhere he noted, "Whatever other objects besides profits or making money there are in farming—and there are others—the item of profit cannot be disregarded. The other purposes and aims of life are more or less conditioned by this factor."[34]

In an attempt to help farmers run their farms as businesses and increase their profits, the federal government sent out an army of advisors to visit family farms and create programs that would demonstrate more effective planting and harvesting techniques and modern methods of farm management. The Smith-Lever Act of 1914, which created a national network of federally supported county agents, was central to this effort. The agents were supposed to help farmers increase their output and revolutionize their marketing practices. Government officials and Country Life activists believed that if these modernization efforts proved successful, they would, in Woodrow Wilson's words, "insure the retention in rural districts of an efficient and contented population." By transforming farm operations and farmers' outlooks, more money could be put in their pockets and more status given to their profession. Farmers finally would enjoy chances for success and wealth equal to those of urban businessmen.[35]

These new approaches to farming, while they often encountered initial resistance, nevertheless were gradually adopted by agriculturalists across the country. Successful farmers who had modernized their operations and become businessmen encouraged discontented men to follow suit. For example, in a magazine interview, prosperous truck farmer Charles Seabrook discussed his youthful discontent and his eventual prosperity. The interview was designed to comfort dissatisfied youths; its title made this apparent: "You don't altogether like your job? Then read this story of Charles Seabrook, who has made a tremendous success at work he used to hate." In the interview, Seabrook recalled his youthful desire for incomes as great as those of his friends in the city, and told how he had achieved them on the farm. Speaking frankly of his envy, Seabrook remarked that "most folks waste a lot of time pitying themselves because they have all the hard work and other folks have things so soft." That is how he had once regarded his situation, "wishing I had almost any other kind of work than the kind I had to do; and thinking that there must be more chances for a man in New York, or Nebraska, or Chicago, or Florida, than there could ever be in a prosaic old place like south Jersey." Gradually, however, Seabrook had learned that his envy was unfounded and that opportunities were waiting for him in his very own fields. "I've learned that the fields a long way from the road always look less stony and greener than the fields alongside. And more rain always seems to fall in the next township than ever falls in yours. The only thing to do is to take what land you've got and *make it be green*, whether it wants to be or not."

Seabrook had found success and fortune in south Jersey by experimenting with new farming techniques. He had built an overhead irrigation system that made his land more fertile and productive. He had gradually converted his family farm into a modern industrial concern by using assembly-line techniques as well as establishing a canning factory and freezing facility on the farm. At one point, he was able to produce five million cans of vegetables and fruits per year. At its largest, Seabrook Farms covered 19,000 acres; this was supplemented with 35,000 acres that he leased from adjoining farmers. While Seabrook's success was extraordinary, he demonstrated that farming could become a modern, commercial, and lucrative venture. Country boys might follow his example and reach the heights of those they envied if they would focus on the commercial potential that farming held, rather than decrying what it lacked.[36] In emphasizing the possibility of gaining financial success on the farm, journalists, county agents, and farmers like Seabrook maintained that young men's preoccupation with profits and advancement was wholly legitimate. No longer was the "rage for sudden wealth" an infection that young men should try to avoid, as Theodore Cuyler had suggested in 1889. Instead, reformers of the 1910s and 1920s regarded rural young men's concern with wealth as natural and unsurprising.

Another way that agricultural advisors sought to combat farmers' envy and their feelings of inferiority was by encouraging them to take on the look of the modern businessman. Young men disdained the traditional appearance of farmers and, like Grant in Hamlin Garland's story, hated the fact that they wore "a two-dollar suit" and spent the day "wadin' around in the mud or sweatin' around in the hay-field," while city men "lay around New York and smoke and wear good clothes and toady to millionaires."[37] To respond to such feelings, many advisors of the 1910s and 1920s suggested that farmers begin to wear business suits. Such attire would bolster their own self-esteem and raise them in the eyes of society as a whole.

While young men on farms were generally eager to buy clothing, their fathers often tried to curb their desires, believing that there was little utility in fancy attire. Rural sociologists wanted to convince these reluctant spenders to become full-fledged consumers, promising them numerous financial and social benefits if they and their families would only assume a more modern look. In 1929, agricultural economist Ellis Lore Kirkpatrick noted, "Generally, farmers are realizing that it pays to keep pace with men of other affairs in the matter of dress and personal appearance." Kirkpatrick contended that "tasteful clothing, accompanied by pleasing personal appearance and habits, is in reality a vital part of one's social life. To the observer clothing . . . is probably the foremost index of the prevailing standard of living. If this be true, farmers cannot afford to dress less well than other people. They must continue to give increasing consideration to clothing as one of the important elements of family living." According to such wisdom, farmers should spend to keep their families happy and to solidify their social position, for the sign of a prosperous and stable farm was not a well-kept barn but a well-dressed farmer.[38]

In addition to advertising one's prosperity and high standard of living, dressing well offered other advantages to the farmer. Professors Wilson Gee and William Henry Stauffer of the University of Virginia noted that in the past, it had been presumed that farm work required only "clothing of the crudest and cheapest sort" and that the farmer's interactions "were of a sort which gave adequate excuse for not 'dressing up.' " This received wisdom was being challenged, however. Gee and Stauffer maintained that farmers should dress up for a number of reasons including their own "psychic" well-being. Perhaps more important, the transformation of farming into a modern business required that farmers appear more like white-collar workers. "With the increasing contacts of the farmer necessitated by the mechanized, urban-ized industrial era, the intelligent farmer recognizes the business advantages of good clothes towards promoting his economic well-being."[39] If farm men wanted to be truly equal to white-collar workers, they needed to look like them. While in the past, advisors like Orison Swett Marden had found virtue in the simplicity of the "plain, threadbare clothes" of farm folk, now fancy clothes were commendable and were the visible symbols of farmers' aspira-tions and modernity. To gain economic prosperity, self-respect, and societal respect, farmers and their families needed to consume.

Essentially the rural sociologists, extension workers, and Country Life activists promised that through farm modernization, the white-collar world of urban men could be made available to farm boys. With more money in their pockets and good suits on their backs, rural men would be able to change the way that they considered their lives and work and in turn alter the way that others perceived them. If they no longer looked old-fashioned, if their work proved profitable, if it was integrated into the modern economy, farmers would have few reasons to envy any longer—or so the rural sociolo-gists, extension agents, and Country Life advisors believed.

The succeeding years of economic tumult and dislocation would prove these advisors wrong. Migrations from the farm continued in subsequent de-cades. Falling prices as well as an ever more alluring and influential com-mercial culture continued to prompt young men and women to leave the farm.[40] Yet while they did not succeed in stemming the rural migration, rural reformers' efforts did have lasting effects. These reformers gave legitimacy to rural men's and women's material desires and assured them—and the wider society—that country people were entitled to all of the pleasures of consumer society. While most farmers had never doubted the legitimacy of their longings, social critics had. The reformers of the 1910s and 1920s dispelled many of the moral concerns about farm people consuming as city folk did, and promoted the idea that the desire for a higher standard of living was laudable.

The changing emotional prescriptions that farm families encountered reflected the dramatic way in which the nation's identity changed between 1890 and 1930. For generations, authors, artists, and politicians had found meaning in America's pastoral landscape. The nation's abundance of land initially seemed to hold out the promise that the United States could avoid the class conflicts and social pathologies endemic to European society. With plentiful land and few luxuries, American farmers would be sheltered from the market, would remain pure and uncorrupted in their tastes, and would in consequence be well equipped for participation in the affairs of the republic. This ideal of America had long been more myth than reality: Farmers had been increasing their marketplace involvement since the eighteenth century, and commercial and specifically consumer motives certainly animated agriculturalists. The agrarian myth was, nevertheless, a vital part of America's national identity.

By the late nineteenth century, however, the foundations of the myth were crumbling. It was very clear that the resentments, envy, and class conflict found in European societies could likewise be found throughout America, and rural districts were no exception. The envy that farm families felt as they contemplated the wealth and creature comforts of city people, and the migrations that such emotions motivated, seemed to contradict the underlying assumption that farmers had simple needs and tastes and were uncorrupted by material desires.

Editorialists, sociologists, and politicians initially responded to farmers' discontent by trying to convince them of the moral value of a life away from commercial temptation. By stifling their envy, farm families might preserve rural society and, some even believed, the moral and civic foundations of the nation. The succeeding generation of advisors, writing in the 1910s and 1920s, saw the nation and its citizens in a very different light. They envisioned America as a commercial power and believed that the way to safeguard the country was not by teaching individuals to repress their commercial and consumer desires but by encouraging them to respond to such instincts. Rural dwellers should buy what they wanted and should keep up with city folk. Farm families should become active participants in commercial society. They should modernize their farming enterprises, produce enough to support the further growth of American cities, and consume enough to keep the furnaces of American factories well stoked. As one editorialist noted in 1924, "The American citizen's first importance to his country is no longer that of citizen but that of consumer." This transformation was surely visible in the altered role of the farmer: Once citizens par excellence, farmers were now to serve the nation by becoming consumers.[41]

Whereas formerly rural culture had been celebrated because it embodied ruggedness, simplicity, self-restraint, and the old-fashioned values of a bygone era, now those concerned with assuaging discontent believed that rural culture must catch up with the modern world. The countryside was no longer to be preserved as a haven from urban and commercial influences. Instead, by the 1920s, those dedicated to solving the problem of farmers' envy and discontent believed that rural people's desires for urban comforts should be encouraged. The culture of American cities must be spread across the countryside. As Carl Taylor noted approvingly in 1927, "Rural people are now a part of the larger community and so will continue to strive for the larger community's standard of living."[42] Advisors like Taylor believed that such striving was desirable, for it would benefit neither city folk nor farmers to stay isolated from each other. Farm people would benefit from increased contact with urban commercial culture by developing new tastes and by demanding a standard of living comparable to that enjoyed by the urban bourgeoisie. In turn, farm families' increased demand for goods, as well as their increased production of food, would support the continued expansion of American industry. In this new vision, country and city were to be ever more linked by a web of commerce and desire.

5. Coming of Age in Consumer Society

In 1920, when she was twelve years old, Louise Rosenfield left her affluent family and their comfortable home in Des Moines, Iowa, and boarded a train bound for Maine. She was headed for summer camp, wearing a brand-new outfit in which she felt "very well dressed." She wore a navy skirt, a white shirt, white socks, "low-heeled shoes, and best of all, a wide-brimmed straw hat decorated with streamers of embroidered ribbons." When the train reached Chicago, she met other girls headed for the same camp. As she sized them up, her satisfaction with her own clothing disappeared. She recalled, "I was completely taken aback. They were wearing heels, silk stockings, girdles, and sophisticated hairdos. I was the unsophisticated girl from the country and completely out of place." Her feelings of inferiority continued. The rest of the girls at camp were "sophisticates from New York and Washington," and Louise found it difficult to bridge the social chasm that separated her from their society. "I felt like an outsider all summer long," she recalled. At the end of her stay at camp, in an attempt to replicate the look of her camping mates and cope with her envy, she replaced her ribbon-trimmed hat (which she now disparaged) with a more stylish beret purchased in a neighboring village. When she returned home, she expected her mother to criticize her for her new purchase, but her mother was unperturbed.[1] Louise's experience was increasingly typical of children growing up in consumer society. Acutely aware of status distinctions and their own relative social standing, middle-class children believed wholeheartedly that the solution to their status anxieties could be found in retail stores, and their parents often supported them in this belief. Children born between 1890 and 1930 developed a strong faith in the power of goods and played a central role in the expansion of American consumer society. As youngsters they developed new emotional habits, habits that stayed with them their entire lives and which they passed on to their own offspring. The emotional style that they developed is widely evident today and continues to sustain the American consumer economy.

Middle-class children's concerns about their own status and their appetite for consumer goods ran counter to many adults' assumptions about the nature of childhood. Bourgeois adults of the period generally regarded childhood as a time of innocence. In this idealized view of youth, adults sheltered children from financial realities, freed them from the need to labor, and protected them from the stiff social competition and status anxieties that so plagued the adult world. While this idealized view was popular, it was hardly accurate.[2] Middle-class children (here defined as under sixteen) growing up in the late nineteenth and early twentieth centuries were acutely aware of the income and relative status of their families, and the differences in wealth and position that separated adults often created sharp cleavages in children's worlds as well.[3] Youngsters with less often envied schoolmates with more, while privileged youth frequently and cruelly flaunted their advantages in order to provoke envy in their poorer acquaintances.

As bourgeois Americans confronted the new pressures and temptations that the expanding consumer economy offered, the occasions for envy multiplied. In the 1890s and 1900s, children observed their parents and friends using consumer goods in their struggle for status, and they often found themselves similarly engaged in social competition. Department stores, magazines, and catalog houses also educated them about desirable products and the social prestige that they offered. The culture of childhood was gradually becoming commercialized. By the 1910s and 1920s, this trend was even more apparent. Movies and advertisements exposed young and old alike to a wider range of goods and lifestyles. The influence of these new media could be felt in the quickening pace of social life, a pace which bourgeois adults and their offspring often struggled to match. Children of the 1920s learned from their parents and from the commercial culture around them that envy, striving, and acquisitive behavior were socially acceptable and became willing participants in the consumer culture.

Some adults worried about children's envy and tried to discourage the emotion and offset the effects of consumer culture. Schoolbook authors, ministers, and psychologists all worked to teach children to restrain their

envy. Even their efforts, however, ultimately would be shaped by the very
market forces they were trying to counteract. While they condemned envy,
educators and child experts, particularly those writing in the 1910s and
1920s, embraced many of the consumer values that earlier generations of
moralists had so strenuously opposed.

Middle-class children then heard many messages about the enticements
of consumer society and the proper ways to regard this bounty. They heeded
only some of the advice they heard, and disregarded many of the lessons
that adults hoped they would follow. In the process, they created a new
model of childhood behavior, one that contemporary youngsters continue to
follow as they confront the temptations of modern consumer culture.

It is impossible to understand how the consumer ethos came to have
such power in the twentieth century without understanding how children became accustomed to assuaging their envy and desire through purchases. The
consumer economy grew not merely because of the activities of adult merchants, advertisers, and shoppers, nor simply as a result of the enhanced productive capabilities of manufacturers. The growth of the consumer society
depended to a great degree on the changing emotional habits of Americans,
and many of these habits were learned during childhood.

Objects and Expressions of Envy

Children have always envied, but the causes of envy have changed over
time. Youngsters growing up between 1890 and 1930 found much to envy in
the bounty of the expanding consumer society, a bounty they could often see
but not always possess. Like their parents, children in the 1890s and 1900s
were exposed to catalogs, mass-circulation magazines, and department stores,
and they often expressed longings for the commercially sold goods they observed. By the 1910s and 1920s they were also tempted by glamorous film
images and modern advertisements, which increased their familiarity with
desirable and expensive toys, houses, parties, and pets. The effects of consumer culture on childhood hopes and dreams became even more pro-
nounced. To a greater degree than earlier generations, these youngsters'
desires and daydreams were shaped by commercial forces. Consumer goods
assumed a new centrality in children's psyches.

All children did not long for the same commercial goods, however.
Contemporary gender roles seem to have shaped desires. According to ob-

servers of the period, little girls were socialized to envy clothes and symbols of prestige, while boys quickly learned to envy the abilities of others as well as toys that inspired lively play. Gail Hamilton described the sexes' different longings in an essay published in a reading book in 1910: "I regret that there are some little girls who can only look with wistful eyes at the fluttering ribbons of their friends, without hope of attaining such delights themselves." In contrast, she told boys they might feel envy because "you have no pony, and are rather bashful, and must work when other boys are at play, and your jacket is short-waisted."[4]

Turn-of-the-century psychological research supported Hamilton's contention that boys and girls envied different things. Pioneering psychologist G. Stanley Hall concluded that girls were more concerned with and envious of possessions while boys were more preoccupied with their abilities. When researcher Anna Kohler asked children if they would save, and what they would save for, if they were given an allowance, she found that girls were more likely than boys to save for clothing and accessories. Only as they reached their teens and became increasingly aware of the demands of social and business life did boys become interested in dressing well. Boys' interest in clothes was less developed than that of girls; they showed a greater desire to save for bicycles, ponies, horses, fishing poles, visits, and parties.[5]

Hall and Kohler both concluded that boys were more interested in activity and experiences, while girls were more concerned with items that conferred status and prestige. They believed that boys desired fishing poles and bicycles not because they were status goods but because they were the means to having an experience. Their conclusions reflect prevailing gender biases of the time. Girls may have longed for dresses for other reasons besides status concerns and may have believed that dresses were the means to certain experiences. Likewise, male interest in bicycles and horses may have been driven as much by a desire for display as by a desire for activity, for boys were certainly attuned to the status attached to particular active possessions. Yet despite the preconceptions about gender that their conclusions reflected and the possible interpretations that they neglected, Hall and Kohler's findings indicate that boys and girls did indeed envy different objects. Their distinct desires illustrate that the socially sanctioned gender roles and ideals of the adult world had penetrated children's consciousness.

Children's desires were shaped not merely by adult gender conventions but also by the adult status system. Children were attuned to the social meaning attached to the possessions and positions of adults. They felt inferior and envious if their parents did not possess elite status symbols. Hall presented evidence of an eleven-year-old girl who longed for expensive carpets, another girl who desired a "carriage with a span of horses," and a seven-year-old girl who wanted bright, high-quality silver. John Dollard, a professor at the Institute for Human Relations at Yale University, described the envy that an anonymous patient of his felt as a child. Growing up in a small industrial town during the first decade of the twentieth century, the patient recalled how he had envied the wealth and elegant lifestyle of a schoolmate, Hanky Bisworth, and longed to have his own parents occupy the exalted social position that Mr. and Mrs. Bisworth enjoyed. Hanky's family owned the "biggest house in town," and this provoked rankling feelings of discontent in the patient. "It was a great, dark red brick house and the informant always walked by it with a certain amount of awe. Would he ever be able to go into a house like that, and why didn't Hanky ever ask him around to play?" The higher status of Hanky's parents made the patient uncomfortable with his family's social rank and heightened his feelings of inferiority. "It was humiliating to notice that there was someone who had a position higher than that of his own parents, those parents who had heretofore seemed so absolute in their prestige."[6]

Even children from affluent circumstances harbored such feelings of inferiority. Nathalie Dana recalled that as a child she was very concerned about the social meaning of her parents' home. Born in 1878, Nathalie was raised in comfort in New York City; nevertheless, she felt greatly inferior to her friend Daisy: "Daisy lived on Madison Avenue, which was correct, while we lived on unfashionable Park Avenue. I was ashamed of the position of our house which I otherwise loved so much." When her family bought a summer cottage in Northeast Harbor, Maine, in 1891, she and her cousin worried that its appearance would hamper their social careers. "Kenneth and I had one disappointment: we had hoped for a lawn which would establish our social status; instead we found a 'turn-around' ornamented by four boulders." Such anecdotes indicate that rather than being a picture of innocence, turn-of-the-century childhood was a realm where the social distinctions of the adult world were clearly present, extremely influential, and often the cause of much pain and anxiety.[7]

While bourgeois children were acutely aware of the status that consumer goods might confer on them and on their families, they usually could not purchase the objects they desired, for they had little income. Children like Nathalie could not control where their families lived or whether they had a lawn; they also lacked the power and resources to purchase smaller personal articles that might fulfill their desires and allay their status anxieties. Historian Viviana Zelizer has likened middle- and upper-class children at the turn of the century to "paupers," while Helen Seymour, an essayist writing for the *Outlook* in 1893, claimed that "servants, bootblacks, and the poorest class are rich in comparison with many young people who are dependent for their pennies." Ironically, poor children who worked frequently had more spending money than children from affluent households. David Nasaw has described the spending habits of working children who often pocketed a portion of their earnings and were thereby able to afford candy, toys, clothes, and nickelodeon shows.[8]

In contrast, middle-class children had less money and thus fewer opportunities for consumer spending. Anna Kohler illustrated the financial dependency of middle-class children in her 1897 study of children's "sense of money." She surveyed four thousand girls and boys in California and discovered that while 72 percent received no regular allowance from their parents, over two-thirds wished to get one. By 1915, some child advisors were recommending that parents give their children allowances, and by 1930 most child-rearing experts agreed that "every child needs an allowance," because the possession of money would inculcate fiscal responsibility and prudential shopping habits. Even with the increased number of children receiving allowances, however, bourgeois youngsters by the end of the period still could not afford all that they desired.[9]

Some middle-class children were tempted to imitate working-class children and become servants or bootblacks in order to earn money. Yet despite their constant celebration of the value of hard work, many middle-class parents objected to their own children working, for it undermined their social status. Using Thorstein Veblen's terms, children's leisure was a conspicuous sign of a middle-class family's secure economic status. Working children or wives, on the other hand, were an indication of a family's inability to live comfortably on the father's salary and a sign of financial instability. William Allen White provoked his father's status anxieties when as a boy he took what his father considered to be a demeaning job. White had traded marbles for a shoeshine kit and was on the street trying to drum up business and shine shoes when his father came upon him and scolded, "Get up from there, Willie—not that, by God! You go home!" Later, his father lectured him, "Now Willie, . . . there are some things you just can't do unless you have to, and you don't have to shine any man's shoes." White concluded,

"It was the only time in all his life that I can remember when he implanted a sense of caste in my heart."[10]

The financial powerlessness of middle-class children drove many to rely on their imagination to supply what they could not actually possess. Children often acted on their envy not by making purchases but through make-believe. Some children told lies as they fantasized about what they had, living aloud their daydreams. Other children acted out their dramas with a greater acknowledgment of their fictive nature. Children have always daydreamed, pretended, and lied; the fantasies that turn-of-the-century youngsters constructed reflected the increasingly important role of consumer goods in their daily lives.

Many observers of child life concluded that envious children who wanted more than they had sometimes told lies in the hope of passing themselves off as something other than they were. Two studies which appeared in the *Pedagogical Seminary* documented children's deceitful behavior. Linus Kline and C. J. France's 1899 study, "The Psychology of Ownership," and G. Stanley Hall and Theodore L. Smith's 1903 study, "Showing Off and Bashfulness as Phases of Self-Consciousness," offer evidence of the ways in which children acted on their envy by lying and pretending.

Hall claimed that when children bragged and lied about things that they did not possess, *"envy and imitation* are frequently motives. Several papers report actual *epidemics* of lying as occurring among groups of children whose sole object seemed to be the attainment of some fancied superiority, conferred by the possession of superior advantages of dress or household furnishings."[11] Kline and France provide a sense of just how widespread these "epidemics" of dishonesty could be. They conducted a survey in which they asked adults to describe "children who wished to own property far in excess of his wants or his ability to use the same aright." Over 80 percent of the 406 responses they received "described a child who would beg, cheat, or steal to get the coveted article." Kline and France reported that these dishonest youths did not seem to be "peculiar" or "exceptional." They could be "anybody's children; the average child." Deceptive behavior was not extraordinary behavior; rather, it was quite ordinary among American children.[12]

In order to appear more affluent than they actually were, many children claimed to own things that they did not possess. Hall described a seven-year-old girl who told a playmate "how many gold rings, watches, and earrings she had and promised the girl to bring her a watch the next day." Another girl, nine years old, "boasted of costly dolls and dresses which she did not possess." A twelve-year-old boy told listeners, "I am going to have a thousand dollars to spend the day the show is here." As Kline and France noted, children sometimes went beyond merely pretending to own goods and lied in order to gain the items they envied. One eight-year-old girl "bought a dress which she charged to her grandmother. Then took it to the dressmaker's and ordered it made up, but she never went after it. Entered another store and ordered two handsome pictures sent home. She went to a milliner's and selected two hats and ordered them trimmed, but never went for them. All these things she charged to her grandmother," although her grandmother apparently had no knowledge of these purchases and had never authorized them. The child had observed and remembered how her family charged goods and had employed the same methods. She had been able, at least temporarily, to carry off her lie and fulfill her desires.[13]

Other children told lies that centered around their families' possessions and position. G. Stanley Hall reported that a seven-year-old girl, shown some newly polished silver, told a listener, "Pooh! my mamma's spoons are always as bright as that and when we polish them they are a hundred times brighter than that." A six-year-old boy boasted of his father's possessions, particularly a special cane. According to Hall, he "said it was very large, all gold, with a lock and key at the head. Everything he happened to see was on that cane." An eleven-year-old girl showed great familiarity with the social significance of particular home furnishings, as she reported "that they had Brussels carpets in every room but the kitchen, where there was a rag carpet. [In reality] the kitchen floor was bare and there were no Brussels carpets."[14]

During the late 1910s and 1920s, as consumer goods came to have even greater significance in social life, competitive pressures on children grew. In 1926 Dr. Adolf Meyer reported in the *Scientific Monthly* that modern social conditions fostered dishonesty in children. He blamed ambitious parents who often encouraged their children's deceitfulness:

in our concentrated and complex city civilization the number of families living beyond their income in order to "keep up" in social position and dignity with other families is also on the increase. Children in such families are quick to be inoculated with the germ of duplicity. As a matter of fact, their parents, in their efforts to throw dust in the neighbors' eyes and thus conceal the family's true economic status, have in all likelihood cautioned their offspring to practice a similar form of deceit.

Meyer claimed that envious children told lies in order to "simulat[e] . . . parental wealth and social position."[15] Lies, although often easily disproved, allowed children to act on their envy, to temporarily transform their lives and their selves into more desirable forms, and to present these fictive selves to the public. These children's actions were not so radically different from the actions of adults who tried to refashion themselves through imitative dressing and thereby equal those whom they envied.

Children expressed their envy in other ways as well. By imitating the small mannerisms of the envied and by play-acting they imagined themselves in better, more affluent, more powerful, and frequently more mature circumstances. Like lying and bragging, play-acting required no money and gave envious children an opportunity to at least momentarily escape their feelings of deprivation. Hall told of a nine-year-old girl who was "very fond of trying to act like someone else. [She] saw a very stylish lady walking down the street. [She] tried to talk just like her, put on so many airs and gestures that she could hardly be understood." Another nine-year-old girl "used to put on a great many airs as she walked, and talk to her doll about the grand way in which they lived. [She] would get into an empty wagon and pretend to drive and would bow condescendingly to those whom she met."[16]

Through lying and through play-acting, children expressed their envy and longings. They often could not buy what they wanted, so they resorted to the means available to them. Such behavior is evidence that middle-class American childhood was not an idyllic democracy but a society in which class lines and distinctions were already becoming fixed.

Lessons in Envy, 1890–1915

Children learned to envy consumer goods through observation. Family and friends provided perhaps the most potent and immediate schooling in the meaning and desirability of commercially sold goods. Historians have often underestimated the degree to which these informal and intimate influences on young people affected their perceptions of and desires for consumer goods, and have focused instead on the power and persuasiveness of merchants and advertisers.[17] While children's longings were indeed influenced by the attractive displays of department stores, they were even more decisively shaped by the way that their parents and playmates used and valued particular objects in daily life.

At the turn of the century, children absorbed the aspirations, desires, and tastes of parents who were adjusting to the growing consumer economy. Parents may have believed they needed to shelter their children from market forces and social competition, yet they themselves were unable to avoid these pressures and sometimes unknowingly taught their children to be sensitive to them as well. They wanted the signs and privileges of higher status and exhibited their longings in front of their children, thereby giving such emotions at least tacit legitimacy. As one magazine writer recalled, his mother "continually impressed upon us children that we were 'as good as anybody,' and in almost the same breath she would urge us to 'get to know the best people.' And by 'best people' she meant those who had the most money, and got their names in the society columns. What I am trying to make clear is that the whole atmosphere of our home was one of strain and worry. We were all striving so hard to succeed." The nameless patient studied by Professor Dollard also vividly recalled his parents' preoccupation with getting ahead. According to Dollard, the parents presented life not "as something to enjoy but rather as a mission in which he was to raise the family prestige."[18]

Adults at the turn of the century not only paid attention to their own social fortunes, but were also very much aware of the ways that their children's behavior, possessions, and appearance reflected family status. The fact that parents were invested in the social life of their children was hardly a secret to the youngsters themselves. Historians Gary Cross and Bernard Mergen have noted that in the late nineteenth century, parents began to show affection for their children in a manner that differed from earlier generations. One way that they displayed their concern and interest was by purchasing factory-made toys for their offspring. In these early days of mass-produced and mass-marketed toys, parents controlled the purse strings and consequently were able to influence the selection of toys. By choosing what toys to buy their children they could exert some control over both their own and their children's social image and identity.[19]

While toys were meant to satisfy children, they also fulfilled adults' social and emotional needs. To use Thorstein Veblen's terms, parents often considered their children to be "vicarious" consumers and symbols of family status.[20] Columnist Filson Young, writing in the *Living Age* in 1912, called children "the victims" of their parents. According to Young, parents were so concerned with their own social ambitions that they did not realize how the gifts and parties that they gave their children actually affected them. Young described the many occasions in which parents unwittingly caused their children to envy.

There are the presents—sources of endless hidden woes and heart-burnings. The cotillion, or the Christmas tree, is crowned by elaborate and expensive gifts that cannot all be equally desirable, and that therefore cannot fail to cause longing, envy, jealousy and disappointment. Have people forgotten how frightfully sensitive children are to anything like social inequality, or how the darts of snobbishness can stab, that they can thus multiply all occasions of them? A child who cannot give to her friends a party as "good" as she received, is to some extent . . . a victim to the selfishness of her elders.[21]

Despite these fears about the harmful effects of too many toys, parents persisted in showering their children with playthings. They offered toys to their children out of love, but they were also often motivated by a desire to establish their own and their household's status. Congressman Sol Bloom of New York recalled that as a young father he was overly generous with gifts for his daughter Vera. Bloom, born in 1870, had risen from humble origins and gloried in his new affluence. He bought luxuries for himself, and when his daughter was born in 1900, he purchased expensive toys and clothes for her. His daughter's lifestyle was a reflection in miniature of his own position, style, and aspirations. In Bloom's eyes, "Nothing was ever too good for Vera. Few things, indeed, seemed to me to be good enough. When I bought a toy, it always had to be the biggest and most expensive. If it was a doll, it had to have real hair, and eyes that opened and closed. If it was a piano, it was a genuine one, even if it had only three or four octaves. Vera had her own pony and cart before she was three." Bloom also wanted his daughter dressed "exclusively in laces and silks. When I tried to buy our child an ermine coat, my wife was so firmly opposed that I became rather sulky. Suppose I *had* bought our two-year-old a sealskin coat just a month before, I argued—we could afford it, couldn't we?" Bloom probed his motives for such extravagance and concluded that he was trying to compensate for deprivations he had experienced growing up in a poor family, perhaps retroactively assuaging his youthful feelings of envy. "Unconsciously, I suppose I was making up to my little girl for my own toyless childhood. I have no doubt that a psychologist would tell me I really bought all those things for myself. I couldn't argue the point, for I certainly derived huge pleasure from Vera's playthings. She, I am sure, would have been just as happy with much simpler toys. I wouldn't have been."[22]

Sol Bloom's love for his daughter was mingled with a desire to display his own financial acumen and social status. Even parents who purchased little for themselves shared this same desire and came to believe that it was a social necessity for their children to possess store-bought toys and other status-marked consumer goods. Viola Goode Liddell, born in 1901 in Alabama, recalled that her father, "unaccustomed to such ease or finery and unmindful of such luxuries for himself, nevertheless, felt it to be his duty to give these things to his children." Her father recognized that the family's status would be reflected in his children's possessions. Viola Liddell believed that "the greatest satisfaction that Father got from this shiny new world of our day was the great pride he felt in possessing it and the great joy he got in giving it to us. That he never became throughly reconciled to it or enjoyed it wholeheartedly for its own sake was probably because he was not born into it."[23]

Children learned to envy and want ever more from the example of their elders. They discovered that the adult social world was filled with rivalry and competition and found that they had a role in forwarding the family's social fortunes. By the early twentieth century, even if some adults—like Viola Liddell's father—did not purchase much for themselves, they believed they must acquire for their children the latest and most fashionable goods. Their offspring would grow up to be adults much accustomed to spending. They learned from their parents that certain possessions had social significance and were worthy of acquisition, and when they became adults in the 1920s and 1930s, they passed on this lesson to their own children.

Children at the turn of the century also learned important lessons about what was enviable from their peers. Nathalie Dana recalled that she discovered the social geography of New York City from her friends and her socially astute cousin, Kenneth. With a friend she would often stroll down Fifth Avenue and steal glances into the fine houses. From her cousin she learned of the deficiencies of own family's lifestyle. Although her family lived in a beautiful house, Nathalie worried about their public image:

I had been proud of our 69th street house until Kenneth, my other social arbiter, had told me that it was in the wrong neighborhood. If we did not live on Murray Hill, which was the ideal spot, we should, at least, be nearer Fifth Avenue. Madison Avenue was socially correct but Park Avenue was too near the East Side Slums. It also worried me that my family carried large packages in the street, and worst of all, they sat on the stoop on summer evenings, passing around soft drinks, like other families in the neighborhood who were not quite the thing. These facts disturbed me greatly when I first became self-conscious.[24]

Affluent children like Kenneth frequently educated less savvy or fortunate children in the social meaning of possessions. Sometimes this education was delivered with a touch of malice, for privileged youngsters often gleefully publicized the particular advantages that they enjoyed and pointed out the shortcomings of their playmates' lifestyles. Hall's study of boasting illustrates children's eagerness to show off. A ten-year-old boy asserted, "My father is richer than your father." A twelve-year-old boy, attuned to the subtle status distinctions between handmade and store-bought toys, told a playmate, "My sled is better than yours; yours was made, mine was bought." Girls' boasts were similar to those of boys. A four-year-old girl proudly informed another child, "Your mamma haint got what my mama's got! My mamma's got a new silk dress." A six-year-old girl cruelly taunted a companion, noting, "It's too bad you can't go down to the seashore. We are all going for two months. Its perfectly elegant there, the band plays all day, we go out walking, dance and are dressed up all the time." Finally, Hall recorded a suspiciously clever exchange between two girls, aged seven and nine, who were desperately trying to outdo one another. Said the seven-year-old, "Our house is grander than yours because we have a cupola on it." Replied her companion, "Oh! that's nothing. I heard pa say this morning we had a mortgage on our house, but I have never seen it myself."[25] For less fortunate children, such exchanges often proved to be powerful—if painful—lessons in the status system. From these day-to-day interactions with family and friends, children gained an awareness of which wardrobe items, toys, and family possessions carried connotations of high status and so came to desire them.

If children learned about the elements of an enviable lifestyle from their parents and peers, they also discovered this through their own encounters with the consumer institutions that were developing and expanding. Like their parents, they read advertisements, catalogs, and magazines and occasionally visited department stores. What they saw and read about whetted their appetites.

By the early twentieth century, advertisements already were adept at introducing new tastes to American children. Although ads had not yet taken on their modern form, which relies on explicit appeals to emotion, they nevertheless cajoled young readers to spend. For example, *St. Nicholas Magazine,* a middle-class children's periodical, published numerous advertisements— some directed at children, some at their parents. The ads aimed at children deliberately tried to stir up youthful longings. A 1913 ad told children that buying things far surpassed the powers of make-believe. The Pine Hill Pony farm pitched its desirable and expensive merchandise by asking children, "Did you ever play horse? Just think what fun it would be with a real Shetland or Welsh Pony." Children could improve on daydreams, the ad suggested, and gain much more satisfaction by fulfilling their desires through purchases. Other ads instructed both parents and children in what was desirable. "Every little girl wants this Toy Range," claimed Western Electric in their advertisement for a tiny stove on which children could actually cook. Through such ads, children learned of new toys and amusements and might also learn that indulging desire was acceptable and morally unproblematic behavior.[26]

Magazines also worked to integrate children into the consumer economy by encouraging them to sell subscriptions and then rewarding sales with desirable commodities. Youngsters might simultaneously learn to be both salesmen and consumers by soliciting new subscribers for various publications. In his memoirs, William Allen White recalled that the premium list of the *Youth's Companion* magazine "opened the doors to so many desirable things: a scroll saw, which Albert Ewing got; Barney and Berry skates, which later I acquired; musical instruments, balls and baseball bats and masks, books of games and magic, dumbbells, boxing gloves—all to be had for new subscribers to the *Youth's Companion*."[27]

Mail-order catalogs and department stores were yet another set of primers that offered children lessons in consumer desire. Daniel Boorstin has observed how influential these catalogs were in training young children, particularly those in rural communities. In addition to relying on the catalogs for pure entertainment, children often learned reading and arithmetic from the "wish-books." Some youngsters merely looked at the pictures, others cut them out and played with them. Catalogs, a fixture in most farming households, thus exposed countless youngsters to the world of goods.[28]

Department store owners likewise diligently worked to expose as many children as possible to their wares. By sponsoring free plays, building extravagant Christmas parks, and celebrating "Children's Day," they were able to bring children into their stores, introduce them to their tempting merchandise, and encourage in them a desire to spend that would last their whole lives. As Harry Selfridge, manager of Marshall Field's proclaimed in 1902, "These children are the future customers of this store, and . . . impressions made now will be lasting." Selfridge was right: The children who wandered into Marshall Field's and other stores did indeed walk out with lasting impressions about consumer spending, impressions they would share with their own offspring in the decades to come.[29]

Children encountered the temptations of the consumer marketplace and became ever more aware of the ways in which possessions fixed social status, but this was not the only lesson they learned from the larger culture. Youngsters at the turn of the century had to sort through mixed and conflicting messages, for sermons, schoolbooks, and parental instructions presented them with a radically different set of emotional imperatives that urged them to contain their longings, repress their envy, and practice self-denial.

The Lessons of Emotional Control, 1890–1915

Children felt the emotional tug of temptation as they contemplated the consumer bounty around them. They also encountered the messages of educators, ministers, reformers, and child-rearing advisors who tried to teach them to resist such temptation and practice emotional restraint. These men and women who urged children to control their envy, while diverse in their professions and approaches, shared a common background and a set of common concerns. Most were Protestant and middle class, and most had been born before 1875. They had come of age before the dramatic expansion of the consumer economy—before the rise of large department stores, mail-order catalogs, mass-circulation magazines, and modern advertising. They were unaccustomed to the material abundance of this new economy and unsettled by the emotions and behaviors that it provoked. They viewed with great alarm the envy that many children were displaying in the face of the new commercial temptations and tried to inculcate in youngsters the same outlooks and virtues that they had been taught decades before. In an effort to reinvigorate the moral traditions that they treasured, these educators, reformers, ministers, and parental advisors attempted to control children's envy by limiting occasions where children would be aware of inequalities and by teaching them to be more sanguine when faced with inequity. Moralists used sermons and magazine columns to encourage these attitudes and character traits in adults and ministers and educators relied on children's textbooks and classroom activities to communicate their message to youth.[30]

At times, the writers and editors of children's readers worked to keep privileged children from flaunting their advantages. They counseled children against vanity, pride, and arrogance, hoping the young would realize that with such feelings of superiority they could hurt themselves and others. "The Peacock," which appeared in *Sheldon's Modern Reader* in 1885 and told of Jane's desire for a fine, trimmed bonnet, carried such a message. Jane's father asked her why she was displeased with her new bonnet. She told him she had hoped for one with an ostrich feather, for "there is not an ostrich feather in the village; and I hoped I should have worn the first one, and mortified the country girls." Jane expressed no qualms about showing off and making the other girls envious. Her father chastised her and observed that she was like a peacock, a bird Jane disliked because it "vainly and proudly" strutted about, showing off its feathers. He told her, "If you hate him [the peacock] for his vanity and pride, although he is only a poor bird . . . how can you expect anything but hatred, if you show off your dress and strut about as he does? The poor bird . . . shows less pride in displaying his own feathers than you do in wishing to display the feathers of an ostrich, or any other borrowed finery." Those like Jane, who harbored prideful feelings, acted from vice and created social strife.[31]

Yet although writers sometimes warned children that they should take care not to excite envy in their playmates, they far more often told envious children to suppress the emotion within themselves. Envious boys and girls learned from reading books and from the larger middle-class culture that if inequalities produced unsettled feelings, those with more were generally not to blame. Children must learn to accept inequality, for disparities in worldly wealth and possessions were inevitable. Many adults recalled hearing this doctrine as children. Nathalie Dana, the daughter of a prominent Episcopalian minister, recalled that as a child she had been taught that "the uneven distribution of wealth was not a matter of concern." While "it seemed a pity that there were so many poor people," Nathalie had been instructed that "this was a part of 'God's own plan.' "[32] Virginia Durr, born in Birmingham, Alabama, in 1903, also recalled learning that "the distribution of wealth was ordained by God. . . . You were born to be either wealthy and wise and rich and powerful and beautiful and healthy, or you were born to be poor and downtrodden and sick and miserable. . . . It was a very comforting thought, you see, because when you saw people starving and poor and miserable, you thought, 'Well, it isn't my fault. I didn't do anything to cause it. God just ordained it this way.' "[33]

Affluent children may have been comforted by such teachings, but the challenge was to make less fortunate children accept these lessons and gracefully resign themselves to living with their deprivations. To that end, schoolbook authors and editors extolled the virtue of contentment to American children as diligently and repeatedly as they did to adults. Although all children's readers contained a wide variety of moral and practical lessons and themes unrelated to envy, the books consistently covered the topic of envy and contentment. Whether students read the *McGuffey Reader*, *Hilliard's Reader*, *Barnes' Reader*, or the *Monroe Reader*, they were sure to encounter treatments of these emotions. Many of these schoolbooks, in fact, contained identical selections on the topic.

Editors tried to adapt the doctrine of contentment to the level of their young readers. *McGuffey's Sixth Eclectic Reader,* published in 1896, illustrated the benefits of contentment with "Discontent—An Allegory." In the short essay written by Joseph Addison, everyone was allowed to exchange his or her burdens, all believing that the loads of their fellows were lighter, but finding them instead to be more burdensome than their own. Eventually, each longed for his or her original burden and learned, with the help of "Patience," "to bear it in a commodious manner." Each character then "marched off with it contentedly, being very well pleased that he had not been left to his own choice as to the kind of evil which fell to his lot." The narrator related that he had learned "never to repine at my own misfortunes, or to envy the happiness of another, since it is impossible for any man to form right judgement of his neighbor's sufferings."[34]

A number of poems taught the lessons of contentment in a more light-hearted format. "The Miller of the Dee," by English poet Charles McKay, appeared quite often in readers. In the poem, a king overheard a miller proclaim, "I envy nobody—no not I, And nobody envies me!" Good King Hal asked why the miller was so contented. The miller replied that he loved his family and friends and possessed all that he needed. When the king took the miller's leave, he declared:

But say no more, if thou'dst be true
That no one envies thee.
Thy mealy cap is worth my crown;
Thy mill my kingdom's fee;
Such men as thou are England's boast,
O Miller of the Dee![35]

Presumably the miller was "England's boast" because he knew his place and was satisfied with it. By accepting his lot in life, rather than struggling to change it, he helped to maintain a peaceful and static social order.[36]

It is revealing that as American textbook editors endeavored to teach contentment and help children control their envy, they repeatedly included the works of European writers that referred to the stratified conditions of social life in England and France and relied on references to kings and nobles. Such works held up as models those who knew and accepted their place in a hierarchical society. Schoolbook editors believed that some of the lessons of the rigid and stratified European class systems might benefit school children in the ostensibly classless United States.

Another lesson that textbook editors hoped children would learn was that wealth could be a burden and that one was better off without it. To foster contentment and diminish the significance of material inequalities, textbook authors often told children that real privileges could be found not among the high and mighty but with the lowly and humble. Moralists compared individuals in both circumstances, and the poorer character—like the Miller of the Dee—inevitably proved superior because of his virtuous contentment.

Young readers might discover this truth through the simple story of "Harry's Riches." Appearing in both the *New McGuffey Fourth Reader* (1901) and the *Character Building Reader: Fourth Year* (1910), the story told of young Harry, who returned home discontented after spending time with his wealthy playmate, Johnny. Johnny lived in an impressive house and rode in the most elegant carriage. He also possessed "a big popgun and a watch, and a hobby horse, and a lot of things." After telling his mother of Johnny's riches, Harry began to cry, exclaiming, "I guess we are very poor, aren't we?" Despite his mother's efforts to convince him otherwise, Harry continued to think himself deprived. Harry's uncle then intervened. He tried to purchase Harry's sense of smell, taste, and hearing. Harry refused, even after being offered thousands of dollars. Having thus been convinced of the priceless gifts that he possessed, he confided to his mother, "Isn't God good to make everyone so rich?"[37]

In addition to celebrating contentment and minimizing the importance of wealth, a third tenet of the doctrine of contentment, found in sermons for both young and old alike, was an affirmation of a divinely ordained Great Chain of Being. Tales that invoked the idea of a Chain of Being were even more common in literature for children than they were for adults. Authors and editors may have chosen such tales because they believed that the talking trees, flowers, and animals who filled the stories would have special appeal for the young. The anthropomorphic creatures learned that although they were small and seemingly insignificant, they had a divinely ordained role to fill in the world's order and that they therefore should not envy others. Such tales also may have served to reinforce the authority of elders by reminding the young of the importance of always knowing their place.

The stories usually centered on creatures in nature who compared themselves with larger, grander, or brighter beings and in consequence wished to be something other than they were. The tales routinely ended with an affirmation of the divine wisdom and order that had put things where they were. These formulaic tales drummed the principles of hierarchy into children's minds. In Sarah Orne Jewett's poem "The Discontented Buttercup," a robin met "a buttercup who wished she were a daisy." The buttercup wanted to change herself because

She always had a passion
For wearing frills around her neck,
In just the daisies' fashion.
And buttercups must always be
The same old tiresome color;
While daisies dress in gold and white,
Although their gold is duller.

The buttercup asked the robin if it could find her a white, daisylike frill to wear about her neck. The bird refused and explained the importance of being true to one's God-given nature. The robin told the buttercup:

"I think you must be crazy:
I'd rather be my honest self
Than any made-up daisy. . . .
Be the best buttercup you can,
And think no flower above you. . . .
We'd better keep our places.
Perhaps the world would all go wrong
With one too many daisies. . . .
Be content with knowing
That God wished for a buttercup
Just here, where you are growing."

As the buttercup learned, too much striving might contravene God's plans and upset the order of the universe.[38]

Innumerable other schoolbook fables reiterated the importance of accepting one's place in the Great Chain of Being and staying contentedly in it rather than struggling to leave it. Henry Van Dyke told the story of the foolish fir tree who longed to replace his needles with utterly unsuitable leaves, but who eventually learned that

... he had been a fool,
To think of breaking the forest rule,
And choosing himself a dress to please
Because he envied the other trees.

Other tales included Ralph Waldo Emerson's fable of an arrogant mountain and a squirrel content with his sphere; the story of two jackdaws, who, dissatisfied with their black feathers, tried to transform themselves into peacocks and pigeons, but came to realize that their borrowed plumage deceived no one and that they had best remain jackdaws; the tale of the wall and the vine in which the vine questioned its purpose and station in the universe and then learned contentment; the lesson of the snowbirds who sang happily despite inclement weather because "God cares for great and small"; the moral of the handful of lowly clay made into a royal pot; the story of the horse and the discontented colt, who at the latter's urging traveled the world looking for the greenest field of all, realizing at the end that the original field in which they were placed was best of all; and the story of the discontented boy who wished himself a bird, and then a cat, and then a dog, before realizing that he was best off as a boy.[39]

By relying on natural imagery, the poems and stories transformed the arbitrary positions, distinctions, and inequalities of society into divinely and beneficently designed relationships. They literally naturalized the social order. Because social positions and inequalities were presented as natural and foreordained, they (at least theoretically) resisted questioning. Such stories offered a deeply conservative ideology and sought to inculcate complacency in their youthful readers. Rather than encouraging children to seek advancement and higher rank, the stories seemed designed to keep all in their assigned places—a strange lesson for a liberal democracy.[40]

Educators also celebrated thrift, another virtue which earlier generations of schoolbook moralists had sought to inculcate in children. By the turn of the century, in the midst of the expanding consumer market, the project of teaching frugality may have seemed more urgent than ever before. For those youngsters caught up in social competition, the temptations for wasteful, imprudent spending were manifold. Many reformers and educators believed that by celebrating the virtues of saving, they could offer children a set of values which would serve as a meaningful alternative to emulation and social competition. They used both reading books and school-sponsored savings programs to inculcate frugality and discourage envy.

Children often read Benjamin Franklin's life story and maxims, for Franklin's writings appeared in many readers. Excerpts from his *Autobiography* and *Poor Richard's Almanack* served to show the folly of emulation and unwise spending. For instance, children might read that "it is as truly folly to ape the rich as for the frog to swell in order to equal the fox," or be asked to consider "of what use is this pride of appearance, for which so much is risked, so much is suffered? It cannot promote health, nor ease pain; it makes no increase of merit in the person; it creates envy; it hastens misfortune." Spending out of vanity, pride, and envy, and attempts at emulation were at best pointless and might even be disastrous.[41]

The School Savings Bank movement offered a concrete opportunity for students to act on the lessons about thrift that they read in their schoolbooks and magazines. School Savings Banks started in France and spread to the United States in the 1870s, flourishing well into the twentieth century. The program allowed students to deposit their small sums in real banks and to earn interest. In 1890 there were 27,430 child depositors nationwide, and three hundred banks were involved. In 1927 close to four million students were depositors in School Savings Banks.

Leaders of the School Bank movement hoped to teach children to save and to limit conspicuous consumption, which might excite envy. Sara Louisa Oberholtzer, national superintendent of School Savings Banks for the Women's Christian Temperance Union, wrote of these goals in 1892. Oberholtzer, born in 1841 and educated in Quaker schools, had grown up in a culture that valued simplicity and that viewed financial profligacy as related to a host of other sins and social problems. As an adult she tried to pass these views on to the next generation. Of the goals of the School Savings Bank program, she wrote, "Extravagant, thoughtless habits, which beget inequality, drunkenness and vice, could not thrive if the population was carefully trained to self-knowledge, self-dependence and economy."[42] The Savings Banks program would, she believed, provide such training.

Whether or not the training in thrift was successful in offsetting envy is unclear. The leaders of the School Savings Bank movement and the writers who preached about thrift certainly thought that it would have this effect, and some children who were taught the necessity of thrift testified that it helped them accept the fact that they could not have all they desired or all that their neighbors had.[43] On the other hand, learning about thrift might merely mean that a child learned how to save for an item that he purchased in order to equal or surpass an envied playmate. As Anna Kohler showed in her study, while children were willing to save, they were often intent on saving for ribbons, laces, sleds, and other nonutilitarian items. Learning how to save might mean merely learning how to delay one's envy-inspired spending.

In addition to reading injunctions against envy in their schoolbooks, children also learned of social prohibitions against the emotion from the child-rearing advice offered to their parents. As professional psychology developed in the early twentieth century, children's envy and rivalry gained new significance in child-rearing literature. The experts condemned envy and advised parents on how to control the emotion in their children.

In the period between 1890 and 1915 the main objective of advice literature was to discourage immorality. Felix Adler's counsel on envy illustrates this tendency. Adler, born in 1851, helped to organize the International Congress of Moral Education and establish the Society for Ethical Culture. In his 1892 book, *The Moral Instruction of Children,* he advised parents to discourage envious behavior by telling children the story of Cain and Abel. Parents should emphasize that both Cain and Abel had faults. Abel was boastful: "In a perfectly innocent way, which yet stung Cain to the quick, he would rattle on to his brother about the increase of his herds, about his plans and prospects, and the pleasant things that people were saying of him. Cain grew jealous of his brother Abel." After telling of Cain's murder of Abel, parents should emphasize that "The moral of the story is: 'Do not harbor evil thoughts in the mind. . . . Cain's sin consisted in not crushing the feelings of envy in the beginning; in comparing his own lot with that of his more favored brother and dwelling on this comparison, until, in a fit of insane passion, he was led on to the unspeakable crime which, indeed, he had never contemplated.' " Adler implied that envy could lead to a host of immoral actions and dreadful consequences if not carefully contained. Other child-rearing experts of the period avoided such dramatic episodes, but nevertheless warned parents that they needed to train their children to control their envy. One advisor suggested that parents teach envious youngsters that their "unfortunate circumstances" need not detract from their "real joy of living." Parents should point out that there were "certain compensating values" which offset their deprivations and which could bring contentment.[44]

In the late nineteenth and early twentieth centuries, American children and their parents were pulled in contradictory directions. Adults and young-sters heard of the moral dangers of envy and the sinfulness of excessive ma-terialism from schoolbooks and advice literature. Yet while many may have worried about the moral implications of the envy they often felt, they never-theless had difficulty controlling their emotions. Parents, told to repress envy in their offspring, found it hard to accomplish this emotional feat them-selves.[45] Children, in their casual interactions with friends and enemies in the schoolyard, in their wanderings through the streets of their hometowns, and in their own families' parlors, observed firsthand the power of consumer goods and found themselves sorely tempted by them.

Children at the turn of the century thus came of age in a society where emotional and moral rules were in a state of flux. Rather than being com-pletely integrated into the consumer culture or as yet largely untouched by it, children faced the challenge of sorting through mixed messages and con-tradictory examples. They felt both the draw of glittering goods and the tug of moral duty. In contrast, children a decade later would find much more co-herence in the culture they encountered, as moral concerns came to be largely drowned out by the siren call of consumerism.

The Commercialization of Childhood, 1915–1930

During the late 1910s and 1920s, America developed into a full-fledged con-sumer society, and American cultural life was transformed. Michael Kam-men has described the 1920s as "the pivotal period when commerce and culture could no longer be tidily compartmentalized." This change affected both the social life of adults and the culture of childhood. The culture that youngsters of the late 1910s and 1920s faced was laden with commercial messages and business ideology, and there was far less debate about the moral implications of consumerism. Parents and peers displayed their envy more publicly; movies and advertisements also encouraged the emotion. Even those reformers and educators who tried to discourage envy frequently did so because of business rather than moral concerns.[46]

Adults noted the quickening pace of social life, which encouraged competitive consumption in the service of social striving. *In The Morality of Spending,* Daniel Horowitz writes that by the 1920s, budget analysts study-ing the middle class believed that "simplicity, higher things, and plain living were giving way to the pressures of reputability, emulation, advertising, and social ambition."[47] Adults transmitted these new concerns to their children, sometimes intentionally and sometimes unknowingly. Psychiatrist James S. Plant, studying children in northern New Jersey in the late 1920s, reported that the social pressures which adults faced had left a mark on their off-spring. In his work at the Essex County Juvenile Clinic in Newark, Plant noted that the residents of suburban New Jersey were exceedingly mobile. Of the children in his district, 78 percent had moved within the previous five years. According to Plant, a geographical move often represented a rise in status. Children's very location then might be changed to accommodate their parents' social aspirations. These aspirations were also visible to children in the social careers of their mothers, who might avidly pursue leisure activi-ties and club membership in order to rub elbows with important neighbors, and in their fathers' long commutes and long hours at work.

According to Plant, children whose parents were engaged in the race for status might themselves become acutely aware of and worried about their own standing relative to other youngsters. Children whose families moved to more socially exclusive areas reported heightened feelings of anxiety and insecurity. "A feeling of insecureness arises when a child is placed in competition with the children of a 'better' neighborhood to which the family's suddenly acquired affluence impels it." While Plant noted that it was difficult to quantify this problem, he reported that the major problem of 80 percent of the children referred to him for treatment was "the insecurity arising from their not having been met with favor in the so-called 'better' neighborhood to which they have recently moved."[48] Plant's evidence sug-gests that the social anxieties of adults were internalized by their children. Following their parents' example, these youngsters often manifested a sharp awareness of status differences and a deep insecurity about their own rank in the social world.

Children might also sense their parents' concerns about social standing when they looked at their own overflowing toy chests. Adults in the late 1910s and early 1920s showered their children with even more toys than had the previous generation of parents. Indeed, the trend that commentators had observed in the early 1900s—that the social needs, envy, and ambitions of adults often dictated the tastes and possessions of children—was only more apparent in succeeding years, as the practice of buying toys for children be-came increasingly common. In 1919, teacher Nora Atwood observed that adults all too frequently competed with each other by loading down their children with conspicuous, high-status possessions. Envious of each other, parents would struggle for social position through their children. Writing in the *Outlook*, Atwood noted, "In some cases there seems to be a kind of rivalry between families, the high aim being to see whose child can boast the largest number of and most expensive toys." According to Atwood, such competition and conspicuous consumption meant that parents spoiled their children's chances for developing a contented spirit and instead filled them with the desire to consume. Atwood claimed that "toys lead either to contentment or discontent. . . . the evil of restlessness, the vacillating disposition, the germ of discontent may all find their birth in a superfluity of toys."[49] Observers of the time recognized that parents were doing more than merely giving material objects to their offspring; they were also providing lessons in the social meaning of things. By giving their children so many toys, parents enhanced their own status, communicated the importance of striving to their children, and encouraged them to want ever more.

Parents found their views on the social meaning of childhood reinforced by advertisements. By the 1920s, advertisers had become more adept at using emotions to sell goods. They focused particular attention on consumers' fears of social failure, their envy of others' success, and their longing for prestige. In pitches they directed toward parents, advertisers reinforced the popular practice of using children as status symbols. As they had in ad campaigns for adult products, advertisers took an existing popular belief, in this case the idea that children had important symbolic functions in adults' struggle for high social status, expanded upon it, and worked to connect it to particular products. Advertisers encouraged adults to buy status-marked goods for their offspring, promising that if they did so, both children and parents would advance socially. Using such tactics, advertisers tried to make children who were well dressed, well shod, and well supplied with toys more enviable, and thereby spur competitive purchasing.

One particularly effective theme that advertisers employed to sell a wide array of products was the belief that what parents bought their offspring in the present would dramatically affect their social futures as adults. If parents bought the correct goods, they might ensure that their sons and daughters were the equals of everyone they met. Implicit in such ads was the idea that the children would not have to envy when they grew up, as their parents so obviously did now. For instance, in an ad entitled "The Boy Next Door," the Calvert School advertised its education. A mother recounted how she had invited a neighboring family over and how the neighbor's son had impressed all with his learning. The nine-year-old remarked to the assembled adults, "Isn't it odd . . . that da Vinci's women are almost always smiling?" The young boy also knew a great deal about Aristotle, botany, zoology, Charlemagne, and other subjects beyond a normal nine-year-old's ken. The boy was a student in the "long-distance system of home instruction" run by the Calvert School of Baltimore. The narrating mother recounted, "I was envious and even jealous of what their son had acquired. By contrast—what our boy had learned was almost nothing." All the mother needed to do, however, was to take the easy step of enrolling her son in the school and her child would have the chance to catch up with the other boy. By implication, the entire family's status would be more secure once the Calvert School's tuition was paid.

Advertisements for musical instruments and equipment played upon similar parental insecurities. A Brunswick phonograph ad showed two children and warned mothers that "in ten years . . . one of these children will be enjoying social advantages which the other can never hope to attain." The disadvantaged child, with no Brunswick phonograph, missed the opportunity for home musical training. On the other hand, those families who purchased a phonograph would be able to give their children "the priceless cultural advantage of basic musical training, the training that will reflect itself so happily in their later social life when they can take their place without embarrassment among people of broad culture." Specifically, such training gave the "subtle advantages of personality which enables some persons to advance so much further, in the keen struggle of life, than those less fortunately endowed." Children's social futures and fates rested on the crucial consumer decisions that their parents made in the present. These advertisements tried to teach parents that they had best make wise consumer decisions if they wanted their children to grow up to be the social, economic, and intellectual equals of their peers. At the same time, however, these ads also consoled parents, counseling that most of their anxieties about their children's futures could be easily resolved through the strategic purchase of goods and services.[50]

Parents, acting on peer example and the urgings of modern advertisements, taught their sons and daughters that they should aspire to higher social position, that they should envy and imitate. The contents of children's toy chests and wardrobes became socially charged, both for parents and for children. As youngsters received presents, parties, and advertised goods from their parents, they also received messages about their own social function and status and the importance of goods in defining this status.

Children found models for consumer behavior in movies as well. By the 1920s, both middle-class children and working-class youths were watching films with great frequency. Movies gave men and women, adults and children, new visual access to the material culture of the wealthy. Such entertainments offered alluring images of appealing stars surrounded by an abundance of consumer goods. Viola Goode Liddell recalled her adolescent desire to look like Norma Talmadge or Mary Pickford. Only upon having her first photographic portrait taken did she come to realize that she did not resemble the stars. As she looked at the photo of herself, she saw her shortcomings and resolved to fix her hair and to avoid wearing hand-me-down clothes. Yale University researchers Frank Shuttleworth and Mark May, commissioned by the Payne Fund to study the effects of movies on youth, found that children who attended movies were far more likely to place great importance on material goods and appearances than those who did not watch movies. Children who attended movies were more apt to agree that "good clothes make the man," "smartly dressed girls are popular," "attractive girls wear smart clothes," and "children would stay away from a party rather than wear shabby clothes."[51] Such findings indicate that children longed for the glamorous way of life that movies presented to them.

The increasing commercialization of culture was even more apparent in the changing formal advice about envy. While children in the late 1910s and the 1920s continued to find in their schoolbooks the same paeans to contentment that youngsters of earlier decades had read, they also encountered a new set of selections that implicitly—and sometimes explicitly—promoted consumerism. Their parents likewise encountered new ideas and methods for child-rearing, ideas that ultimately encouraged the development of consumerist values.

The editors of children's readers began to include selections that encouraged children to buy status goods. While in many readers, editors continued to include the old stories about fishes and flowers learning contentment, they also seemed to recognize that these moral tales no longer quite fit the social realities of the times. Many of the schoolbook editors and writers active in the 1920s had been children in the 1880s and 1890s and were accustomed to the consumer abundance that department stores, advertisements, and movies displayed. They considered this abundance to be a benefit to society because it seemed to offer all Americans the opportunity for a higher standard of living. Accordingly, these authors presented consumer activity, envy, and discontent in a far different light from their predecessors.

Some schoolbooks, for instance, explicitly encouraged their youthful readers to shop so long as they did so wisely and resisted overly popular fads and trends. In the *Home and Country Reader*, published in 1918, home economist Isabel Bevier offered shopping tips to students. Born in 1860, Bevier had grown up before emulative spending was widely accepted, and she continued to condemn it well into the twentieth century. She disliked imitation luxury goods and discouraged her readers from trying to resolve their envy by purchasing such items. Nevertheless, she made some accommodation to the modern consumer economy and did not condemn spending, so long as purchases were made with judgment and taste. "Avoid pretentious things," she wrote. "If real lace cannot be afforded, sham lace ought not to be allowed. Muslin curtains are better adapted to the purpose and much prettier than sham lace ones. Get simple things, few things, durable things." In succeeding pages, however, Bevier showed signs of succumbing to the new consumerist ethic. She advised her readers that "two-toned green paper with a cream ceiling, weathered oak furniture and woodwork, with Oriental rugs or American ones in shades of brown and a little red, make a satisfactory living room." A parlor, she told her students, should contain "delicately upholstered furniture, the rare vase or bit of favrile glass. Oriental rugs with their mellowed tones will harmonize with almost any color." Bevier believed that a properly furnished home was filled with fine ornaments, good upholstery, and costly carpets, and she tried to inculcate similar expensive tastes in her students.[52]

In his 1923 *English for Boys and Men*, Homer J. Smith offered even more encouragement to spenders, and in the process, he redefined the meaning of thrift. He argued that thoughtful spending could improve individuals' material conditions as well as aid their personal development. He reminded readers that while learning to save money was important, learning to spend it wisely was also an important skill to develop. Materialism did not seem to hold the same dangers for Smith as it had for earlier writers; instead, it held great potential. He wrote, "Thrift seeks the best." Thrift, however, was not "miserable hoarding." Instead, it was "discriminating and studied expenditure in the rational gratification of wants. It does not mean purchasing only cheap things—indeed, the thrifty man usually buys the best. The thrifty man, however, studies his wants; he rules out the tawdry and superfluous, and he purchases those things that contribute to his permanent efficiency or that aid his future development." Implicit in the essay's message was the assumption that spending was not an inherently immoral activity; indeed, spending could be a force for progress. It was only unwise purchasing habits that needed to be reformed. This was a significant change from the earlier readers, which had urged students to guard their money rather than to spend it.[53]

Some schoolbook authors went even further and encouraged students not merely to consume but to actively cultivate a discontented spirit. For instance, a selection in the textbook *Economic Civics*, published in 1921, criticized the complacency which many felt with their current standard of living. The book's author, Ray Osgood Hughes, worried that some people were not participating fully in the consumer economy and did not display an appropriate interest in improving themselves or their conditions. If they were to experience envy, however, they might progress. Hughes declared, "Let these same ignorant people once . . . become acquainted with the pleasures and luxuries that some folks have in abundance. Immediately discontent sets in, and a striving for higher and better things may follow. And then gradually from this, a new contentment comes. . . . This higher kind comes from realizing what one ought to have and knowing that one is actually making progress toward gratifying those needs. In many cases, then, a certain discontent is almost desirable."[54] The new wisdom, offered to adults and children alike, held that individuals should act on their envy in order to gain contentment, because true contentment came from possessing what one truly wanted. Hughes suggested that those who acted on their envy did more than just secure their own satisfaction; they also were benefactors of the larger society. Envy spurred social progress and led to a higher standard of living for all. These schoolbooks maintained that discontent, envy, and materialism, traits once considered sins, were now to be regarded as emotional traits and character attributes worthy of cultivation. A materialistic and commercial ethos had seeped into children's readers just as it had so many other sectors of American culture.

The child-rearing advice that parents read also took on a commercial flavor during the late 1910s and 1920s. First, the advice itself was mass-marketed. According to some estimates, by the 1930s, 90 percent of mothers and 65 percent of fathers in the professional class read child-rearing advice.[55] Additionally, the content of the advice was increasingly commercialized. The advice books continued to preach the same message: Children should be taught to conquer their envy. There were, however, significant changes in both the rationale for repressing envy and the methods for training children to do so. Whereas child-rearing advisors of the 1890s warned of the moral perils of envy, experts of the 1920s focused much more attention on the societal hazards of envy, and the moralistic content of their advice gradually dropped away.

By the 1920s, child-rearing experts concurred that envy should be discouraged not because it made children sinful, as earlier generations of child advisors had warned, but because it might lead to character flaws that would surface in adulthood. Indeed, Peter Stearns and Daniel Rodgers have suggested that the child-rearing practices of this period were especially suited to corporate needs, for they were designed to produce adults who matched the culture of the white-collar world. Stearns claimed that the authors of the advice literature in the 1920s hoped to create "emotionally undifferentiated adults, capable of rational control," and therefore adapted to modern working conditions. Child advisors encouraged parents to inculcate in their children the values and habits that would allow them to grow up to be well-adjusted, well-integrated members of a corporate society.[56]

To be a well-adjusted member of corporate society, individual children had to learn to quell their competitive instincts and to work as a team. Child-rearing experts therefore told parents that not only must they discourage envy but they must encourage their children to take joy in others' successes, to practice cooperation, and to lose gracefully rather than to express envy at another's triumph. Such advice mirrored almost exactly the new behavior that corporations were coming to demand of their white-collar workers. In 1929 Douglas A. Thom, director of the Habit Clinic of Boston, instructor in psychiatry at Harvard Medical School, and director of the Division of Mental Hygiene for Massachusetts, argued that if a child grew up without conquering his or her envy, he or she would be maladjusted as an adult. Using the words *envy* and *jealousy* interchangeably, as would become common in the twentieth century, he wrote, "Later in life this emotion [jealousy] causes an inability to share the joys of others, and makes it impossible to see others succeed without manifesting open resentment." Thom, born in 1887, was representative of the new cohort of child-rearing experts: Seemingly unconcerned with moral questions, he condemned envy because it did not mesh with the needs of the modern economy and society.[57]

These emotional prescriptions matched those offered to white-collar men in the 1920s. Both men and their children should learn to love their endeavors for their own sake, renounce competition, and work for the good of the group rather than for individual advancement. As child-rearing advisor Benjamin C. Gruenberg noted, children's "satisfaction with competitive rivalry should be gradually transferred from personal rivalry to group rivalry, with its demand for subordination, for self-control, for cooperation, for admiration and for loyalty." This was necessary because "we are coming to see that cooperation will probably turn out better for society as a whole than will unrestrained competition."[58]

If the child-rearing experts of the 1920s were hoping to shape the rising generation of children into less competitive beings, some of their colleagues in psychiatry and psychology were providing evidence of the damage that unrestrained social striving had done to past generations of children. According to their clinical research, envy and competition were social acids that dissolved the ties between people and left individuals isolated, unstable, and fundamentally scarred. Yale Professor John Dollard described his patient, who had been taught as a child to be socially competitive. Dollard suggested that while it was hard to establish absolute causality, it seemed likely that the feelings of "discontent . . . rebellion and hatred" which the patient felt as an adult might have their origins in his exposure as a child to excessive striving and competitiveness. Dollard noted that as an adult, his patient eagerly sought his own social advancement. Rather than celebrating such mobility and individual initiative, Dollard noted that his patient's efforts to advance himself were based on drives that were fundamentally neurotic: "Tendencies to outdo others, to humiliate others and to revenge oneself upon others can be displayed amply under the competition which leads to the securing of higher status."[59] Dollard's discussion was not meant to serve as advice to parents but was intended for a more academic audience; nevertheless, his conclusions manifested the same fears of overly competitive behavior. In an age when the economy was increasingly dominated by large corporations rather than rugged individualists running independent businesses, cooperation was fast replacing competition as the new ideal of social behavior for old and young alike. Just as children's readers reflected the increasing influence of the consumer economy, so parenting advice accommodated the needs of corporate capitalism. Whereas once reading books and parenting advice had tried to stand outside of the marketplace and had urged readers to resist materialism, by the 1920s the literature for both children and adults was far more responsive to and shaped by market concerns.

The other significant change in advice to parents was its increasing reliance on consumer goods to teach social lessons. A number of psychologists began to describe toys as important tools for guiding children's development. Rather than being corrupting objects that encouraged an immoral love of material things, they argued, toys could teach crucial lessons.

Sidonie Gruenberg, president of the Child Study Association, offered this new viewpoint. Gruenberg was born in 1881, and like other psychologists of her generation, she had grown up in the burgeoning consumer economy. She was therefore more accustomed to a rich material life and less worried about its corrupting effects. She argued that children's actions and emotions should not be judged as moral or immoral, nor should youngsters be required to repress their desires. They needed to play and should not face "repressive penalties imposed by an arbitrary puritanism which suspects every desire and impulse of being Satanic." She affirmed the central values of the consumer ethic, arguing that the desire for pleasure and for things was not immoral. As historian William Leach notes, it was no coincidence that in 1928 Macy's Department Store hired her to lecture to parents on the important developmental role of play. Her advice represented exactly the ethic that merchants hoped the American populace would develop.[60]

Gruenberg and her husband, Benjamin, also supported the idea that the possession of certain consumer goods was necessary to a child's adjustment. They counseled parents that they should purchase items like silk stockings for their offspring so that they might fit in with other children. While they should discourage extravagance, parents should not make their children conspicuous by depriving them of popular articles that other children possessed. Parents should not "insist upon the virtue of privation and self-sacrifice as having intrinsic merit for everybody and under all circumstances." The Gruenbergs implied that parents should help their children navigate the social system. They needed to recognize that their offspring's popularity and social acceptance depended, at least to some degree, on ownership of the right objects.[61]

The new view of toys and clothes as valuable tools for socialization was visible in the emerging literature on sibling rivalry, a problem which child experts of the 1920s began to emphasize. Child-rearing experts told parents that to minimize rivalry, they should give extra toys to youngsters who might otherwise feel envious, deprived, or excluded. For instance, if a child was celebrating a birthday, his parents should be careful to provide his siblings with gifts as well. Rather than teaching children to repress envy and to accept inequality, adults were to make sure that no one felt neglected or passed over.[62] Child advisors seemed to be undermining their stated goal of teaching children not to envy, for they implied that the way for children to overcome their covetousness was not through self-control but through increased materialism. This ambiguous message, that the problem of envy could be solved by providing more goods to children, was repeated throughout American culture, and ultimately this emotional ethic, rather than the older lessons of self-control and repression, would carry the day.

By the 1920s, middle-class children had become integrated into the consumer society. Surrounded by examples of envious behavior, children became accustomed to pursuing what they desired—and what they desired were consumer goods. There was no part of American culture unaffected by the powerful new values of consumer society, no cultural preserve off limits to market forces. During the late nineteenth century, bourgeois Americans had conceived of their children as pure beings, existing in a world quite separate from the pressures of commerce and competition. While this vision had always been more myth than reality, it became even less accurate by the 1920s. Bourgeois childhood was not separate from commercial forces, but in many ways it was defined by them. Even the textbook authors and child-rearing experts who sought to restrain children's envy and shield youth from the commercial world, had accepted this new reality and had come to rely on consumer goods as a means for reaching these goals.

Just as bourgeois childhood was coming to be defined by commercial forces, so the success of consumer society became increasingly dependent on children. Those Americans who grew up between 1890 and World War I were exposed early to the charms of consumerism. Their children, who were born in the late 1910s and the 1920s, were the first to be raised from the cradle on up in a commercial environment. Surrounded by mass-produced toys, dressed in store-bought clothes, these children read advertisements and magazines, wandered through stores, and attended movies. They learned the habits of consumerism and continued to practice them as adults. Perhaps most fundamentally they developed a style of emotional comportment that differed from earlier generations. They learned that their envy and longings need not be repressed but should instead be indulged. It would be this widely accepted emotional style that would enable the consumer society to expand and would sustain it into the future.

A powerful example of this new attitude toward envy and the way it supported consumer spending came from a small girl in Alabama. She articulated the very principles that the moralists who taught thrift and contentment had opposed and that the merchants, advertisers, salesmen, and even the modern child experts hoped the public would follow. An Alabama minister reported that "a little girl in one of my church schools was asked the other day, What was the Tenth Commandment? The reply was 'Thou shalt not covet.' When asked what covet meant, she replied, 'not to want other folks things, but to get Sears, Roebuck Catalogue and buy for yourself.' "[63] The girl believed that she could assuage her envy not by repressing it but by purchasing what she wanted. Envy was no longer a sin, and marketplace behavior no longer had to match moral dictates. The consumer ethos had become so influential that it could be found in all parts of American cultural life, even the Sunday school classroom.[64] The children who so ardently longed for new toys, clothes, and family wealth unabashedly expressed the emotions and accepted the values that supported consumerism. They would grow into a generation of adults who considered spending to be morally unproblematic and believed that all were entitled to—and should pursue—the bounty of consumer society.

Conclusion

In 1899, long before many Americans accepted such ideas, Robert Ellis Thompson, a professor of political economy at the University of Pennsylvania, proclaimed, "It is a benefit to spread a discontent with ugliness in dress, house and furniture. The peddler and the storekeeper are missionaries of civilization, and through their labor we have reached the point at which the poorest are no longer content with what once satisfied the most opulent. But much remains to be done." He pointed to the "large sections of the American people" who "are still very poor consumers and make small demands upon the industries of the country." In order to raise the standard of living for such people, "a just discontent with the paltry ways they have of living" must be diffused throughout the country. Thompson, aware that he was advocating a morally controversial position about consumption, confided to his readers that they need not worry about the moral effects of their envy and discontent. He claimed that they would not be "less men, but more, for learning to want and to enjoy more than they do."[1]

This view, that Americans would become better people if they only felt sufficient discontent and desire, bucked conventional wisdom about the basis of morality. Traditionally, Americans had believed that only through asceticism and restraint might one improve morally. Thompson's claim, that men and women's physical circumstances and moral condition would be improved when they became good consumers, presaged the increasing acceptance of envy, discontent, and materialism that would develop in the twentieth century.

By 1930, Thompson's ideas had become commonplace in the United States. Bourgeois Americans of all ages had become accustomed to indulging their desires and acting on their envy. They had come to think of envy and discontent as emotions which indicated that they had aspirations, taste, and a desire for a higher standard of living. Rather than seeing envy as a sin and consumer activity as a threat to their moral integrity, Americans believed that they could better themselves through spending. They also believed that they could make themselves happier by making purchases. The way to gain true contentment was not to accept deprivations but to act on their envy and pursue the things they longed for. These new interpretations of envy, discontent, and contentment which consumers and merchants developed in the 1910s and 1920s continue to shape consumer behavior in our own time.

Modern consumers accept not only the emotional codes that their grandparents and great-grandparents developed, but their larger social implications as well. They believe that all Americans, regardless of their location, age, or sex, have a right to purchase what they want. Sumptuary laws, formal or informal, have largely disappeared from American culture. There are few people who are presumed to live outside of the thrall of consumer society, few who are expected to be satisfied with merely peering through the show windows instead of entering into America's retail stores. No longer do moralists try to prevent farmers from looking like city folk, nor do they worry when middle-class women and men dress themselves like far wealthier people. Children, their pockets filled with allowance money, are also recognized as ready consumers. While many parents and child psychologists still worry about children consuming, few believe that it is possible to insulate them from the world of goods, and few are surprised when they display envy, consumer desire, and competitive tendencies at a relatively tender age.

Modern consumers also accept and act on the idea that they can at least partially transform their identities through purchases. Such an idea offended nineteenth-century moralists, who believed that the self was a static, God-given essence that existed apart from the worldly activities of getting and spending. Since the 1910s and 1920s this traditional notion of the self has faced a stiff challenge from a more malleable conception of personal identity. Americans today have great faith that they can give themselves "makeovers"—that they can turn themselves into who they long to be if only they can have access to the right clothes, accessories, and cars.

These influential ideas about the self, spending, and the emotions arose out of the dramatic transformations of turn-of-the-century society. The Victorian moral order began to crumble in the face of assaults leveled at it by

Darwinists, psychologists, sociologists, and modern economists. A more secularized understanding of social life, the causes and nature of inequality, and human behavior gradually gained strength. The new consensus that emerged in the early twentieth century held that inequality was not necessarily natural, social life was not divinely ordered, human behavior sprang from external influences as well as internal ones, and consequently individuals could not always control their instincts and emotions. Such a perspective revolutionized the way that Americans perceived envy. If social inequality was not providentially ordained but instead arbitrary, then struggling to leave one's position carried no moral onus. If men and women had strong desires and aggressions, perhaps controlling them was not always possible or beneficial for either the individual or society. Finally, if envy spurred consumer spending, raised the national standard of living, and supported economic growth, shouldn't the emotion be cultivated rather than discouraged?

The material and social conditions of American life also created a climate that was more accepting of envious behavior. As America became more urbanized, many men and women realized that even if conventional moral dictates condemned acting on envy, emulating the wealthy, and thereby changing one's identity, the circumstances of life certainly accommodated such behavior. With accessible and affordable imitation goods at hand, it was easy to emulate the rich, and there seemed to be little harm in pursuing the material objects that one longed for. With what seemed to be an ever-expanding pool of goods, it appeared that no one suffered if an envious woman purchased a coat just like a rich woman's. There seemed to be no scarcity, no net loss in the material world, but instead a boundless abundance that would never run out and from which all could and should partake.

The hope that Thompson expressed in 1899, that all Americans eventually would learn to consume and would strive to get what they envied, has largely come to pass. In the last few decades, however, other voices have questioned the wisdom that has supported and driven so much consumer spending for over a century. With limited natural resources and with frequently limited incomes, can Americans continue to cultivate a spirit of discontent with their current belongings? Should they continue to long for and pursue what they have not yet attained? Is it really laudable to encourage people to feel discontent with their own belongings and envy of other people's? The "luxury fever" or "affluenza" that has beset middle America has come under attack once again.[2]

The difficulty lies in escaping the pattern of conspicuous and competitive consumer spending. The envy and desire for material equality that besets modern Americans and that causes them to seek more things has roots stretching back into the nineteenth century. While it is a worthy goal to seek and develop a new model for consumer behavior in the twenty-first century, such a model will require Americans to cultivate not merely new spending habits but also new emotional habits.

Notes

Introduction

1. "An Early Lesson," *Saturday Evening Post* 7 (December 11, 1897): 5.
2. "The Best-Dressed Woman in the World," *Ladies' Home Journal* 40 (January 1923): 24.
3. I follow Stuart Blumin's criteria for determining middle-class identity. He argues that five types of social experiences were crucial to middle-class formation and identity: work, consumption, residential location, formal and informal voluntary association, and family organization strategy. Following this model, I include workers engaged in the professions of both the "old" middle class—farmers, "free professionals," and independent businessmen—as well as members of the "new" middle class who generally worked in salaried positions at large corporations or institutions. Since both rural and urban middle-class families were examined, the residential location of those studied varied, and it was not always possible to discern where families lived. The general pattern of family organization for the urban middle class was an employed husband and a wife and children who did not work outside of the home. Consumer habits were something the subjects shared (or wanted to share), and their distinctive patterns will be examined throughout this book. Only occasionally was I able to find information about subjects' membership in voluntary organizations. See Stuart Blumin, "The Hypothesis of Middle-Class Formation in Nineteenth-Century America: A Critique and Some Proposals," *American Historical Review* 90 (1985): 299–338. See also Stuart Blumin, *The Emergence of the Middle Class: Social Experience in the American City, 1760–1900* (New York: Cambridge University Press, 1989), p. 11.
4. For discussion of the criticism and halting acceptance of emulative spending among the working class, see Daniel Horowitz, *The Morality of Spending: Attitudes Toward the Consumer Society in America, 1876–1940* (Baltimore: Johns Hopkins University Press, 1985), pp. 59, 65–66, 123, 131–32. For a discussion of the expanding role of African Americans in the consumer economy, see Robert E. Weems Jr., *Desegregating the Dollar: African-American Consumerism in the Twentieth Century* (New York: New York University Press, 1998); Paul K. Edwards, *The Southern Urban Negro as a Consumer* (1932; rpt., College Park, Md: McGrath, 1969), pp. 98–99. See also James Twitchell, "Two Cheers for Materialism," in *The Consumer Society Reader*, ed. Juliet B. Schor and Douglas B. Holt (New York: New Press, 2000), p. 283; Eric Foner, *The Story of Freedom* (New York: W. W. Norton, 1998), p. 278.
5. Agnes Repplier, "The Divineness of Discontent," *Atlantic Monthly* 131

(June 1923): 724–34. On the theoretical connection between envy and discontent, see Solomon Schimmel, *The Seven Deadly Sins: Jewish, Christian, and Classical Reflections on Human Nature* (New York: Free Press, 1992), p. 79. On the use of religion to discourage envy, see Helmut Schoeck, *Envy: A Theory of Social Behavior,* trans. Michael Glenny and Betty Ross (New York: Harcourt, Brace, and World, 1969), pp. 2, 132–33.

6. *Christian Advocate* 101 (July 15, 1926): 874.

7. John Brooks, *Showing Off in America: From Conspicuous Consumption to Parody Display* (Boston: Little, Brown, 1981), pp. 17–18; Richard M. Huber, *The American Idea of Success* (New York: McGraw-Hill, 1971), pp. 186–90.

8. George M. Foster, "The Anatomy of Envy: A Study in Symbolic Behavior," *Current Anthropology* 13 (April 1972): 165–202, esp. 167–68. Foster argues that envy is particularly evident in limited goods economies.

9. William Allen White, *The Autobiography of William Allen White,* 2nd ed., ed. Sally Foreman Griffith (Lawrence: University Press of Kansas, 1990), p. 329.

10. Social scientists have frequently focused on the ill will, malice, and anger that envious individuals display. Many have seen these emotions as inseparable from the experience of envy and claim that the envious invariably wish for the downfall of those whom they envy. Yet as psychiatrist Philip Spielman points out, this ill will "seems to be the most variable ingredient in the compound effect of envy." Certainly such malice was less evident in the context of the expanding consumer economy where scarcity was disappearing. Philip M. Spielman, "Envy and Jealousy: An Attempt at Clarification," *Psychoanalytic Quarterly* 40 (January 1971): 60, 62, 76–77.

11. Peter N. Stearns, *Battleground of Desire: The Struggle for Self-Control in Modern America* (New York: New York University Press, 1999), pp. 113–16; Horowitz, *Morality,* pp. 163–65; Hal Barron, *Those Who Stayed Behind: Rural Society in Nineteenth-Century New England* (New York: Cambridge University Press, 1984), pp. 41–42; T. J. Jackson Lears, *No Place of Grace: Antimodernism and the Transformation of American Culture, 1880–1920* (New York: Pantheon Books, 1981), pp. 37–40; Frederick Lewis Allen, *Only Yesterday: An Informal History of the 1920s* (1931; rpt., New York: Harper and Row, 1964), pp. 73–101.

12. Garet Garrett, "This Is Well Being," *Saturday Evening Post* 198 (December 26, 1925): 16–17.

13. Here I follow Peter L. Berger's definition of secularization in *The Sacred Canopy: Elements of a Sociological Theory of Religion* (Garden City, N.Y.: Doubleday, 1969), p. 107.

14. Lewis H. Lapham, *Money and Class in America: Notes and Observations on the Civil Religion* (New York: Ballantine, 1989), p. 70; Daniel Bell, *The Cultural Contradictions of Capitalism* (New York: Basic Books, 1976), p. 22.

15. Envy is the feeling an individual experiences when another possesses what he or she desires. Today it is often confused and conflated with jealousy, but historically the two terms have conveyed very different meanings. While the envious individual longs for what he does not have, the jealous person feels that his or her

existing relationships or possessions are threatened by another. Some commentators have maintained that envy is the emotion of those with less, who want the privileges of the elites, while jealousy is the emotion of the upper classes, who feel that they must defend their possessions and status from the aspiring lower classes. For discussions and definitions of envy, see Peter N. Stearns, *Jealousy: The Evolution of an Emotion in American History* (New York: New York University Press, 1989), pp. 10–11; Foster, "The Anatomy of Envy," pp. 166–68; Schoeck, *Envy,* 12–13, 46–61; Spielman, "Envy and Jealousy," pp. 60, 62, 76–77.

16. Admittedly, not all bourgeois consumer spending sprang from a desire to emulate; likewise, not all emulation was motivated by envy. Consequently, this book focuses attention not on all types of consumer activity but specifically on those instances where envy was the clear and documented motivation for emulative purchasing. The historical connections between envy, emulation, and consumerism are both tangled and contested. Some historians and sociologists have maintained that consumer spending is not motivated by a desire to imitate the upper classes. Other scholars have argued the opposite, claiming that a widespread desire for the refined luxury goods of the elites has been a main factor in industrialization and the development of mass production. According to this school of thought, envy stoked the fires of the factories that were turning out imitation luxury goods. For examples of the opposing views, see Colin Campbell, *The Romantic Ethic and the Spirit of Modern Consumerism* (Oxford: Basil Blackwell), pp. 52–53; Lori Anne Loeb, *Consuming Angels: Advertising and Victorian Women* (New York: Oxford University Press, 1994), pp. 158–66; Neil McKendrick, John Brewer, and J. H. Plumb, *The Birth of a Consumer Society: The Commercialization of Eighteenth-Century England* (Bloomington: Indiana University Press, 1982), pp. 9–99; Richard Bushman, *The Refinement of America: Persons, Houses, Cities* (New York: Knopf, 1992), pp. 406–10; Richard Ohmann, *Selling Culture: Magazines, Markets, and Class at the Turn of the Century* (New York: Verso, 1996), pp. 90, 147.

17. See, e.g., William Leach, *Land of Desire: Merchants, Power, and the Rise of a New American Culture* (New York: Vintage, 1993); Roland Marchand, *Advertising the American Dream: Making Way for Modernity, 1920–1940* (Berkeley: University of California Press, 1985); Daniel Boorstin, *The Americans: The Democratic Experience* (New York: Vintage, 1973), pp. 89–157; Ohmann, *Selling Culture;* T. J. Jackson Lears, *Fables of Abundance: A Cultural History of Advertising in America* (New York: Basic Books, 1994); Jennifer Scanlon, *Inarticulate Longings: The Ladies' Home Journal, Gender, and the Promises of Consumer Culture* (New York: Routledge, 1995); Ellen Gruber Garvey, *The Adman in the Parlor: Magazines and the Gendering of Consumer Culture, 1880s to 1910s* (New York: Oxford University Press, 1996); Loeb, *Consuming Angels;* Elaine Abelson, *When Ladies Go-A-Thievin': Middle-Class Shoplifters in the Victorian Department Store* (New York: Oxford University Press, 1989); Lizabeth Cohen, *Making a New Deal: Industrial Workers in Chicago, 1919–1939* (New York: Cambridge University Press, 1990); Roy Rosenzweig, *Eight Hours for What We Will: Workers and Leisure in an Industrial City, 1870–1920* (New York: Cambridge University Press, 1983); Kathy Peiss,

Cheap Amusements: Working Women and Leisure in New York City, 1880 to 1920 (Philadelphia: Temple University Press, 1985).

18. Scholarship related to this topic includes T. J. Jackson Lears, "From Salvation to Self-Realization: Advertising and the Therapeutic Roots of the Consumer Culture," in *The Culture of Consumption: Critical Essays in American History, 1880–1980,* ed. Lears and Richard Wightman Fox (New York: Pantheon, 1983), pp. x–xi, 1–38; Peter N. Stearns, "Consumerism and Childhood: New Targets for American Emotions," in *An Emotional History of the United States,* ed. Stearns and Jan Lewis (New York: New York University Press, 1998), pp. 396–413; Stearns, *Battleground of Desire,* pp. 119–23, 148–53, 334–35.

19. Mary Stewart Cutting, "Concerning Comfort," *Harper's Bazaar* 43 (November 1909): 1076.

20. Edward Bok, "At Home with the Editor," *Ladies' Home Journal* 8 (September 1891): 10, emphasis added.

21. Joseph H. Appel, *My Own Story, Illustrating the Spirit and Service of Big Business* (New York: Platt and Peck, 1913), pp. 87, 88, 91–99, 116–17, 133–34, 143.

22. Theodore Roosevelt to Liberty Hyde Bailey, August 1, 1908, Liberty Hyde Bailey Collection, Cornell University Archives, Collection #21/2/1400, box 4, folder 2.

Chapter 1

1. "Why Are We American Women Not Happy, by an American Mother," *Ladies' Home Journal* 18 (December 1900): 22.

2. Bernard Barber and Lyle Lobel," 'Fashion' in Women's Clothes and the American Social System," *Social Forces* 31 (December 1952): 124–31; Max Weber, "Class, Status, Party," in *From Max Weber: Essays in Sociology,* ed. H. H. Gerth and C. Wright Mills (New York: Oxford University Press, 1958), pp. 186–93; Anthony Giddens, "The Class Structure of Advanced Societies," in *Social Stratification: Class, Race, and Gender in Sociological Perspective,* ed. David B. Grusky (Boulder, Colo.: Westview Press, 1994), pp. 131–40.

3. Daniel Boorstin, *The Americans: The Democratic Experience* (New York: Random House, 1973), pp. 101–9, 118–29; Michael Schudson, *Advertising, the Uneasy Persuasion: Its Dubious Impact on American Society* (London: Routledge, 1993), p. 151; William Leach, *Land of Desire: Merchants, Power, and the Rise of a New American Culture* (New York: Random House, 1993), pp. 20–21; David Cohn, *The Good Old Days: A History of American Morals and Manners as Seen Through the Sears Roebuck Catalogs 1905 to the Present* (New York: Simon and Schuster, 1940), pp. 538–39.

4. Helen Woodward, *The Lady Persuaders* (New York: I. Obloloensky, 1960), pp. 42–54.

5. Barber and Lobel, " 'Fashion' in Women's Clothes," p. 130.

6. Leach, *Land of Desire,* pp. 24, 272–73; "The Future of the Chain Store," ca.

1927, pp. 16–19, Research Reports, reel 38, J. Walter Thompson Company Archives, Hartman Center for Sales, Advertising, and Marketing History, Duke University Library (hereafter JWT).

7. Helen Jay, "How I Manage to Be Happy Though a Busy Housewife," *Ladies' Home Journal* 8 (October 1891): 10.

8. Thorstein Veblen, *Theory of the Leisure Class* (New York: New American Library, 1953), pp. 68–69; Katherine C. Grier, *Culture and Comfort: Parlor Making and Middle-Class Identity, 1850–1930* (Washington, D.C.: Smithsonian Institution Press, 1997), pp. 27–28. Grier's evidence that the middle classes learned of upper-class tastes through such auctions is drawn mainly from mid-nineteenth-century sources. James Thompson, "The Ideal Kitchen," *Ladies' Home Journal* 13 (December 1895): 36; "Inside of a Hundred Homes," *Ladies' Home Journal* 14 (November 1897): 6–7; "Looking into Other Women's Homes, *Ladies' Home Journal* 31 (September 1914): 25–28; Mary Hoffman, *The Buying Habits of Small-Town Women* (Kansas City, Kans.: Ferry-Hanly Advertising Co., 1926), pp. 11–12.

9. "Standards," *Christian Advocate* 65 (November 6, 1890): 736.

10. Helen Jay, "How I Manage to Be Happy," p. 10.

11. Mara Millar, *Hail to Yesterday* (New York: Farrar and Rinehart, 1941), p. 56.

12. Craig Roell, *The Piano in America, 1890–1940* (Chapel Hill: University of North Carolina Press, 1989), pp. 22–28.

13. James Woolf, "The Problem of Creating Desire," *J. Walter Thompson News Bulletin,* no. 85 (April 1922): 5, News Bulletin Series, Newsletter Collection 1922–1931, box 1, JWT. The Wanamaker version appeared in Edward S. Babcox, "Milestones in Advertising," *Advertising and Selling* 22 (October 1912): 26.

14. See Louise Bolard More, *Wage-earners' Budgets: A Study of Standards and Cost of Living in New York City* (New York: Henry Holt, 1907), p. 139, quoted in Andrew Heinze, *Adapting to Abundance: Jewish Immigrants, Mass Consumption, and the Search for American Identity* (New York: Columbia University Press, 1990), p. 138; "The Baldwin Piano Company Consumer Investigation," January 1930, pp. 2–3, 7, 12, Research Reports, reel 195, JWT; Arthur Loesser, *Men, Women, and Pianos: A Social History* (New York: Simon and Schuster, 1954); Roell, *The Piano.*

15. Harriet Lane Levy, *920 O'Farrell Street* (Garden City, N.Y.: Doubleday, 1947), p. 147.

16. "Standards," p. 736; G. Stanley Hall and Theodore Smith, "Showing Off and Bashfulness as Phases of Self-Consciousness," *Pedagogical Seminary* 10 (June 1903): 174–75; William Allen White, *The Autobiography of William Allen White,* 2d ed., ed. Sally Foreman Griffith, (Lawrence: University Press of Kansas, 1990), pp. 11–12; Joseph Appel, "Reaching Women Through Advertising," in *Library of Advertising: Methods of Appeal, Outdoor, Street Car, and Miscellaneous Advertising, Mediums, and Publications,* ed. A. P. Johnson (Chicago: Cree, 1911), p. 27; "Kent-Costikyan Investigations, East and Midwest," 1921, pp. 3, 4, 8, 10, 13, 14, 33, 47, Research Reports, reel 196, JWT.

17. Juliet Virginia Strauss, "When a Man Thinks of a Woman as a Pretty Fool, The Third of the Series: The Woman Who Frets over Things," *Ladies' Home Journal* 29 (January 1912): 16.

18. Paul Boyer, *Urban Masses and Moral Order in America, 1820–1920* (Cambridge, Mass.: Harvard University Press, 1978), pp. 4–5. Karen Halttunen, *Painted Ladies and Confidence Men: A Study of Middle-Class Culture in America, 1830–1870* (New Haven, Conn.: Yale University Press, 1982), pp. 35–36; Veblen, *Theory of the Leisure Class,* p. 71.

19. Hortense Odlum, *A Woman's Place* (New York: Scribner's, 1942), pp. 179, 181, 8–9.

20. Louis W. Flaccus, "Remarks on the Psychology of Clothes," *Pedagogical Seminary* 13 (March 1906): 76. Flaccus, a "sometime fellow" at Clark University, based his study in part on responses to a questionnaire that G. Stanley Hall had designed and circulated. Linus Kline and C. J. France, "The Psychology of Ownership," *Pedagogical Seminary* 6 (December 1899): 462–63.

21. Ida M. Tarbell, "A Woman and Her Raiment," *American Magazine* 74 (August 1912): 472, 474.

22. Mrs. James Farley Cox, "The Council Chamber: A Special Talk with Girls," *Ladies' Home Journal* 20 (June 1903): 18.

23. Virginia Allen Durr, *Outside the Magic Circle,* ed. Hollinger F. Barnard (New York: Simon and Schuster, 1985), p. 42.

24. Claudia B. Kidwell and Margaret C. Christman, *Suiting Everyone: The Democratization of Clothing in America* (Washington, D.C.: Smithsonian Institution Press, 1974), pp. 135–51.

25. Tarbell, "A Woman and Her Raiment," pp. 470–71.

26. Millar, *Hail to Yesterday,* 103.

27. Kidwell and Christman, *Suiting Everyone,* pp. 135–51; Cohn, *The Good Old Days,* pp. 355–56; "The Ideas of a Plain Country Woman," *Ladies' Home Journal* 29 (January 1912): 32; Albert Atwood, "Are We Extravagant?" *Saturday Evening Post* 192 (January 3, 1920): 116; Paul K. Edwards, *The Southern Urban Negro as a Consumer,* reprint (1932; rpt.,College Park, Md.: McGrath, 1969), pp. 66–67.

28. Dorothy Rodgers, *A Personal Book* (New York: Harper and Row, 1977), p. 57.

29. Newell LeRoy Sims "Hoosier Village: A Sociological Study With Special Reference to Social Causation" (Ph.D. diss., Columbia University, 1912), p. 91. See also Albert Blumenthal, "A Sociological Study of a Small Town" (Ph.D. diss, University of Chicago, 1932), p. 170.

30. "Kent-Costikyan Investigation: Boston, Springfield, Hartford, Pittsburgh, Harrisburg, Philadelphia," 1921, pp. 13, 14, 47, Research Reports, reel 196, JWT.

31. Account History, January 18, 1926, in Chesebrough Pond's Inc., Account Files, pp. 2–6, 8, box 3, JWT; Kathy Peiss, *Hope in a Jar: The Making of America's Beauty Culture* (New York: Henry Holt, Metropolitan Books, 1998), p. 137. Boorstin discusses the rise of brand names in *The Americans: The Democratic Experience,* pp. 146–48.

32. Another factor that many believed contributed to Penney's low prestige was the chain's now famous black and yellow store fronts. Many regarded the stores' exteriors as garish. "Don't know much about Penney's, but think that the yellow and black front is hideous," reported one consumer. "J. C. Penney Company Investigation Among Consumers in Ashtabula Ohio, Auburn New York, Little Falls, New York, Rome, New York, Summary of Findings," July 1928, Summary, pp. 1–9; Ashtabula, pp. 1–2; Little Falls, 1; Rome, p. 2, all in Research Reports, reel 197, JWT.

33. Barber and Lobel, " 'Fashion' in Women's Clothes," p. 128. Just as elites worried about bourgeois women who were getting too uppity, so the middle class worried about members of the working class who were striving to enter the bourgeoisie. Historian Daniel Horowitz has described how many middle-class reformers condemned members of the working class who seemed to be buying the same goods (or the same sorts of goods) as their social betters. He contends that much of their condemnation was linked to a fear that middle-class Anglo Americans were being displaced by more recent immigrants who were gaining power and status. Daniel Horowitz, *The Morality of Spending: Attitudes Toward the Consumer Society in America, 1875–1940* (Baltimore: Johns Hopkins University Press, 1985), pp. 125–33.

34. See, e.g., Leach, *Land of Desire,* pp. 191–94. In contrast, David Shi and Daniel Horowitz have paid considerable attention to the widespread moral concerns about consumerism at the turn of the century. Shi has described the nineteenth-century roots of the reaction against emulation, status seeking, and materialism. See David Shi, *The Simple Life: Plain Living and High Thinking in American Culture* (New York: Oxford University Press, 1985), pp. 100–125. Horowitz, in *The Morality of Spending*, has examined how moralists of various stripes reacted to the expansion of consumer society.

35. The Epistle of Paul the Apostle to the Philippians 4:11; Solomon Schimmel, *The Seven Deadly Sins: Jewish, Christian, and Classical Reflections on Human Nature* (New York: Free Press, 1992), p. 79.

36. Elzira A. Whittier, "Contentment," *Christian Advocate* 170 (October 17, 1895): 670.

37. Barbara Welter, "The Cult of True Womanhood, 1820–1860," *American Quarterly* 18 (Summer 1966): 151–74; Edward Bok, "At Home with the Editor," *Ladies' Home Journal* 8 (September 1891): 10.

38. "Standards," p. 736.

39. Ann Douglas, *The Feminization of American Culture* (New York: Knopf, 1977), 223, 225.

40. "The Secret of Content," *Christian Advocate* 67 (February 4, 1892): 70.

41. Mrs. Margaret Bottome, "The King's Daughters," *Ladies' Home Journal* 13 (November 1896): 18. This is a continuation of a long tradition of using the promise of heavenly rewards to neutralize envy. For further discussion of this theme, see Helmut Schoeck, *Envy: A Theory of Social Behavior,* trans. Michael Glenny and Betty Ross (New York: Harcourt, Brace, and World, 1969), pp. 2, 132–33.

42. Karen Halttunen, in *Confidence Men and Painted Women*, pp. 56–91,

traces the concern with sincerity in dress to the early nineteenth century, when Americans living in rapidly growing cities began to fear that they were the victims of hypocrisy in a society of strangers. Katherine Grier described the preoccupation with sincere furnishings in *Culture and Comfort*, pp. 108–11.

43. Bok, "At Home with the Editor," 10.

44. Alice Preston, "Simplicity in Living—Especially at Christmas," *Ladies' Home Journal* 25 (December 1907): 28.

45. Orison Swett Marden, "Keeping Up Appearances," *Christian Advocate* 79 (November 19, 1904): 181.

46. "An $1800 City Brick House," *Ladies' Home Journal* 15 (January 1898): 15.

47. Halttunen, *Confidence Men and Painted Women*, pp. 56–91.

48. Ruth Ashmore, "The Small Faults of Girls," *Ladies' Home Journal* 12 (December 1894): 26.

49. "In an Editorial Way," *Ladies' Home Journal* 24 (February 1907): 5. It is clear that these fears about women's supposedly frivolous and potentially ruinous spending habits have a long history. See, e.g., Stuart Blumin, *The Emergence of the Middle Class: Social Experience in the American City, 1760–1900* (New York: Cambridge University Press, 1989), pp. 185–86.

50. Agnes Surbridge, *The Confessions of a Club Woman* (New York: Doubleday, Page, 1904), pp. 8, 38, 61.

51. Laura A. Smith, "The Girl in the Small Town: How She Can Best Succeed in the City," *Ladies' Home Journal* 23 (October 1906): 24.

52. Tarbell, "A Woman and Her Raiment," p. 469.

53. Juliet Strauss, "When a Man Thinks of a Woman," p. 16. This same concern was evident in other expanding consumer societies. See Mariana Valverde, "The Love of Finery: Fashion and the Fallen Woman in Nineteenth-Century Social Discourse," *Victorian Studies* 32 (Winter 1989): 169–88.

54. Reginald Wright Kauffman, *The Girl That Goes Wrong* (New York: Macaulay, 1914), 25–37. For another account, see *The Social Evil in Syracuse: Being the Report of an Investigation of the Moral Condition of the City Conducted by a Committee of Eighteen Citizens* (Syracuse, N.Y., 1913), p. 56.

55. Elizabeth Hawes, *Fashion Is Spinach* (New York: Random House, 1938), pp. 119–20.

56. Robert S. Lynd and Helen Merrell Lynd, *Middletown: A Study in American Culture* (New York: Harcourt Brace, 1929), p. 83.

57. Roland Pertwee, "Chic and Dominant: American Women Are a Revelation of Charm and Command," *Ladies' Home Journal* 41 (October 1924): 20.

58. In *The Morality of Spending*, pp. 134–65, Horowitz has shown how economists, sociologists, and budget experts of the 1920s and 1930s came to see emulative consumerism as acceptable.

59. Shi, *The Simple Life*, p. 217; Charles F. McGovern, "Sold American: Inventing the Consumer, 1890–1940" (Ph.D. diss., Harvard University, 1993), pp. 12–28.

60. T. J. Jackson Lears, *No Place of Grace: Antimodernism and the Trans-*

formation of American Culture, 1880–1920 (New York: Pantheon Books, 1981), pp. 7–12.

61. Peter Stearns, *Battleground of Desire: The Struggle for Self-Control in Modern America* (New York: New York University Press, 1999), pp. 113–16; Horowitz, *The Morality of Spending,* pp. 163–65; Hal Barron, *Those Who Stayed Behind: Rural Society in Nineteenth-Century New England* (Cambridge: Cambridge University Press, 1984), pp. 41–42; Lears, *No Place of Grace,* pp. 37–40; Frederick Lewis Allen, *Only Yesterday: An Informal History of the 1920s* (1931, rpt., New York: Harper and Row, 1964), pp. 73–101.

62. John Brooks, *Showing Off in America: From Conspicuous Consumption to Parody Display* (Boston: Little, Brown, 1981), pp. 17–18. Richard M. Huber, *The American Idea of Success* (New York: McGraw-Hill, 1971), pp. 186–190. See also, Irving Bacheller, *Keeping Up with Lizzie* (New York: Harper, 1911).

63. Woods Hutchinson, "The Sin of Homeliness: The Duty of Every Woman to Be Well Dressed," *Saturday Evening Post* 183 (March 25, 1911): 45.

64. "Extravagance as a Virtue," *Current Opinion* 54 (January 1913): 51–52. Patten's speech sparked a heated debate.

65. "The Best-Dressed Woman in the World," *Ladies' Home Journal* 40 (January 1923): 24.

66. "The Confessions of a Businessman's Wife," *American Magazine* 109 (May 1930): 62, 64, 158–62; "The Confessions of a Businessman's Wife," *American Magazine* 109 (June 1930): 63, 153, 156; "The Confessions of a Businessman's Wife," *American Magazine* 110 (July 1930): 55, 56, 151.

67. Lynd and Lynd, *Middletown,* pp. 81, 82n.

68. Lary May, *Screening Out the Past: The Birth of Mass Culture and the Motion Picture Industry* (New York: Oxford University Press, 1980), p. 203; Kathy Peiss, "Making Faces: The Cosmetics Industry and the Cultural Construction of Gender, 1890–1930," *Genders* 7 (Spring 1990): 143–49; "Motion Picture Autobiographies," Motion Picture Research Council Papers, Hoover Institution, quoted in Peiss, *Hope in a Jar,* pp. 192–93. See Frank K. Shuttleworth and Mark May, "The Social Conduct and Attitudes of Movie Fans," in W. W. Charters, *Motion Pictures and Youth: The Payne Fund Studies* (New York: Macmillan, 1933), p. 58.

69. Mabel A. Elliott and Frances E. Merrill, *Social Disorganization* (New York: Harper, 1934), p. 644.

70. Cohn, *The Good Old Days,* pp. 524–25; Roland Marchand, *Advertising the American Dream: Making Way for Modernity, 1920–1940* (Berkeley: University of California Press, 1985), pp. 4, 127, 6.

71. Albert Leffingwell, "The Gentle Reader," *J. Walter Thompson News Bulletin,* no. 86, May 1922, p. 2, News Bulletin Series, Newsletter Collection, 1922–1931, box 1, JWT. Marchand explores this issue in some depth in his chapter "Advertisements as Social Tableaux," in *Advertising the American Dream.*

72. Frances Maule, "The Snob Appeal," *J. Walter Thompson News Bulletin,* no. 96, March 1923, pp. 11–14, News Bulletin Series, Newsletter Collections, 1922–1931, box 1, JWT.

73. Stanley Resor, "Personalities and the Public: Some Aspects of Testimonial Advertising," *J. Walter Thompson News Bulletin*, no. 138, April 1929 pp. 1–2, News Bulletin Series, Newsletter Collection, 1922–1931, box 1, JWT.

74. Marchand, *Advertising the American Dream*, pp. 217–22; "The Andrew Jergens Co., Woodbury's Facial Soap National Campaign, 1926," pp. 1–6, Account Files, Andrew Jergens Account Histories 1916–1926, Box 1 of 21, JWT; *Vogue*, September 15, 1928, p. 123, in Chesebrough Pond's, Domestic Ads, 1926–28, box 9, JWT; Andrew Jergens Co., Woodbury Facial Soap, in Domestic Advertisement Collection, Andrew Jergens Co., 1915–1935, Box 1, JWT; Pond's Extract Company, January 18, 1926, Chesebrough Pond's Inc., Account Histories in Account Files, box 3, JWT; "Domestic Ads, Simmons Mattresses, 1927–28, 1930, 1974–77," Small Box "s," JWT; Maule, "The Snob Appeal," pp. 11–14; Account History, January 18, 1926, in Chesebrough Pond's Inc., Account Files, pp. 2–6, 8, box 3, JWT.

75. *Saturday Evening Post*, 190 (April 7, 1917): 135.

76. *Ladies' Home Journal* 36 (April 1919): 184.

77. *Saturday Evening Post*, 194 (November 19, 1921): 49; *Ladies' Home Journal* 42 (November 1925): 132.

78. *Ladies' Home Journal* 41 (May 1924): 64.

79. Michael Schudson argues that the goal of advertisements is mainly to convince consumers to change brands of a product that they already use. At this they may have some success, whereas the goal of convincing consumers that they need an entirely new item is a more difficult one to achieve. See Schudson, *Advertising, the Uneasy Persuasion*, pp. 9–10, 26–27.

80. "Re: Notes on the Woodbury Investigation in Boston," part 2, Consumer Interviews Given in Detail, p. 8, interview no. 82, May 22, 1923, Research Reports, reel 45, JWT; "Report on the Woodbury's Facial Soap Investigation Among Minnesota University Girls," 1925, p. 30, Research Reports, reel 45, JWT.

81. "The Pond's Extract Company Consumer Investigation in Columbus, Ohio," November 1927, p. 41, Research Reports, reel 52, JWT; "The Pond's Extract Company Consumer Investigation in Providence, Rhode Island, and Chester, Pennsylvania, June 1927, pp. p-43, c-39, Research Reports, reel 52; JWT; "The Pond's Extract Company Consumer Investigation in Circleville, Ohio, and the Farming Sections" November, 1927, pp. 39, 40, 28, 29, Research Reports, reel 52, JWT.

82. "Report on Woodbury's Facial Soap Investigation among Minnesota University Girls," September 1925, p. 24, Research Reports, reel 45; "Woodbury's Facial Soap Investigation among Wisconsin University Girls," May 1925, p. 22, Research Reports, reel 45; "Investigation among Chicago University Girls," May 1925, pp. 21–22, Research Reports, reel 45; "Memo to Miss Lewis from Research Department Informal Summary of Returns from McGill," August 5, 1926, Research Reports, reel 45; "Woodbury's Facial Soap Investigation among Smith College Girls," January 1925, p. 14, Research Reports, reel 45, JWT.

83. Michael Schudson has concluded that ads generally do not create new fears or new needs so much as they play upon and provoke the consumer's exist-

ing insecurities and anxieties. See Schudson, *Advertising, the Uneasy Persuasion,* 207, 248.

84. William Leach makes a similar point about department stores and pleasure in "Transformations in a Culture of Consumption: Women and Department Stores, 1890–1925," *Journal of American History* 71 (September 1984): 319–42.

Chapter 2

1. Bernard Baruch, *Baruch: My Own Story* (New York: Henry Holt, 1957), p. 98.

2. Mark Sullivan, *The Education of an American* (New York, Doubleday, Doran, 1938), p. 98.

3. T. J. Jackson Lears, *No Place of Grace: Antimodernism and the Transformation of American Culture, 1880–1920* (New York: Pantheon Books, 1981), p. 37.

4. Carole Srole, " 'A Position That God Has Not Particularly Assigned to Men': The Feminization of Clerical Work, 1869–1915" (Ph.D. diss., University of California, Los Angeles, 1984), p. 2; C. Wright Mills, *White Collar: The American Middle Classes* (New York: Oxford University Press, 1951), p. 65. For a different view of class status and white-collar work, see Ileen A. DeVault, *Sons and Daughters of Labor: Class and Clerical Work in Turn-of-the-Century Pittsburgh* (Ithaca, N.Y.: Cornell University Press, 1990), p. 95.

5. Will Payne, "Those Contented Clerks: The Broad Line Between Making Good and Making Money," *Saturday Evening Post* 181 (February 6, 1909): 6.

6. Srole, " 'A Position That God Has Not Particularly Assigned to Men,' " pp. 119–21.

7. R. R. Shuman, "The Malcontent in Office Organization," *Iron Trade Review,* August 15, 1901, quoted in DeVault, *Sons and Daughters of Labor,* p. 157.

8. Isaac F. Marcosson, *Before I Forget: A Pilgrimage to the Past* (New York, Dodd, Mead, 1959), pp. 26–27.

9. Louis Brownlow, *A Passion for Politics: The Autobiography of Louis Brownlow, First Half* (Chicago: University of Chicago Press, 1955), pp. 188, 317–24.

10. "On Success in Business: Practical Talks by Practical Men," *Saturday Evening Post* 171 (July 23, 1898): 58; "Abundantly Satisfied," *Christian Advocate* 75 (September 6, 1900): 1449.

11. "The Sin That Everybody Commits and How I Cured Myself of It," *American Magazine* 88 (September 1919): 27; "I Nearly Died of Envy!" *American Magazine* 101 (June 1926): 47.

12. Lears, *No Place of Grace,* pp. 47–58; T. J. Jackson Lears, "From Salvation to Self-Realization: Advertising and the Therapeutic Roots of the Consumer Culture, 1880–1930," in *The Culture of Consumption: Critical Essays in American History, 1880–1980,* ed. Richard Wightman Fox and T. J. Jackson Lears (New York: Pan-

theon, 1983). See also Tom Lutz, *American Nervousness, 1903: An Anecdotal History* (Ithaca, N.Y.: Cornell University Press, 1991).

13. George Beard, *American Nervousness: Its Causes and Consequences* (New York: G. P. Putnam, 1881), p. 122.

14. "Nerves a National Ailment," *Saturday Evening Post* 179 (March 30, 1907): 16; "The Autobiography of a Neurasthenic," *American Magazine* 71 (December 1910): 231.

15. "I Nearly Died of Envy," pp. 46–47, 157–58.

16. Baruch, *My Own Story,* pp. 97–98.

17. Thorstein Veblen, *The Theory of the Leisure Class* (1899; rpt., New York: New American Library, 1953), pp. 120–21; Carole Turbin, "Collars and Consumers: Changing Images of American Manliness and Business," in *Beauty and Business: Commerce, Gender, and Culture in Modern America,* ed. Philip Scranton (New York: Routledge, 2001), p. 91.

18. Walter Creedmoor, "The Problem of Life in New York," *Munsey's Magazine* 27 (July 1902): 636.

19. William Allen White, *The Autobiography of William Allen White,* 2d ed., ed. Sally Foreman Griffith (Lawrence: University Press of Kansas, 1990), p. 99.

20. J. W. Erlich, *A Life in My Hands: An Autobiography* (New York: G.P. Putnam, 1965), p. 39.

21. Will Irwin, "The Spending Jag in New York," *Saturday Evening Post* 185 (December 14, 1912): 9.

22. Warren Susman, "Personality and the Making of Twentieth-Century Culture," in *Culture as History: The Transformation of American Society in the Twentieth Century* (New York: Pantheon Books, 1984), pp. 271–85.

23. "Dominant Envy," *Harper's Weekly* 47 (May 30, 1903): 914–15.

24. "Grains of Gold," *Saturday Evening Post* 77 (November 27, 1897): 13; "The Treatment of Envy," *Nation* 64 (January 7, 1897): 5–6.

25. Albert O. Hirschman, "The Changing Tolerance for Income Inequality in the Course of Economic Development," in *Essays in Trespassing: Economics to Politics and Beyond* (Cambridge: Cambridge University Press, 1981), pp. 39–58. Hirschman would not agree completely with my analysis, for he defines envy only in the resentful sense, not in the aspirational sense.

26. "Our El Dorado," *Munsey's Magazine* 8 (January 1893): 473.

27. "How to Be Happy," *Christian Advocate* 79 (November 17, 1904): 14.

28. "The Path to Contentment," *Independent* 72 (April 18, 1912): 855–56.

29. Mills, *White Collar,* p. 217; Daniel Rodgers, *The Work Ethic in Industrial America, 1850–1920* (Princeton, N.J.: Princeton University Press, 1979), pp. 1–29.

30. Orison Swett Marden, *Architects of Fate; or Steps to Success and Power* (New York: Success, 1897), pp. 115, 117, 119.

31. "In Love with Your Job," *Saturday Evening Post* 181 (November 28, 1908): 18.

32. Charles Richard Dodge, "Riches and the Pursuit of Happiness," *Craftsman,* 11 (November 1906): 237.

33. Srole, " 'A Position That God Has Not Particularly Ordained for Men,' " pp. 99, 122–23, 182; Olivier Zunz, *Making America Corporate, 1870–1920* (Chicago: University of Chicago Press, 1990), pp. 33, 148; Daniel Rodgers, *The Work Ethic in Industrial America*, p. 27; *White Collar,* pp. 219–29; Eric Foner, *The Story of Freedom* (New York: W. W. Norton, 1998), pp. 142–43.

34. Alexis de Tocqueville most famously described American restlessness in his *Democracy in America*, ed. J. P. Mayer, trans. George Lawrence (New York: Doubleday, 1969), pp. 535–38. More recently James M. Jasper, in *Restless Nation: Starting Over in America* (Chicago: University of Chicago Press, 2000), has argued that restlessness is an ingrained part of the American character.

35. "The Royal Road to Happiness," *Saturday Evening Post* 171 (September 24, 1898): 200.

36. Phillips Brooks, "The Duty of the Christian Business Man," *Perfect Freedom* (Boston: Charles E. Brown, 1893), p. 75.

37. "The Passion for the Steady Job," *Saturday Evening Post* 176 (October 17, 1903): 12.

38. Robert Waters, "A Chapter on Ideals," *Christian Advocate* 59 (August 28, 1884): 566. See also "Robert Waters," *Appleton's Cyclopaedeia of American Biography,* vol. 6 (New York: D. Appleton, 1889), p. 387.

39. "Letter to the Editor," *Saturday Evening Post* 172 (September 2, 1899): 155.

40. "What Makes Life Worth Living," *Saturday Evening Post* 171 (October 1, 1898): 216.

41. "Insatiable Aspirations," *Christian Advocate* 77 (March 5, 1902): 374.

42. W. F. Tillett, "The Content of Poverty," *Christian Advocate* 76 (September 19, 1901): 1493.

43. T. H. Huxley, *Evolution and Ethics,* in *Evolution & Ethics: T.H. Huxley's Evolution and Ethics with New Essays on Its Victorian and Sociobiological Context*, ed. James Paradis and George C. Williams (Princeton, N.J.: Princeton University Press, 1989), p. 85.

44. Waters, "A Chapter on Ideals," p. 566.

45. "The Passion for the Steady Job," p. 12.

46. "What Makes Life Worth Living," p. 216.

47. "Maxims That Have Made Millions," *Saturday Evening Post* 172 (July 2, 1899): 52; Russell Sage, "The Gospel of Saving," *Saturday Evening Post* 173 (December 8, 1900): 10; "Economy for Young Men," *Christian Advocate,* 59 (April 10, 1884): 10.

48. Orison Swett Marden, "Keeping Up Appearances," *Christian Advocate* 79 (November 10, 1904): 1819.

49. Perriton Maxwell, "The Poor Richard Papers: The Importance of Being Well-Dressed," *Saturday Evening Post* 171 (March 18, 1899): 607.

50. Walter Creedmoor, "The Problem of Life in New York: How a Young Man of Moderate Income Can Live in the Metropolis Most Satisfactorily, and Qualify Himself for Business and Social Success," *Munsey's Magazine* 27 (August 1902): 780; "The Problem of Life in New York," *Munsey's Magazine* 27 (July 1902): 634–37.

51. Roland Marchand, *Advertising the American Dream: Making Way for Modernity, 1920–1940* (Berkeley: University of California Press, 1985), pp. 208–17; *Saturday Evening Post* 181 (September 19, 1908): 33; *Saturday Evening Post* 184 (October 14, 1911): 1; *Saturday Evening Post* 181 (March 27, 1909): 35; *Saturday Evening Post* 182 (October 30, 1909): 27; *Saturday Evening Post* 181 (April 24, 1909): 37.

52. Charles P. Steinmetz, "The World Belongs to the Dissatisfied," *American Magazine* 85 (May 1918): 39; "Charles Proteus Steinmetz," *Dictionary of American Biography*, vol. 9, ed. Dumas Malone (New York: Scribner's, 1964), pp. 565–66.

53. John B. Kennedy, "Go Fast, Young Man, Go Fast: An Interview with Cyrus H. K. Curtis," *Colliers* 76 (November 21, 1925): 24.

54. "Cyrus H. K. Curtis," *National Cyclopaedia of American Biography*, vol. 24 (New York: J. T. White, 1935), pp. 26–27.

55. M. K. Wisehart, "Henry Ford Talks to Young Men," *American Magazine* 108 (August 1929): 44–45.

56. "Ford, Henry," in *National Cyclopaedia of American Biography*, vol. 38 (New York: J. T. White, 1953), pp. 1–4.

57. Clark Davis discusses corporate efforts to make workers more loyal to the company during this period. See Clark Davis, *Company Men: White-Collar Life and Corporate Cultures in Los Angeles, 1892–1941* (Baltimore: Johns Hopkins University Press, 2000), pp. 42, 47.

58. Joseph H. Appel, *My Own Story, Illustrating the Spirit and Service of Big Business* (New York: Platt and Peck, 1913), pp. 87, 88, 91–99, 116–17, 133–34, 143.

59. "The Value of Stability," *Saturday Evening Post* 195 (June 16, 1923): 28.

60. "The Routine Worker," *Saturday Evening Post* 195 (June 30, 1923): 22.

61. "Great Oaks from Little Acorns," *Saturday Evening Post* 195 (June 9, 1923): 26.

62. "The Sin That Everybody Commits," pp. 118, 131.

63. "I Nearly Died of Envy," pp. 46, 160.

64. "The Sin That Everybody Commits," pp. 118, 131; "I Nearly Died of Envy," pp. 46, 160; "Why I Quit Thinking About Myself," *American Magazine* 103 (April 1927): 29, 137–38, 140–42;

65. Dale Carnegie, *How to Win Friends and Influence People* (1936; rpt., New York: Simon and Schuster, 1964), pp. 58–66.

66. Susman, "Personality and the Making of Twentieth-Century Culture," pp. 271–85; Peter N. Stearns, *Battleground of Desire: The Struggle for Self-Control in Modern America* (New York: New York University Press, 1999), pp. 110, 175; Angel Kwolek-Folland, *Engendering Business: Men and Women in the Corporate Office, 1870–1930* (Baltimore: Johns Hopkins University Press, 1994), pp. 53–54.

67. Stearns, *Battleground,* p. 160.

68. See Stearns, *Battleground,* pp. 154–65; Edmund Wilson, "The Best People," *Scribner's* 91 (March 1932): 153–60.

69. Walter E. Weyl, "The New Wealth," *Harper's Magazine* 132 (March 1916): 610.

70. Robert Lynd and Helen Lynd, *Middletown: A Study in Contemporary American Culture* (New York: Harcourt Brace, 1929), pp. 81, 162, 239.

71. *Saturday Evening Post,* 202 (July 20, 1929): 105.

72. *Saturday Evening Post,* 197 (December 6, 1924): 157.

73. *Saturday Evening Post* 197 (March 28, 1925): 116–17.

74. *Saturday Evening Post* 196 (April 26, 1924): 49.

75. Roland Marchand also noted this trend. He quotes Francesco Nicosia and Robert Mayer, who observed that gradually a "deflection of the success ethic from the sphere of production to that of consumption" occurred. See Marchand, *Advertising the American Dream,* p. 222; Lynd and Lynd, *Middletown,* pp. 80–82.

Chapter 3

1. Theodore Roosevelt to Liberty Hyde Bailey, August 1, 1908, Liberty Hyde Bailey Collection, Cornell University Archives, Collection #21/2/1400, box 4, folder 2.

2. Herbert Quick, "The Women on the Farms," *Good Housekeeping* 57 (October 1913): 426–36. The U.S. Census Department categorized as rural those people who lived in towns with fewer than 2,500 residents. Department of the Interior, Census Office, *Report on Population of the United States at the Eleventh Census: 1890, Volume I, Part I, Population* (Washington, D.C.: Government Printing Office, 1890), p. lxix.

3. J. H. Kolb and E. deS. Brunner, *A Study of Rural Society* (Boston: Houghton Mifflin, 1940), 206; C. E. Lively and Conrad Tauber, *Rural Migration in the United States,* Works Progress Administration Research Monograph 19 (Washington, D.C.: Government Printing Office, 1939), pp. xv, 13, 14–16; David Danbom, *The Resisted Revolution: Urban America and the Industrialization of Agriculture, 1900–1930* (Ames: Iowa State University Press, 1979), pp. 134–35; Dennis Gilbert and Joseph A. Kahl, *The American Class Structure: A New Synthesis,* 4th ed. (Belmont, Calif.: Wadsworth, 1993), pp. 66–67; C. Wright Mills, *White Collar: The American Middle Classes* (New York: Oxford University Press, 1951), pp. 3–20; Lewis Corey, *The Crisis of the Middle Class* (New York: Colcivi, Friede, 1935), pp. 137–40.

4. William Allen White, *The Autobiography of William Allen White,* 2d ed., ed. Sally Foreman Griffith (Lawrence: University Press of Kansas, 1990), p. 13.

5. Daniel Boorstin, *The Americans: The Democratic Experience* (New York: Random House, 1973), pp. 119–45; Joel Benton, *Harper's Weekly* 39 (October 26, 1895): 1026.

6. White, *Autobiography,* p. 329.

7. Mary Hoffman, *Buying Habits of Small-Town Women* (Kansas City: Ferry-Hanly Advertising, 1926), pp. 11–13.

8. Ernest R. Groves, "Suggestion and City-Drift," in *Rural Manhood* 7 (April 1916): 46–52.

9. Lary May, *Screening Out the Past: The Birth of Mass Culture and the Mo-*

tion Picture Industry (New York: Oxford University Press, 1980), pp. 163–65; William Harrison Hays, "Supervision from Within," in *The Story of the Films*, ed. Joseph Kennedy (New York: A. W. Shaw, 1927), pp. 33–40, quoted in May, *Screening Out the Past*, p. 236.

10. Albert Blumenthal, "A Sociological Study of a Small Town" (Ph.D. diss., University of Chicago, 1932), pp. 385–86, 399.

11. Hal Barron, *Mixed Harvest: The Second Great Transformation in the Rural North, 1870–1930* (Chapel Hill: University of North Carolina Press, 1997), pp. 156, 193–94, 206; Mary Neth, *Preserving the Family Farm: Women, Community, and the Foundations of Agribusiness in the Midwest, 1900–1940* (Baltimore: Johns Hopkins University Press, 1995), pp. 201–4. Ronald Kline also discusses the way rural people reacted to, resisted, and sometimes altered urban technologies. They often used such technologies in ways quite different from urban people. See Ronald Kline, *Consumers in the Country: Technology and Social Change in Rural America* (Baltimore: Johns Hopkins University Press, 2000). For discussions of capitalism in the countryside, see Richard Hofstadter, *The Age of Reform: From Bryan to F.D.R.* (New York: Knopf, 1955), pp. 37–40; Joyce Appleby, "Commercial Farming and the 'Agrarian Myth' in the Early Republic," *Journal of American History* 68 (March 1982): 833–49; David Blanke, *Sowing the American Dream: How Consumer Culture Took Root in the Rural Midwest* (Athens: Ohio University Press, 2000), pp. 1–65. Allan Kulikoff has articulated the connection between consumer desire and market orientation of farmers in the early nineteenth century. See Allan Kulikoff, "The Transition to Capitalism in Rural America," *William and Mary Quarterly*, 3d ser., 46 (January 1989): 120–44.

12. Marquis W. Child, *The Farmer Takes a Hand: The Electric Power Revolution in Rural America* (Garden City, N.Y.: Doubleday, 1952), p. 35. See also Jack Doyle, *Lines Across the Land: Rural Electric Cooperatives, The Changing Politics of Energy in Rural America* (Washington, D.C.: Environmental Policy Institute, 1979), p. 4; Paul T. Cherington, "Some Recent Changes in the Rural and Small-Town Market," *J. Walter Thompson News Bulletin*, no. 114, July 1925, News Bulletin Series, Newsletter Collection, box 1, JWT; Ellis Lore Kirkpatrick, *The Farmer's Standard of Living,* (New York: Century, 1929), pp. 242–43; Kline, *Consumers in the Country,* pp. 5, 87–112, 114–15, 285–98.

13. Blumenthal, "Sociological Study," p. 144.

14. Thorstein Veblen, *The Theory of the Leisure Class* (1899; rpt., New York: New American Library, 1953), p. 72.

15. Blumenthal, "Sociological Study," pp. 104–5

16. Newell LeRoy Sims, "Hoosier Village: A Sociological Study with Special Reference to Social Causation" (Ph.D. diss., Columbia University, 1912), p. 92. See also Neth, *Preserving the Family Farm,* 193–94.

17. Neth, *Preserving the Family Farm,* pp. 11–12, 193, 250–52; John M. Gillette, *Rural Sociology* (New York: Macmillan, 1922), p. 380; personal communication with Hazel Stover, March 16, 2001; Truman S. Vance, "Why Young Men

Leave the Farm," *Independent* 70 (March 16, 1911): 555, 556; O. Latham Hatcher, *Rural Girls in the City for Work: A Study Made for the Southern Woman's Educational Alliance* (Richmond: Garrett and Massie, 1930), pp. 37, 42–43; Paul Landis, *Rural Life in Process* (New York: McGraw-Hill, 1940), p. 410; Florence Ward, *Farm Women's Problems,* USDA Circular 148, November 1920, quoted in Catherine McNicol Stock, *Main Street in Crisis: The Great Depression and the Old Middle Class on the Northern Plains* (Chapel Hill: University of North Carolina Press, 1992), p. 150.

18. Joel Benton, *Harper's Weekly* 39 (October 26, 1895): 1026; Wilson Gee and William Henry Stauffer, *Rural and Urban Living Standards in Virginia,* Institute for Research in the Social Sciences, Institute Monograph no. 6 (Charlottesville: University of Virginia, Institute for Research in the Social Sciences,1929), p. 8.

19. Quick, "The Women on the Farms"; E. L. Morgan and Henry J. Burt, "Community Relations of Rural Young People," Missouri Agricultural Experiment Station Research Bulletin no. 110, October 1927, pp. 16–26; Lively and Tauber, *Rural Migration in the United States,* p. 14; Pitirim Sorokin and Carle C. Zimmerman, *Principles of Rural-Urban Sociology* (New York: Henry Holt, 1929), p. 546; Kolb and Brunner, *A Study of Rural Society,* p. 222; Gillette, *Rural Sociology,* p. 379.

20. "The Ideas of a Plain Country Woman," *Ladies' Home Journal* 30 (February 1913): 32; USDA, Office of the Secretary, Domestic Needs of Farm Women, Report 104 (Washington, D.C.: Government Printing Office, 1915), p. 43, quoted in Kline, *Consumers in the Country,* p. 1; Kulikoff, "The Transition to Capitalism," pp. 120–44; Blanke, *Sowing the American Dream,* pp. 1–65; Roy Hinman Holmes, "The Passing of the Farmer," *Atlantic Monthly,* October 1912, reprinted in *The Rural Community, Ancient and Modern,* ed. Newell LeRoy Sims (New York: Scribner's, 1920), p. 378; Hatcher, *Rural Girls,* p. 58. As the club manager indicated, when rural young women decided to migrate to cities, their feelings were tangled and their motives mixed. Yet while a variety of feelings and circumstances may have factored into women's evaluations of farm life, envy was certainly an emotion with which many women struggled as they weighed the choice between city and country.

21. USDA, "Average Clothing Expenditures of 86 Farm Families of Franklin County, Vermont, Preliminary Report, 1927," in Kirkpatrick, *The Farmer's Standard of Living,* pp. 103–5; USDA, "Present Trends in Home Sewing," Misc. Pub. no. 4, 1927, in Kirkpatrick, *The Farmer's Standard of Living,* pp. 116–19.

22. "Lulu Rutenber Bartz," in Anne McCall and Mary Jane Henderson, *Fragments of Yesterday: A Collection of Childhood Memories in Delaware County from 1892–1929* (Deposit, N.Y.: Courier, 1993), p. 60.

23. Mary Timothy, *The Growing Years: A Family Story* (Salt Lake City: Utah Printing Company, 1961), pp. 192, 199.

24. Annie Pike Greenwood, *We Sagebrush Folks* (1934; rpt., Moscow: University of Idaho Press, 1988), pp. 4, 311–17.

25. For more examples, see Blumenthal, "Sociological Study," p. 398; Louise Rosenfield Noun, *Journey to Autonomy: A Memoir* (Ames: Iowa State University

Press, 1990), pp. 23–24; Cyrenus Cole, *I Remember I Remember: A Book of Recollections* (Iowa City: State Historical Society of Iowa, 1936), p. 68; Paul Landis, *Rural Life in Process* (New York: McGraw-Hill, 1940), pp. 138–39.

26. Gillette, *Rural Sociology,* p. 95.

27. "Recreation" [not identified—probably analysis of responses to Commission on Country Life surveys], pp. 6–7, Liberty Hyde Bailey Papers, Cornell University Archives, Collection #21/2/1400, box 4, folder 4–17.

28. Hatcher, *Rural Girls,* p. 34; Blumenthal, "Sociological Study," pp. 44–45.

29. E. L. Morgan and Henry J. Burt, "Community Relations of Rural Young People," *Missouri Agricultural Experiment Station Research Bulletin,* no. 110, October 1927, pp. 24–25, 30.

30. Neth, *Preserving the Family Farm,* pp. 250–52.

31. "Why Young People Leave Rural Sections for the City," quoted in Hatcher, *Rural Girls,* p. 56.

32. Martha Foote Crow, *The American Country Girl* (New York: Frederick A. Stokes, 1915), p. 7; Danbom, *The Resisted Revolution,* p. 47; Hal Barron, *Those Who Stayed Behind: Rural Society in Nineteenth-Century New England* (Cambridge: Cambridge University Press, 1984), pp. 41–48; Neth, *Preserving the Family Farm,* pp. 102–6.

33. Ruth Ashmore, "The Country Girl," *Ladies' Home Journal* 10 (July 1893): 10.

34. Ruth Ashmore "The Girl in a Small Community," *Ladies' Home Journal* 12 (March 1895): 16.

35. Helen Burgess, "Her Tailor-Made Gown," *American Magazine* 30 (September 1890): 369–72.

36. Ashmore, "The Country Girl," p. 10.

37. Helen Jay, "The Social Life of a Farmer's Wife," *Ladies' Home Journal* 12 (May 1895): 22.

38. Mrs. James Speers, "If I Were a Country Girl," *Rural Manhood* 6 (November 1915): 375–77.

39. Roderick Nash, *Wilderness and the American Mind* (New Haven, Conn.: Yale University Press, 1967), pp. 67–82; Michael Kammen, *Mystic Chords of Memory: The Transformation of Tradition in American Culture* (New York: Knopf, 1991), pp. 44–45.

40. Carl C. Taylor, "Where Does the Farmer Get the Standard by Which He Measures His Life and Living?" in *Farm Income and Farm Life*, ed. Dwight Sanderson (New York: University of Chicago Press for the American Country Life Association, 1927), pp. 65–66.

41. Danbom, *The Resisted Revolution,* pp. 84–86; Neth, *Preserving the Family Farm,* pp. 107–8, 124, 196–97; Barron, *Those Who Stayed Behind,* pp. 41, 49; Kline, *Consumers in the Country,* pp. 7, 9–10, 12–14.

42. Crow, *The American Country Girl,* p. 263.

43. Gillette, *Rural Sociology,* p. 508.

44. Laura Amos, "As a Student Sees Farm Life," in *Farm Youth: Proceedings*

of the Ninth National Country Life Conference, Washington D.C., 1926 (New York: University of Chicago Press for the American Country Life Association, 1926), pp. 22–23.

45. "Mary Meek Atkeson," in *Who's Who of American Women* (Wilmette, Ill.: Marquis Who's Who, 1958); Mary Meek Atkeson, *The Woman on the Farm* (New York: Century, 1924), pp. 134, 138–39.

46. Kolb and Brunner, *A Study of Rural Society,* p. 175; Research Department Reports, Small Town and Rural Investigation (Questionnaires by Mail) Among Subscribers to *People's Home Journal,* 1925, box 2 of 2, Reports, 1925, 1936, 1954, n.d., Printed Material 1923, p. 65, JWT. See also Barron, *Mixed Harvest,* pp. 198–99.

47. "Elementary Garment Making: A Manual for Junior Extension Workers In Clothing," *Cornell Junior Extension Bulletin,* Bulletin 2, December 1918, Cornell University Archives, Collection #23/2/749, box 46. Extracts from Annual Report, 1924, Extension Service in Home Economics, New York State College of Agriculture at Cornell University, Ithaca, N.Y., School of Home Economics; Cornell University Archives, Collection #23/2/749, box 24, folder 1; Marilyn Irvin Holt, *Linoleum, Better Babies, and the Modern Farm Woman, 1890–1930* (Albuquerque: University of New Mexico Press, 1995), p. 147.

48. Atkeson, *The Woman on the Farm,* pp. 131–39; Neth, *Preserving the Family Farm,* p. 123.

49. Kirkpatrick, *Farmer's Standard of Living,* pp. 138–39.

50. Neth, *Preserving the Family Farm,* pp. 122–24, 192–94.

51. Crow, *The American Country Girl,* pp. 346–47.

52. Chester T. Crowell, "Why the Young People Leave the Farm," *Independent,* 101 (February 14, 1920): 237–38.

53. Morgan and Burt, "Community Relations of Rural Young People," pp. 43, 74–75. See also Landis, *Rural Life in Process,* pp. 452–56.

54. Hatcher, *Rural Girls,* pp. 34, xv.

Chapter 4

1. Edgar Lee Masters, *Across Spoon River: An Autobiography* (1936; rpt., New York: Octagon Books, 1969), p. 79.

2. Pitirim Sorokin and Carle C. Zimmerman, *Principles of Rural-Urban Sociology* (New York: Henry Holt, 1929), p. 402.

3. Theodore L. Cuyler, "Moral and Spiritual Dangers of Young Men," *Christian Advocate* 64 (January 31, 1889).

4. Richard Hofstadter, *The Age of Reform: From Bryan to F.D.R.* (New York: Alfred A. Knopf, 1955), pp. 37–40; Joyce Appleby, "Commercial Farming and the 'Agrarian Myth' in the Early Republic," *Journal of American History* 68 (March 1982): 833–49; Allan Kulikoff, "The Transition to Capitalism in Rural America," *William and Mary Quarterly,* 3d ser., 46 (January 1989): 120–44; David Blanke,

Sowing the American Dream: How Consumer Culture Took Root in the Rural Midwest (Athens: Ohio University Press, 2000), pp. 12–65.

5. Charles Dillon, "Education and Discontent," *Outlook* 91 (April 10, 1909): 831, 830.

6. Truman S. Vance, "Why Young Men Leave the Farm," *Independent* 70 (March 16, 1911): 555, 556.

7. E. L. Morgan and Henry J. Burt, "Community Relations of Rural Young People," *Missouri Agricultural Experiment Station Research Bulletin,* no. 110, October 1927, pp. 5–77.

8. William L. Bowers, *The Country Life Movement in America, 1900–1920* (Port Washington, N.Y.: Kennikat Press, 1974), p. 9; "The Political Menace of the Discontented," *Atlantic Monthly* 78 (October 1896): 449.

9. Liberty Hyde Bailey, "Why Do the Boys Leave the Farm?" *Century Magazine* 76 (July 1906): 411, 412, 414; John Gillette, *Constructive Rural Sociology* (New York: Sturgis and Walton, 1913), p. 71.

10. John Bookwalter, *Rural Versus Urban* (New York: Knickerbocker Press, 1910), pp. 247, 248; Paul L. Vogt, *Introduction to Rural Sociology* (New York: D. Appleton, 1917), p. 103; John Gillette, *Rural Sociology* (New York: Macmillan, 1922), pp. 264–65; David M. Kennedy, *Freedom from Fear: The American People in Depression and War, 1929–1945* (New York: Oxford University Press, 1999), p. 22.

11. Bruce Barton, "You Don't Altogether Like Your Job? The Story of Charles Seabrook," *American Magazine* 91 (May 1921): 34, 35, 114, 117–18.

12. Henry J. Fletcher, "The Drift of Population to the Cities: Remedies," *Forum* 19 (October 1895): 739; Gillette, *Constructive Rural Sociology,* p. 131; Gillette, *Rural Sociology,* p. 95; Ernest Groves, *The Rural Mind and Social Welfare* (Chicago: University of Chicago Press, 1922), pp. 58, 73; Sorokin and Zimmerman, *Principles of Rural-Urban Sociology,* pp. 41, 42.

13. Albert Blumenthal, "A Sociological Study of a Small Town" (Ph.D. diss., University of Chicago, 1932), pp. 44–45, 260–61.

14. Walter P. Chrysler in collaboration with Boyden Sparkes, *Life of an American Workman* (New York: Dodd, Mead, 1950), p. 51.

15. Florence Elizabeth Ward, "The Farm Family: Its Contribution to the Nation," in *The Country Life of the Nation,* ed. Wilson Gee (Chapel Hill: University of North Carolina Press, 1930), pp. 111–12.

16. Henry Wallace, *Letters to the Farm Boy* (New York: Macmillan, 1900), p. 40.

17. Hamlin Garland, *Main Traveled Roads: Six Mississippi Valley Stories* (New York: Rinehart, 1954), p. 70.

18. Hamlin Garland, *A Son of the Middle Border* (New York: Macmillan, 1924), pp. 177, 200, 205, 365–66. While the events Garland recounts occurred in the 1870s and 1880s, they were representative of the farm sentiment of succeeding generations. His *Main Traveled Roads,* first published in 1891, was extremely popu-

lar and controversial. The book's supporters argued that it was an accurate portrayal of farm life. See *A Son of the Middle Border*, p. 415.

19. H. E. Wilkinson, *Memories of an Iowa Farm Boy* (Ames: Iowa State University Press, 1994), pp. 107, 152–54.

20. "The Political Menace of the Discontented," p. 449.

21. Roy Hinman Holmes, "The Passing of the Farmer," *Atlantic Monthly* (October 1912), reprinted in *The Rural Community, Ancient and Modern*, ed. Newell LeRoy Sims (New York: Scribner's, 1920), pp. 378–79; Gillette, *Constructive Rural Sociology* (New York: Macmillan, 1922), pp. 105–6.

22. Wilkinson, *Memories*, p. 84; Paul Landis, *Rural Life in Process* (New York: McGraw-Hill, 1940), pp. 138–39.

23. John Bell, "From the Man Who Holds the Plow," *Outlook* 91 (April 10, 1909): 826; *Farm Youth: Proceedings of the Ninth National Country Life Association, Washington, D.C., 1926* (Chicago: University of Chicago Press for the American Country Life Association, 1926), pp. 64–65; Gillette, *Rural Sociology*, p. 490; Edmund de S. Brunner, Gwendolyn Hughes, and Marjorie Patten, *American Agricultural Villages* (New York: George H. Doran, 1927), pp. 150–51.

24. Edwin Osgood Grover, "The Country Boy's Creed," *Rural Manhood* 3 (April 1912).

25. Fletcher, "The Drift," p. 745.

26. Orison Swett Marden, *Architects of Fate; or, Steps to Success and Power* (New York: Success: 1897), pp. 93, 94, 423.

27. Wallace, *Letters to the Farm Boy*, pp. 42, 44.

28. "Where Are the Americans?" *Munsey's Magazine* 12 (January 1895): 442.

29. Isaac F. Marcosson, "Why the American Farmer Is Rich," *Munsey's Magazine* 46 (November 1911): 168.

30. William Bowers, in *The Country Life Movement in America, 1900–1920*, pp. 28–29, argued that within the Country Life movement there was a heated debate between those who tried to develop farming as a business and those who sought to preserve it as a lifestyle emblematic of noncommercial values. He maintained that the divided ideology and the divergent approaches were institutionalized through the founding, in 1919, of the National Country Life Association, which emphasized the significance of farming as a way of life, and the establishment, in 1920, of the American Farm Bureau Federation, which focused on farming as a business and which ultimately outlived the Country Life movement. On the goal of farm modernization, see Ronald Kline, *Consumers in the Country: Technology and Social Change in America* (Baltimore: Johns Hopkins University Press, 2000), p. 2.

31. Danbom, *The Resisted Revolution*, pp. 85–86, 144; Hal S. Barron, *Those Who Stayed Behind: Rural Society in Nineteenth-Century New England* (Cambridge: Cambridge University Press, 1984), 48–50; Mary Neth, *Preserving the Family Farm: Women, Community, and the Foundations of Agribusiness in the Midwest, 1900–1940* (Baltimore: Johns Hopkins University Press), pp. 97–99, 216–27; Catherine McNicol Stock, *Main Street in Crisis: The Great Depression and the Old Middle*

Class on the Northern Plains (Chapel Hill: University of North Carolina Press, 1992); Kline, *Consumers in the Country,* p. 13.

32. Barron, *Those Who Stayed Behind,* p. 50.

33. Dillon, "Education and Discontent," pp. 830–31.

34. Gillette, *Rural Sociology,* pp. 179, 191.

35. Neth, *Preserving the Family Farm,* pp. 97–121, 193–213, 217–19; Danbom, *The Resisted Revolution,* pp. 72–74.

36. Barton, "You Don't Altogether Like Your Job?" pp. 34–35, 114, 118–118; "Charles Seabrook," *National Cyclopaedia of American Biography,* vol. 53 (New York: J. T. White, 1971), p. 240; "Charles Seabrook," *Who Was Who in America with World Notables,* vol. 4, *1961–1968* (Chicago: Marquis Who's Who, 1968), p. 844. Stock maintains that it was not until the 1930s that managerial capitalism was fully introduced into American agricultural operations. See Stock, *Main Street in Crisis,* p. 208.

37. Garland, "Up the Coule," in *Main Traveled Roads,* p. 70.

38. Ellis Lore Kirkpatrick, *The Farmer's Standard of Living* (New York: Century, 1929), pp. 101, 105–12, 121.

39. Wilson Gee and William Henry Stauffer, *Rural and Urban Living Standards in Virginia,* University of Virginia Institute for Research in the Social Sciences, Institute Monograph no. 6 (Charlottesville: University of Virginia Institute for Research in the Social Sciences, 1929), p. 31.

40. Neth, *Preserving the Family Farm,* pp. 264–66; Stock, *Main Street in Crisis,* p. 89.

41. Samuel Strauss, "Things Are in the Saddle," *Atlantic Monthly* 134 (November 1924): 579. See also Eric Foner, *The Story of Freedom* (New York: W. W. Norton, 1998), p. 151. In a similar vein, Charles McGovern discusses the way consuming came to be described as a particularly American and democratic activity. See Charles McGovern, "Sold American: Inventing the Consumer, 1890–1940" (Ph.D. diss., Harvard University, 1993), pp. 62–156.

42. Carl Taylor, "Where Does the Farmer Get the Standard by Which He Measures His Life and Living?" in *Farm Income and Farm Life,* ed. Dwight Sanderson (New York: the University of Chicago Press for the American Country Life Association, 1927), p. 66.

Chapter 5

1. Louise Rosenfield Noun, *Journey to Autonomy: A Memoir* (Ames: Iowa State University Press, 1990), pp. 23–24.

2. Philippe Aries, *Centuries of Childhood: A Social History of Family Life,* trans. Robert Baldick,(New York: Knopf, 1962), pp. 110, 119. See also Joan Jacobs Brumberg, *Fasting Girls: The History of Anorexia Nervosa* (New York: New American Library, Plume Books, 1989), pp. 126–28.

3. Although defining children as individuals under the age of sixteen is somewhat arbitrary, it seems to accord with the way turn-of-the-century Americans defined

childhood. Those working to regulate child labor, for instance, used sixteen as the dividing line between childhood and adulthood. See Russell Friedman, *Kids at Work: Lewis Hine and the Crusade Against Child Labor* (New York: Clarion Books, 1994), pp. 1, 22–23; John Spargo, *The Bitter Cry of Children* (New York: Macmillan, 1906), pp. 148–53, 163–67, reprinted in Richard Hofstadter, *The Progressive Movement, 1900–1915* (Englewood Cliffs, N.J.: Prentice-Hall, 1963), pp. 39–44.

4. Gail Hamilton, "The Inequalities of Fortune," in *The Character Building Readers—Sixth Year: Fidelity and Justice* ed. Ellen Kenyon-Warner (New York: Hinds, Noble, and Eldredge, 1910), pp. 152–59. Gail Hamilton was the pen name of Mary Abigail Dodge (1833–1896), who edited the midcentury children's magazine *Our Young Folks*. See "Mary Abigail Dodge," *Dictionary of American Biography*, vol. 3 (New York: Scribner's, 1959), p. 350.

5. G. Stanley Hall and Theodore L. Smith, "Showing Off and Bashfulness as Stages of Self-Consciousness," *Pedagogical Seminary* 10 (June 1903): 171; Anna Kohler, "Children's Sense of Money," *Studies in Education* 1 (March 1897): 323–31.

6. Hall and Smith, "Showing Off" p. 173; John Dollard, "The Life History in Community Studies," *American Sociological Review* 3 (1938): 733–34.

7. Nathalie Dana, *Young in New York: A Memoir of a Victorian Girlhood* (Garden City, N.Y.: Doubleday, 1963), pp. 64–65, 76–77.

8. Viviana Zelizer, *Pricing the Priceless Child: The Changing Social Value of Children* (New York: Basic Books, 1985), pp. 5, 103, 112; Helen B. Seymour, "Money Matters With Young People," *Outlook* 48 (September 23, 1893): 553, quoted in Zelizer, *Pricing the Priceless Child*, p. 103; David Nasaw, *Children of the City: At Work and at Play* (Garden City, N.Y.: Anchor Press, Doubleday, 1985), pp. 130–37.

9. Anna Kohler, "Children's Sense of Money," p. 324; William Byron Forbush, *Guidebook to Childhood* (Philadelphia: G. W. Jacobs, 1915), pp. 155, 246–50; Thomas D. Eliot, "Money and the Child's Own Standards of Living," *Journal of Home Economics,* 24 (January 1932): 2; Francis Frisbie O'Donnell, "Every Child Needs an Allowance," *Parents Magazine* 5 (March 1930): 18–19, 38–40; Gary Cross, *Kid's Stuff: Toys and the Changing World of American Childhood* (Cambridge: Harvard University Press, 1997), p. 51; David I. Macleod, *The Age of the Child: Children in America, 1890–1920* (New York: Twayne, 1998), 18.

10. Thorstein Veblen, *The Theory of the Leisure Class* (New York: New American Library, 1953), p. 54; William Allen White, *The Autobiography of William Allen White,* 2d ed., ed. Sally Foreman Griffith (Lawrence: University Press of Kansas, 1990), p. 20. For further evidence of the pride families took from the fact their children did not work, see Brumberg, *Fasting Girls,* pp. 126–27.

11. Hall and Smith, "Showing Off," p. 174, emphasis in the original.

12. Linus Kline and C. J. France, "The Psychology of Ownership," *Pedagogical Seminary* 6 (December 1899): 452, 454.

13. Hall and Smith, "Showing Off," pp. 174–75; Kline and France, "The Psychology of Ownership," p. 453.

14. Hall and Smith, "Showing Off," pp. 174–75.

15. Adolf Meyer, "The Lies That Children Tell," *Scientific Monthly* 23 (December 1926): 522, 526, 527.

16. Hall and Smith, "Showing Off," pp. 176–77.

17. William Leach, "Child-World in the Promised Land," in *The Mythmaking Frame of Mind: Social Imagination and American Culture,* ed. James Gilbert, Amy Gilman, Donald M. Scott, and Joan W. Scott (Belmont, Calif.: Wadsworth, 1993), pp. 209–38; William Leach, *Land of Desire: Merchants, Power, and the Rise of a New American Culture* (New York: Random House, Vintage, 1993), pp. 85ff.

18. "Why I Quit Thinking About Myself," *American Magazine* 103 (April 1927): 137; Dollard, "The Life History in Community Studies," p. 357.

19. Cross, *Kids' Stuff,* p. 8; Bernard Mergen, "Made, Bought, and Stolen: Toys and the Culture of Childhood," in *Small Worlds: Children and Adolescents in America 1850–1950,* ed. Elliot West and Paula Petrik (Lawrence: University Press of Kansas, 1992), p. 88.

20. Veblen, *Theory of the Leisure Class,* pp. 69–70. (Veblen does not discuss children but describes wives as "vicarious" consumers; the term seems appropriate to bourgeois children as well.)

21. Filson Young, "Children's Parties," *Living Age* 272 (Feruary 17, 1912): 431.

22. Sol Bloom, *The Autobiography of Sol Bloom* (New York: Putnam, 1948), pp. 174–75.

23. Viola Goode Liddell, *With a Southern Accent* (Norman: University of Oklahoma Press, 1948), pp. 67–68.

24. Dana, *Young in New York,* p. 99.

25. Hall and Smith, "Showing Off," pp. 172–73. The wit of the remark about the cupola may indicate that adult reporters shaped or altered the children's actual remarks.

26. Loose advertisements in *St. Nicholas Magazine* 40, pt. 1, nos. 3–6 (1913): 23, 30, 42 (Cornell University Library Annex); St. Nicholas advertisements in *St. Nicholas Magazine* 43 (November 1915–April 1916): 47.

27. White, *Autobiography,* p. 29.

28. Daniel Boorstin, *The Americans: The Democratic Experience* (New York: Random House, 1973), p. 129. For other accounts of children playing with paper dolls cut from catalogs see the reminiscence of Annis Hume Hillis of Hamden, New York, in Anne McCall and Mary Jane Henderson, *Fragments of Yesterday: A Collection of Childhood Memories in Delaware County, 1892–1929* (Deposit, N.Y.: Courier, 1993). p. 63; see also a customer letter to Sears reprinted in David Cohn, *The Good Old Days: A History of American Morals and Manners as Seen Through the Sears Roebuck Catalogs 1905 to the Present* (New York: Simon and Schuster, 1940), 574.

29. Leach, *Land of Desire,* pp. 328–38; Miriam Formanek Brunell, *Made to Play House: Dolls and the Commercialization of American Girlhood, 1830–1930.* (New Haven, Conn.: Yale University Press, 1993), pp. 160–84; Harry Selfridge,

"Children's Day," from "Notes Concerning Subjects of Talks Made by H.G.S. to Department Heads . . . , as compiled by Waldo Warren, 1901–1906," Marshall Field Archives, Chicago, September 25, 1905, quoted in Leach, "Child-World in the Promised Land," p. 214.

30. David McClelland, studying many of the same children's readers as those examined here, concluded that stories in the readers were rich historical sources because they tended to "reflect the motives and values of the culture" and presented these values less subtly and more directly than adult literature. Additionally, children's schoolbooks were valuable because they were written and deemed "appropriate for all children to read, not just those from a special social class." David C. McClelland, *The Achieving Society* (Princeton, N.J.: Van Nostrund, 1961), p. 71.

31. "The Peacock," in *Sheldon's Modern School Fourth Reader* (New York: Butler, Sheldon, 1885), pp. 40–42; For another example, see Hans Christian Andersen, "The Conceited Apple Branch," in Stanley Firman and Ethel Maltby, *The Winston Fourth Reader* (Philadelphia: J. C. Winston, 1918), pp. 13–18.

32. Dana, *Young in New York,* p. 4.

33. Virginia Allen Durr, *Outside the Magic Circle: The Autobiography of Virginia Allen Durr,* ed. Hollinger F. Barnard (New York: Simon and Schuster, 1985), p. 32.

34. Joseph Addison, "Discontent—An Allegory," in *McGuffey's Sixth Eclectic Reader* (New York: American Book Company, 1896), pp. 300–301.

35. Charles McKay, "The Miller of the Dee," in *Barnes National Reader* (New York: A. S. Barnes, 1884), pp. 177–78.

36. See also Edna Henry Lee, *The Lee Readers: Fourth Book* (New York: American Book Company, 1912), p. 213; Howard Copeland Hill and Rollo LaVerne Lyman, *Reading and Living* (New York: Scribner's, 1924), pp. 220–21; John Manly, Edith Rickert, and Nina Leubrie, *Good Reading: Fourth Reader* (New York: Scribner's, 1927), pp. 180–81.

37. "Harry's Riches," in *The New McGuffey Fourth Reader* (New York: American Book Company, 1901), pp. 70–74. See also Ellen Kenyon-Warner, *The Character Building Readers, Fourth Year: Thoughtfulness and Devotion* (New York: Hinds, Noble, and Eldredge, 1910), p. 227. This theme is a continuation of an eighteenth-century pattern documented by Isaac Kramnick in *Republicanism and Bourgeois Radicalism: Political Ideology in Late Eighteenth-Century England and America* (Ithaca, N.Y.: Cornell University Press, 1990), p. 127.

38. "The Discontented Buttercup," in Kenyon-Warner, *The Character Building Readers, Fourth Year,* pp. 103–4.

39. Henry Van Dyke, "The Foolish Fir Tree," in *Reading and Living*, ed. Hill and Lyman, pp. 436–39; See also Ellen Kenyon-Warner, *Character Building Readers, Second Reader: Courage* (New York: Hinds, Noble and Eldredge, 1910), pp. 54–61; Ralph Waldo Emerson, "Fable," in *Our Country's Reader*, ed. Leonard Lemmon (Dallas: Southern, 1903), pp. 76–77; Kenyon-Warner, *The Character Building Readers: Fourth Year,* p. 125; "The Two Jackdaws Who Pretended," in *The*

Kendall Series of Readers, Third Reader, ed. Calvin Kendall and Marion Paine Steven (Boston: D. C. Heath, 1918), pp. 16–18; "The Vine and the Wall," in Kenyon-Warner, *The Character Building Readers, Sixth Year,* p. 72; "What the Snowbirds Said," in *Harper's Third Reader* (New York: American Book Company, 1888), pp. 205–8; Henry Van Dyke, "A Handful of Clay," in Hill and Lyman, *Reading and Living,* pp. 406–9; Manly, Rickert, and Leubrie, *Good Reading,* p. 64; Charles Love Benjamin, "The Discontented Boy," *St. Nicholas* (November 1898): 71–72.

40. Daniel Rodgers has noted a similar conservative tone in the children's stories and advice manuals of the early to mid-nineteenth century. Daniel Rodgers, "Socializing Middle-Class Children: Institutions, Fables, and Work Values in Nineteenth-Century America," *Journal of Social History* 13 (Spring 1980): 354–64.

41. Benjamin Franklin, "The Way to Wealth," in *Williams Choice Literature: Book Two* (New York: Sheldon, 1898), pp. 234–35. The quotations originally appeared in *Poor Richard Improved, 1758.* See *Benjamin Franklin: Writings,* ed. J. A. Leo Lemay (New York: Library of America, 1987), p. 1300.

42. Sara Louisa Oberholtzer, "School Savings Banks," *Annals of the American Academy of Political and Social Science* 3 (July 1892): 18, 20–21, 22. See also Carobel Murphy, *Thrift Through Education* (New York: A. S. Barnes, 1929), p. 9; "Oberholtzer, Sara Louisa," in *Who Was Who: A Companion Biographical Reference Work to Who's Who in America,* vol. 4 (Chicago: Marquis-Who's Who, 1968), p. 712.

43. Ethel Spencer, *The Spencers of Amberson Avenue: A Turn-of-the-Century Memoir* (Pittsburgh: University of Pittsburgh Press, 1983), p. 126.

44. "Felix Adler," *National Cyclopaedia of American Biography,* vol. 23 (New York: J. T. White, 1933), pp. 98–99; Felix Adler, *The Moral Instruction of Children* (New York: D. Appleton, 1892), pp. 116–20; William Byron Forbush, *Guidebook to Childhood* (Philadelphia: G. W. Jacobs, 1915), pp. 331–32; "Forbush, William," in *Who Was Who,* vol. 1 (Chicago: Marquis, 1943), p. 411. In examining these advice books I have tried to separate discussions of what was traditionally called jealous behavior from discussions of the envy of possessions, abilities, and opportunities of others. Peter Stearns has noted that experts increasingly came to conflate the meanings of jealousy and envy, and in the case of child-rearing advice I agree. Stearns, "Girls, Boys, and Emotions," pp. 36–74; Stearns, "The Rise of Sibling Jealousy in the Twentieth Century," in *Emotion and Social Change: Towards a New Psychohistory,* ed. Carol Z. Stearns and Peter N. Stearns (New York: Holmes and Meier, 1988), pp. 193–222.

45. Jay Mechling discussed the frequent gap between advice to parents and parents' actual behavior. See Jay E. Mechling, "Advice to Historians on Advice to Mothers," *Journal of Social History* 9 (fall 1975): 44–63; see also Rodgers, "Socializing Middle-Class Children," pp. 354–64.

46. Michael Kammen, *American Culture, American Tastes: Socal Change and the 20th Century* (New York: Knopf, 1999), p. 53.

47. Daniel Horowitz, *The Morality of Spending: Attitudes Towards the Con-*

sumer Society in America, 1875–1940 (Baltimore: Johns Hopkins University Press, 1985), p. 148.

48. James S. Plant, "Sociological Factors Challenging the Practice of Psychiatry in a Metropolitan District," *American Journal of Psychiatry* 8 (January 1929): 705–16.

49. Nora Atwood, "Children and Toys," *Outlook* 122 (May 7, 1919): 27–29.

50. Roland Marchand, *Advertising the American Dream: Making Way for Modernity, 1920–1940* (Berkeley: University of California Press, 1985), pp. 206–35; *Parents' Magazine* 6 (August 1931): 6; *Saturday Evening Post,* 195 (January 20, 1923): 86–87.

51. Robert Lynd and Helen Lynd, *Middletown: A Study in Contemporary American Culture* (New York: Harcourt Brace, 1929), pp. 81, 82n; Liddell, *With a Southern Accent,* pp. 80–81; Frank Shuttleworth and Mark May, "The Social Conduct and Attitudes of Movie Fans," in W. W. Charters, *Motion Pictures and Youth* (New York: Macmillan, 1933), pp. 7–9, 58; Kathy Peiss, "Making Faces: The Cosmetics Industry and the Cultural Construction of Gender, 1890–1930," *Genders* 7 (March 1990): 143–69, esp. p. 155.

52. Isabel Bevier, "Coloring and Furnishing the Home," in *The Home and Country Readers: Book Four,* ed. Mary A. LaSelle (Boston: Little Brown, 1918), pp. 52–57.

53. Homer J. Smith, *English for Boys and Men* (Boston: Allyn and Bacon, 1923), p. 106.

54. Ray Osgood Hughes, *Economic Civics* (Boston, 1921), pp. 16–17.

55. Cross, *Kids' Stuff,* p. 124.

56. Peter N. Stearns, "Consumerism and Childhood: New Targets for American Emotions," in *An Emotional History of the United States,* ed. Stearns and Jan Lewis (New York: New York University Press, 1998), pp. 396–413; Stearns, "Girls, Boys, and Emotions," 37–39, 64, 66; Rodgers, "Socializing Middle-Class Children," pp. 354–64. Stearns makes a similar observation about the match between child-rearing advice and corporate needs.

57. Douglas A. Thom, *Everyday Problems of the Everyday Child* (New York: D. Appleton Century, 1929), p. 179; "Thom, Douglas," in *Who Was Who,* vol. 3 (Chicago: Marquis-Who's Who, 1966), p. 848.

58. Benjamin C. Gruenberg, "Rivalry and Competition," in *Guidance of Childhood and Youth: Readings in Child Study, Compiled by the Child Study Association of America,* ed. Gruenberg (New York: Macmillan, 1926), pp. 95–98. Sociologist Arlie Hochschild has noted that there often is great similarity between parents' work and children's roles. Arlie Russell Hochschild, *The Managed Heart: Commercialization of Human Feeling* (Berkeley: University of California Press, 1983), p. 156.

59. Dollard, "The Life History in Community Studies," p. 735. Others explored this theme in later years. See, e.g., Karen Horney, *The Neurotic Personality of Our Times* (New York: W. W. Norton, 1937), pp. 80–82, 178–79; Evelyn Ellis, "Social Psychological Correlates of Upward Social Mobility Among Unmarried Career Women," *American Sociological Review* 17 (October 1952): 558–63.

60. Sidonie Gruenberg, *Your Child Today and Tomorrow* (New York, 1912), pp. 32, 43–46, *Sons and Daughters* (New York: H. Holt, 1916), pp. 145, 235, 312, and unpublished autobiography, pp. 121–23, in Sidonie Gruenberg Papers, Library of Congress, all quoted in Leach, "Child-World in the Promised Land," pp. 232–34.

61. Sidonie Gruenberg and Benjamin C. Gruenberg, *Parents, Children, and Money: Learning to Spend, Save, and Earn* (New York: Viking Press, 1933), pp. 8–9.

62. Stearns, "Girls, Boys, and Emotions," pp. 36–74; Stearns, "Sibling Jealousy in the Twentieth Century," pp. 193–222; Stearns, "Consumerism and Childhood," pp. 396–413.

63. Quoted in Cohn, *The Good Old Days*, 576.

64. For another account of how materialism infiltrated the Sunday school classroom, see Dorothy Rodgers, *A Personal Book* (New York: Harper and Row, 1977), pp. 19–20.

Conclusion

1. Robert Ellis Thompson, "The Folly of False Contentment," *Saturday Evening Post* 171 (May 13, 1899):730.

2. Robert H. Frank, *Luxury Fever: Why Money Fails to Satisfy in an Era of Excess* (New York: Simon and Schuster, Free Press, 1999); John de Graaf, David Wann, and Thomas H. Naylor in association with Redefining Progress, *Affluenza: The All-Consuming Epidemic* (San Francisco: Berrett-Koehler, 2001); Juliet Schor, *Do Americans Shop Too Much?* (Boston: Beacon Press, 2000), pp. 3–36.

Index

Acknowledgments

There are many people and institutions who helped me during the long process of writing this book. My graduate school advisors helped me launch this project and continued to take an interest in it long after their formal obligations ended. Michael Kammen has been a tremendous mentor whose understanding of American cultural history has shaped and influenced my own. He has been unstintingly generous with his advice and friendship. He read multiple early drafts of this work, and it benefited from his careful editing, thoughtful suggestions, and keen historical sense. Joan Jacobs Brumberg has been my other chief mentor on this project. Her insightful comments on early drafts helped me to think about gender and class in new and valuable ways. Her encouragement and warmth have meant a great deal to me through the years. Stuart Blumin and Isaac Kramnick provided me with important ways of thinking about the material and ideological implications of envy in a liberal capitalist society. I also appreciated their good advice and collegiality.

Daniel Horowitz tirelessly and patiently read countless drafts of this work. He has been incredibly generous with his time and his advice. His suggestions have strengthened and refined this book, and I am deeply indebted to him.

Kathy Peiss first introduced me to the scholarship on consumer culture in a seminar she taught as a visiting faculty member at Cornell University. She set me to thinking about consumer culture's effects on American mores. Susan Porter Benson, David Nasaw, Peter Stearns, and Joanne Meyerowitz read versions of Chapter 5, and their suggestions helped me to refine my argument. An anonymous reader of the entire manuscript also offered valuable comments.

Other scholars along the way helped me to discover the pleasures of history. Karl Weintraub introduced me to the study of the history of culture and showed me its many complexities and wonders. Edward Cook, Ronald Inden, and Mark Kishlansky offered excellent guidance and direction as I pursued this interest. Terry Cox, Judith Carithers, Maggie Cantrall, Michael Kayse, and Gail Spong Jaroski taught me important early lessons about history and writing, lessons I continue to use many years later.

Several institutions supported this project. Fellowships from Cornell University and the Mellon Foundation provided needed financial assistance as I wrote my dissertation. Additionally research was supported in part by a fellowship from the Henry Murray Research Center at Radcliffe College. A travel grant from Duke University's Special Collections Library enabled me to use their collection on sales, advertising, and marketing history.

My colleagues at Clark University, particularly Doug Little, Drew McCoy, and Janette Thomas Greenwood, provided excellent feedback on this project when I presented my work there. Randall Kindleberger, my colleague at the University of Maine at Machias, commented on drafts of this project and provided good advice and warm and treasured friendship. My colleagues at Weber State University have helped me as I completed the project. Richard Sadler, dean of the College of Social Sciences, supported my research and helped to defray some of the costs associated with it. Lee Sather, chair of the history department, and my colleagues William Allison, James Dolph, Sara Dant Ewert, Stephen Francis, Oliver Griffin, Henry Ibarguen, LaRae Larkin, Greg Lewis, Kathryn MacKay, Gene Sessions, John Sillito, and Richard Ulibarri have made teaching at Weber State a pleasure. Natalie McBride and Angela Hales provided excellent secretarial work. David Ferro, Lauren Fowler, Marjukka Ollilainen, Peter Vernezze, Eric Amsel, Frank Guliuzza, Russell Burrows, and Thomas Kuehls, all of Weber State, also provided discussion and friendship throughout the process of writing this book. Thom Kuehls deserves special thanks for reading and commenting on portions of this manuscript and for offering good advice. Jennifer Ritterhouse of Utah State University read portions of this manuscript and has my thanks as well. Thanks to Kathryn MacKay for proofreading.

Very special thanks to Christine Y. Todd.

Several libraries and librarians enabled me to complete my research. I thank the librarians at the Olin and Mann Libraries at Cornell University, the Joseph Regenstein Library at the University of Chicago, the Gutman Library at Harvard University, the Marriott Library at the University of Utah, and Stewart Library at Weber State University. Special thanks to Jacqueline Reid of Duke University's John W. Hartman Center for Sales, Marketing, and Advertising History for helping me find materials during my visit to Durham, for sending me copies of the Butterick and Palmolive ads that appear in this book, and for granting me permission to use them. At the University of Chicago, Sherry Byrne and Sandra Applegate found a way for me to reproduce advertisements. At Weber State University, Debbie Stephenson and the staff of the interlibrary loan department were amazingly quick in locating needed books, Clark Taylor helped me reproduce images, and Sandra Andrews helped make things go smoothly.

I owe a great deal to Peter Agree, editor at the University of Pennsylvania Press. I have benefited from his experience and skill as an editor. From the beginning, he helped me think about the shape this book should take, and along the way he has shown tremendous patience during the many years it took me to complete it. I am grateful to him for having faith in the project and in me. Thanks also to the editorial staff at the University of Pennsylvania Press, including Erica Ginsburg, Elaine Otto, Laurel Frydenborg, and Audra Wolfe.

Finally, I am indebted to my family. My grandmother Clara Stover Jipson, now deceased, and my great-aunt Hazel Stover offered me firsthand insight into life in rural Iowa in the early twentieth century and excited my interest in the period. Andres Fernandez, Lisa Fernandez, and Richard Remnick, my brothers- and sister-in-law, have always been generous and supportive. James and Renate Fernandez offered me anthropological perspectives on envy, thoughtful discussions, citations, and encouragement. I could not ask for better in-laws. My sister Elizabeth Matt Turner, my brother-in-law Jonathan Turner, and their family have taken an interest in this project and have helped me keep a sense of perspective.

To my parents, Barbara Jipson Matt and Joseph Matt, I owe so much. They nurtured my interest in history, read drafts of this work, asked provocative questions, sent citations, and above all, always sent their love. Their unfailing support through good times and bad has made all the difference.

Finally, my husband, Luke Fernandez, has helped me in ways too various to count. He has seen this project evolve from a dissertation proposal to a finished book. His queries, editorial advice, and distinctive perspective have left their mark. Even more, his love and humor have made me happy.